The
FOOD
BIBLE

The
FOOD
BIBLE

JUDITH WILLS

WHITE OWL

AN IMPRINT OF PEN & SWORD BOOKS LTD.
YORKSHIRE – PHILADELPHIA

This new, fully revised and updated edition
published in 2019 by White Owl Books
An imprint of Pen & Sword Books Ltd
Yorkshire – Philadelphia

Text copyright © 1998, 2002, 2006, 2007, 2019
Judith Wills

Hardback ISBN: 9781526725059
Paperback ISBN: 9781526761224

Printed and bound by Replika Press Pvt. Ltd.

Design: Paul Wilkinson.

Pen & Sword Books Limited incorporates
the imprints of Atlas, Archaeology, Aviation,
Discovery, Family History, Fiction, History,
Maritime, Military, Military Classics,
Politics, Select, Transport, True Crime, Air
World, Frontline Publishing, Leo Cooper,
Remember When, Seaforth Publishing, The
Praetorian Press, Wharncliffe Local History,
Wharncliffe Transport, Wharncliffe True
Crime and White Owl.

For a complete list of Pen & Sword titles
please contact:
PEN & SWORD BOOKS LIMITED
47 Church Street, Barnsley, South Yorkshire,
S70 2AS, United Kingdom
E-mail: enquiries@pen-and-sword.co.uk
Website: **www.pen-and-sword.co.uk**

Or
PEN AND SWORD BOOKS
1950 Lawrence Rd, Havertown, PA 19083, USA
E-mail: Uspen-and-sword@
casematepublishers.com
Website: **www.penandswordbooks.com**

Contents

INTRODUCTION 6

Introduction

When the first edition of this book was published twenty years ago, I started my introduction 'What you eat and what you drink really are vital parts of what you are – and what you will become. From before you are born all the way into old age, sustenance isn't just survival, it is your strength, your size, your short-term health, your long-term health, and — all other factors being equal— the length and quality of your life.'

As I write today, twenty years later, those words are still true. But so much else has changed in the world of food and health that when I sat down to begin the revision of *The Food Bible* for its timely new publication, I realised that the world of nutrition is perhaps more baffling for the average person who just wants to go and buy some decent – and hopefully healthy – food each week than it has ever been.

If you want to enjoy food but also feel secure in the knowledge that at least most of it is a good choice, health-wise, which do you believe? The media headlines you read last week that declared that butter's good for you after all – or the study reported this week, suggesting saturated fat is still the 'baddie'...??

And as for how to tell the difference between a poor food fad and a concept worth building on, that's little easier. The twenty-first century saw the birth of the idea of 'superfoods' but who talks about them now? If you never eat a goji berry or make yourself a wheatgrass juice does it matter? Good news – the answer is NO.

Twenty years ago, veganism was more or less dismissed as a ridiculous niche notion – now it's become mainstream, whilst meat-eating is beginning to be the no-go area for many more of us, along with a lot of the carbohydrates that formed the backbone of the typical 'healthy' low-fat diet of the day when my first edition was published.

'Clean' eating was all the thing when I started this new edition – but even before I've finished, it's been castigated by many experts. Alternate day fasting and the Amazonian Rainforest Diet are some of the ideas still popular as I write – but I can more or less assure you that next week, or next year, they'll probably be forgotten, or in disgrace.

But there is a solution to the great nutrition confusion that may be forcing many of

us into an 'I don't care' stance with our glass of wine (ok yesterday but not today...) our hunk of artisan cheese (bad last week, good this)... and a slice of home-made bread (dark rye fine, white wheat maybe not so fine, last week and this week too...).

Part of the problem is too much information coming at you from too many directions. But you need to know that many headline-grabbing food 'facts' are studies based on just a handful of humans, or, often, mice, and conducted over a very short time. We need only pay attention to those studies that have been carried out on thousands of people over a reasonable time scale. Or better still, go for what are called 'overviews' – studies analysing all the work done on a particular topic over a number of years.

We also need to take with a pinch of salt (very bad 20 years ago, now, maybe not so bad) any study or advice funded by an interested party. The 'meat cures diabetes' one funded by a country's meat producers council, for example.

I expect you know that every country has its version of a department of health within which there will be officials deciding on the nation's food and health policy and such things as recommended daily amounts of nutrients. And I expect you are also aware that there is eating advice on the website of every organisation representing the major and less major diseases of today. The advice from governments and these organisations is more reliable than most. But it can be out of date, as the wheels of consensus-reaching within both types of organisation tend to move very, very slowly.

But you're thinking now, 'I can't cope with all this – I have to work/raise kids/enjoy myself.'

Quite – and that's where this book comes in handy. Because I've spent a year, as I did when I first wrote it, revising every single page, every line and word, to bring you an unbiased reference to food and health for all the family.

I've ignored too-small and biased research, I've used my common sense, remained as impartial as possible (having nothing but this book to sell) and set out to tell you what really matters, and nothing more nor less.

I hope this new *Food Bible* will become a go-to, not only for every person wanting to protect and improve their health and lifespan but also, like the first edition, that it will be on the shelves of teachers, students and professionals.

I also hope that eating well for you does not just mean eating healthily but that you will enjoy choosing food, preparing your food, and eating your food. Good healthy meals can always be delicious, appealing meals – and perhaps that is the most important message of all.

SECTION ONE

Food for a balanced diet

T he health experts are always telling us that we ought to eat a balanced diet. But what exactly does that mean, and how do you know you're achieving the correct balance? Most of us, for example, still fall well short of eating enough of the healthier carbohydrates; and many of us who try to follow a diet very low in fat may be doing just as much harm to our health as those who eat a high-fat diet.

Then there's the advice to eat 'five a day' of fruit and vegetables. What is a portion? And which fruits and veg can be included? Many people haven't got a clue. Do you know that some fats vital to our well-being aren't all that easy to find in a typical diet? And did you know that many of us in the UK fall short of at least some of the vitamins and minerals our bodies need? And what about the other nutrients you hardly ever hear about? The microscopic elements in food that aren't vitamins or minerals but have similar potential for boosting our health.... 'good' bacteria, for instance, or phytochemicals. What exactly are they, where do you get them, and how much do you need?

Here is where you will find out all you need to know about 'a balanced diet', in a way that you can understand. Pictured overleaf is a perfect day's eating for an average woman, containing all the carbohydrates, fat, protein, vitamins, minerals, fibre and micronutrients that are needed, in all the right quantities. Using this as our blueprint, we go on to see how you can achieve your own perfect diet.

That's the beauty of food today – there is so much available in so much variety you can eat 'a balanced diet' without compromising your own needs. Section One sets out the foundation of your own diet for health and well-being and shows how to give your body the fuel it needs for life.

The Building Blocks of a Healthy Diet

A DAY'S PERFECT EATING

What you see on these pages is a perfect day's healthy eating according to the guidelines that appear on the next 65 pages. The meals and snacks contain the ideal amounts of calories, carbohydrates and fat (for a female aged from 35-54) and the ideal balance of the different types of carbs and fats, too. The day's eating also has more than adequate levels of protein, fibre, vitamins, minerals, plant chemicals and other micronutrients as well as around

nine portions of fruit and vegetables.

Taken together, the breakfast, lunch, supper, snack and milk allowance give a total of:

* 2,104 calories
* 79.1g total fat (33.8% of day's energy intake)
* 19.1g of saturated fat (8.2% of day's energy intake)
* 30.2g monounsaturated fat (13% of day's energy intake)
* 22.8g polyunsaturated fats (9.6% of day's energy intake)
* 2.3g EPA + DHA and 90.8g protein (17% of day's energy intake)
* while salt content is 3.4g, just over half the amount the UK says is a healthy daily maximum
* Add in several glasses of water and use the milk as a drink on its own or with a couple of cups of tea/coffee – both now known to be healthy drinks.

BREAKFAST

100g raspberries, 30g rolled oats, 10g chopped walnuts, 2 tsp sunflower seeds, 1 tbsp milled flaxseed, 1 tbsp pumpkin seeds, 2 chopped dried apricots, 150g fat free natural bio yogurt, 1 large banana.

LUNCH

30g each red lettuce leaves and dark green Cos leaves, 10g rocket, 15g baby spinach, 10 watercress, half a small red onion, 2 cherry tomatoes, 1 hard-boiled egg, 100g cooked weight Puy lentils, a dressing of 2 tsp extra virgin olive oil and ½ tbsp balsamic vinegar, 45g slice dark rye bread with 7g butter from grass-fed cows.

SNACKS/EXTRAS

1 apple, 1 orange, 200ml semi-skimmed milk.

SUPPER

115g farmed salmon, dry-fried, 150g cooked brown rice, 80g each broccoli and kale, 40g mangetout, 100g sweet potato, 1 small red pepper, 1 small fresh red chilli, 1 clove crushed garlic, 5g grated fresh ginger, all vegetables and spices stir-fried in 1 tbsp extra-virgin cold-pressed rapeseed oil.

YOU NEED ENERGY!

At the most basic level, what your body needs to live is energy – energy to breathe, to move, to function, to power itself, for repair and growth. Like machines, we need an outside source of energy, which is what we eat and drink.

That energy is measured in kilocalories (popularly just called calories). In these days of metrication, energy is also sometimes measured in kilojoules and 1 kilocalorie = 4.18 kilojoules.

When you expend energy you 'burn up' calories, and when you eat you add fuel to your energy store. The amount of energy or calories your body needs in a day depends on your size, age, proportion of muscle to fat, activity levels and many other factors.

However, guidelines called Estimated Average Requirements (EARs) have been laid down by the UK Department of Health's (DoH) Scientific Advisory Committee on Nutrition, and they are set out in the table below. (EARs for children, teenagers and the elderly appear in Section Three.)

In order to maintain a reasonable and stable body weight, energy (food) intake and energy expenditure need to be balanced. Too little intake and too much expenditure can result in weight loss and being too thin, too much intake and too little expenditure can result in weight gain (from the surplus calories converting themselves into body fat) and eventual obesity. More about maintaining the correct energy balance appears later in Section Four, Food for Weight Control.

All food and drink containing calories can supply you with energy, and calories can come in the form of carbohydrate, fat, protein or alcohol. Hardly any foods contain only one of these elements, the main exceptions being oils, which contain nothing but fat, and pure sugar, which contains nothing but carbohydrate. Most foods are a mixture of more than one element (along with combinations of the vitamins and minerals). For example, bread is high in carbohydrate, but also contains protein and fat; whole milk and nuts contain carbohydrate, fat and protein; meat is a mixture of protein and fat; and so on.

The Food Charts at the end of the book give the protein, fat and carbohydrate content of over 300 items, along with the other elements important for good health. Reading the next few pages will help you interpret these charts.

The ideal macronutrient (the scientific term for our major nutrients – carbs, fat, protein) proportions for a healthy diet are frequently debated worldwide, and here we will look at the advice not only from the UK but also from the World Health Organisation – whose Nutrition Guidance Expert Advisory Group is taking over five years to formalise a revised set of recommendations on diet and health –

Estimated Average Requirements for Energy for Adults SACN 2011		
Age	**Males** (kcals per day)	**Females** (kcals per day)
19-24	2772	2175
25-34	2749	2175
35-44	2629	2103
45-54	2581	2103
55-64	2581	2079
65-74	2342	1912
75+	2294	1840

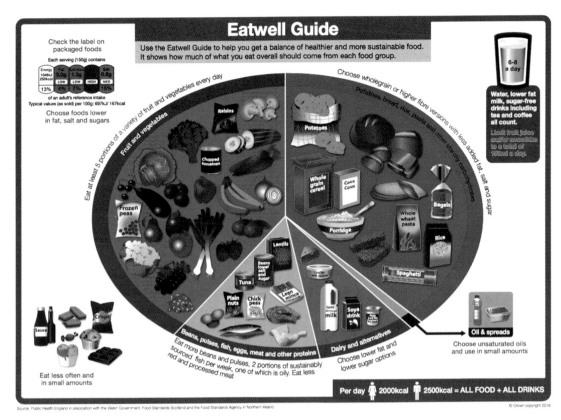

Eatwell Guide

Use the Eatwell Guide to help you get a balance of healthier and more sustainable food. It shows how much of what you eat overall should come from each food group.

Check the label on packaged foods

Each serving (150g) contains

Energy 1046kJ 250kcal	Fat 3.0g	Saturates 1.3g	Sugars	Salt 0.9g
13%	LOW 4%	LOW 7%	HIGH	MED 15%

of an adult's reference intake
Typical values (as sold) per 100g: 697kJ/ 167kcal

Choose foods lower in fat, salt and sugars

Eat at least 5 portions of a variety of fruit and vegetables every day

Fruit and vegetables

Raisins

Chopped tomatoes

Frozen peas

Choose wholegrain or higher fibre versions with less added fat, salt and sugar

Potatoes, bread, rice, pasta and other starchy carbohydrates

Potatoes

Whole grain cereal

Cous Cous

Whole wheat pasta

Porridge

Bagels

Rice

Lentils

Spaghetti

Beans lower salt and sugar

Tuna

Plain nuts

Chick peas

Lean mince

Lower salt beans

Semi milk

Soya drink

Beans, pulses, fish, eggs, meat and other proteins
Eat more beans and pulses, 2 portions of sustainably sourced fish per week, one of which is oily. Eat less red and processed meat

Dairy and alternatives
Choose lower fat and lower sugar options

6-8 a day

Water, lower fat milk, sugar-free drinks including tea and coffee all count.

Limit fruit juice and/or smoothies to a total of 150ml a day.

Oil & spreads

Choose unsaturated oils and use in small amounts

Sauce

Crisps

Eat less often and in small amounts

Per day 2000kcal 2500kcal = ALL FOOD + ALL DRINKS

Source: Public Health England in association with the Welsh Government, Food Standards Scotland and the Food Standards Agency in Northern Ireland
© Crown copyright 2016

and other renowned organisations, to help us make informed choices when it comes to the 'perfect' diet.

ENERGY-GIVING CARBOHYDRATES

Health departments from most countries agree that the majority of your calorie intake should come from carbohydrates. One reason is that carbs are easily converted into glucose – the fuel for all your body activity and energy requirements – and many carbs are also important sources of a range of other nutrients and fibres that we need for health. However, there is still not quite complete agreement on the exact amount we need.

The DoH guidelines for carbohydrates are fairly conservative. The last (2015) report from their

The Eatwell Guide

This colour chart was published by Public Health England in revised version in 2016 and claims to show in simple form a healthy balanced diet. While it has its limitations, it may be a useful quick reference tool for most of us.

Scientific Advisory Committee on Nutrition (SACN) said, 'It is recommended that the dietary reference value for total carbohydrate should be maintained at an average population intake of approximately 50% of total dietary energy.'

Many other countries have higher recommended carbohydrate levels (e.g. USA up to 65% for adults) and the World Health Organisation's (WHO) last advice was 55-75% of our total calorie intake should come from carbohydrates but they say 'A wide range of intakes, as a proportion of total energy intake, is compatible with low risk of chronic diseases' and are currently updating their guidelines which are tipped to be lowered to 50%.

Certainly, levels of up to 50% of your total daily calorie intake are likely to be good for your health but for a truly healthy carb intake it is crucial to choose the right types of carbohydrate and cut back on, or avoid, the rest.

TYPES OF CARBOHYDRATE

There are two main sorts of carbohydrate - starches and sugars. At the moment, around 60% of the carbohydrates that we eat are starches, and about 40% are sugars.

Starchy foods are plant-based foods such as grains, bread, potatoes, pulses, pasta and rice. Vegetables, nuts and seeds also contain starch in varying amounts. The carbohydrates in these foods are called polysaccharides.

Sugars are either intrinsic, such as those found in fruits (and called fructose) and vegetables, which are part of the cellular structure of the food, or 'free' sugars, which SACN defined in its 2015 report as, 'All monosaccharides and disaccharides (the chemical name for sugars) added to foods by the manufacturer, cook or consumer, plus sugars naturally present in honey, syrups and unsweetened fruit juices.'

Milk contains a free sugar, lactose, naturally present in milk and milk products, which is grouped with the intrinsic sugars for nutrition purposes and excluded from the free sugars definition.

Although a recent report from the World Health Organization recommends that free sugars can be eaten in moderation (5-10% of total calories) as part of a healthy diet, they are the one type of carbohydrate for which the DoH has set an upper intake limit, at 5% of total daily calorie intake for anyone age 2 and above. One reason for this limit is that more and more research indicates that high consumption of free sugars is a major cause of obesity as well as tooth decay and other health problems, including raised blood pressure. A diet high in sugary, fatty snack foods may also be low in essential nutrients.

It is all too easy to consume more

free sugars than you may think, as they feature in very many manufactured foods - even savoury ones – and drinks.

It is the complex, unrefined or minimally refined carbohydrates that should form the bulk of your healthy diet. These are the plant foods such as brown rice, oats, barley, whole-grain bread, vegetables and fruits, pulses, nuts and seeds, which not only supply your body with an easily converted form of energy but which also contain a whole range of other vital nutrients including fibre, protein, healthy fats, vitamins, minerals, phytochemicals and pre- and probiotics, and tend to be low on the Glycaemic Index (see page 210). They also have few health drawbacks.

Refined carbohydrates, such as white rice, white pasta and white flour, contain less of these elements, although they can still be worth eating in some circumstances.

Many common manufactured high-carb products, such as mass-produced cakes, packet puddings and biscuits, have lost much of their natural fibre, vitamins, minerals and phytochemicals, and may also contain high levels of the less healthy types of fat and free sugars and are often high in calories and are therefore worth cutting right down on in your diet.

FOODS FOR FIBRE

Plant foods of all types are our only source of dietary fibre, which is an important part of a healthy balanced diet. The various different compounds which can all be classed as 'fibre' may have different benefits – they can help prevent heart disease, stroke, diabetes, weight gain and some cancers, and can also improve digestive health and,

Recommended Daily Carbohydrate intakes for Adults UK*

Total Carbohydrate, average: 50% of total calorie intake

Example
Men (age 35-44) 350g
Women (age 35-54) 280g

Free Sugars, not more than: 5% of total calorie intake

Example
Men (age 35-44) 35g maximum
Women (age 35-54) 28g maximum

* Dietary Reference Values

researchers are beginning to discover, may have many other powers.

Fibre is not easily absorbed by the digestive system, passing undigested through the small intestine and reaching the colon where the different types are fermented or partially fermented by bacteria. SACN 2015 says, 'The term 'dietary fibre' refers to either some or all of the constituents of non-digestible carbohydrates.'

Fibre is often further divided into *insoluble* and *soluble* although it was suggested over ten years ago that the terms should be phased out, because of problems defining exactly what each of these are. However, in layman's terms, the tags can be useful. Most plant foods contain both types, but proportions vary.

Insoluble fibre is mainly *cellulose* and *lignin* and is found in all plants. Good sources are grains, especially wheat, corn and rice, vegetables and pulses.

Insoluble fibre is important for avoiding constipation and haemorrhoids. Taken with sufficient fluids, a high insoluble fibre diet increases stool bulk, speeds the passage of stools through the bowel, may help prevent or ease diverticulitis

Recommended daily fibre intakes, UK	
Age	**g**
2-5	15
5-11	20
11-16	25
17 and over	30

Selected good sources of fibre*	Total fibre (g)/100g
Pot barley (hulled barley), dry weight	17.3
Haricot beans, dry weight	15.3
Red kidney beans, dry weight	15.2
Shredded Wheat	12.0
Dried figs	9.8
Hazelnuts, shelled	9.7
Soya beans, dry weight	9.3
Wholewheat pasta, dry weight	9.2
Dried apricots	7.3
Prunes, stoned	7.1
Avocado	6.7
Wholemeal bread	6.0
Parsnips	4.9
Peas, frozen	4.5
Brussels sprouts	3.8
Kale	3.6
Pears	3.1
Savoy cabbage	3.1
Oranges	2.4

* Fibre figures from USDA Nutrient Database 28th edition. This list is not comprehensive; it simply represents a selection of sources of fibre.

and irritable bowel syndrome, and some research indicates it may help to prevent bowel cancer although this is a subject of debate. It also (with extra fluids) helps us to feel full and thus may be of help to people wanting to eat less.

All types of soluble fibre slow down the time it takes your body to absorb sugar from food. This helps prevent blood sugar 'spikes' – an important consideration for diabetics, and a potential help in controlling food intake. Soluble fibre also binds with fatty acids, flushing them out of the body and helping to lower cholesterol. There are various types of soluble fibre, such as pectin (good sources are citrus fruits and apples), *glucans*, (oats, barley and rye) and *arabinose* (pulses).

Resistant starch is a soluble fibre found in unripe bananas, oatmeal, peas and beans, for example, and is particularly beneficial in increasing the feeling of fullness and increasing insulin sensitivity. *Inulin* (chicory, onion, globe artichoke) acts as a prebiotic in the gut, having a beneficial effect on the microbiome and immune system (see Gut Health pages 151–153).

How much fibre is enough?
In Western countries, most of us still don't get enough fibre in our diets, the average intake in the UK being approximately 18g a day. The DoH recommends 30g for both men and women from the age of 17, though recommended amounts vary across the world.

One problem in measuring fibre in foods, and how much we need, is that fibre analysis methods vary across the world and this produces varying figures of exactly how much fibre foods do contain, which is why you will see different figures depending upon where you look. Amounts on food labels may not be quite the same as those in the UK and USA databases, for example. In time, hopefully this problem will be resolved.

It is always best to get your fibre naturally, from high-fibre foods, if possible, rather than from supplements. If you do use a supplement to boost fibre intake, cardio-vascular-friendly oat bran has a more positive impact on health in trials than wheat bran, which can reduce the body's absorption of certain minerals.

The Food Charts (pages 262–331) list total fibre content for a wide range of foods. Neither the UK Composition of Foods or the USA Nutrient Database list soluble fibre figures for foods. This seems to be because recent research finds that accurate measures aren't possible. For this reason, I haven't included any either, but I've flagged up good sources in the Notes (last column) in the Food Charts.

FATS

In dietary terms, fat was the wicked witch of the late twentieth century. Every time we grabbed a fatty snack, we felt guilty. Similarly, high-cholesterol foods were items to be eaten when no-one was looking. But, since the first edition of *The Food Bible* was published in 1999, much has altered.

Even conservative national departments of health, for whom the word 'cautious' was invented, have, in recent years, been altering their advice to populations about fat intake. For example, since 2015, the USA official advice has no upper limit in grams of fat intake a day, nor of cholesterol. The only fat it advises us to limit is saturated fat.

So what changed? Here's what you need to know.

THE COMPOSITION AND WORK OF FATS

Fat is made up mainly of fatty acids and glycerol, along with some other compounds – fatty acids being by far the largest component (glycerol comprises roughly 3% of total fat energy intake; glycerol is naturally present as a building block of fats and you do not need to be concerned about intake).

The fatty acids can be divided into three main groups – saturated, polyunsaturated and monounsaturated. All fat-containing foods contain all three types of fatty acid, but in varying proportions.

When people say, for instance, that butter is a saturated fat that is not really true. Certainly, the majority (67%) of the fat in butter is saturated, but it also contains 25% monounsaturated fat and even a little polyunsaturated. Beef, another food that people typically think of as containing saturated fat, contains virtually as much monounsaturated fat as saturated, at 43%.

There is also another type of fat – trans fat – which we look at in more detail on page 22.

Fat is mainly used by the body as energy – it contains 9 calories a gram, over twice as many as either carbohydrate or protein. If you eat more fat than your body can use for energy needs, however, it stores itself in the body as adipose tissue (fat!). This can later be converted into energy if needed.

A small amount of fat is needed because it carries the fat-soluble vitamins A, D and E (see pages 29–32). Polyunsaturated fats are also needed to supply essential fatty acids (see overleaf) and fats have other roles to play. Some types may protect your heart by improving the balance of cholesterol levels. Your body also utilizes fat to regulate your temperature and hormone production, and to help the production of digestive enzymes.

HOW MUCH FAT SHOULD WE EAT?

In recent decades the medical advice on fats was similar across the Western

Selected foods high in saturates, per 100g

	Saturates (g)	Total fat (g)
Coconut oil	82.5	99.1
Creamed coconut block	58.5	68
Suet, animal	56.0	100
Butter	53.5	80
Suet, vegetable	45.0	88
Lard	41.0	100
Hard margarine	35.0	80
Mascarpone cheese	30.5	46
Cream cheese	30.0	48
Double cream	30.0	48
Crème fraîche, full-fat	26.5	40
Stilton cheese	22.5	36
Cheddar cheese, full-fat	21.5	34
Chocolate	18.5	31
Fried bacon, lean and fat	16.0	41
Shortcrust pastry	10.0	28
Pork pie	10.0	27
Potato crisps	9.0	37
Minced beef	7.0	16
Lamb shoulder, roast	6.5	14

world – that we should limit total fat intake for health. The UK Department of Health chose 33% or less, the USA and the World Health Organisation (WHO) chose 30%, and this was because evidence at the time linked a high fat diet with cardio-vascular disease as well as some forms of cancer, diabetes, obesity and other ills.

The idea was that a generally low-fat, high carbohydrate diet was the healthiest one. But the consensus of opinion is changing as more recent and more sophisticated research finds that low-fat diets may not be as good for health as previously thought and that if the right fats are chosen, a higher-fat diet may be positively good for you.

As we've seen, the USA's recently released dietary guidelines for 2015-2020 do not even mention an upper limit for total fat intake in their Key Recommendations. The WHO is currently considering their 'less than 30% of total energy' guideline and may amend this before long. However, the UK lags behind – the Department of Health still recommends a total fat limit of 35%, and NICE, the institution that forms much of the DoH opinion, still recommends eating less unsaturated oil when reducing total fat intake. The values in the table here – an amalgamation of advice from the major world organisations and departments of health – give a rough idea of a reasonable balance of the fats to aim for based on current consensus.

So, let's look at the types of fat mentioned above and see which are best for health and which are less good.

SATURATED FAT

This is the kind of fat that is usually solid at room temperature and is found in largest quantities in animal produce such as meat, cheese, cream, milk, eggs, butter and lard, and in milk chocolate and many manufactured pies, pastries, cakes and biscuits. Currently our saturated fat intake is about 12-14% (depending on age group) of our total calorie intake.

The consensus of opinion amongst the medical profession is that a diet high in saturates is proven to raise your 'bad' (LDL) cholesterol and put you at higher risk of heart disease (for more on diet and heart disease see page 132).

A diet high in saturated fat has also been linked with high blood pressure, and other ailments and problems, including cancer and obesity.

Most bodies recommend that we eat no more than 10% of our total calories as saturates. The UK Department of Health says 11%; the American Heart Association reduces this to 5-6%, while the UK's NHS says women should limit saturates to 20g a day and men to 30g a day.

However, not everyone agrees that saturated fat is such a baddie. For example, in 2016 in two large studies it was found that full fat milk can help protect against diabetes and that full fat, not low-fat, dairy helps with weight control. Various studies have refuted the idea that saturates cause disease, and others suggest that replacing saturates in the diet with simple (refined) carbohydrates is even worse for health. There is recent evidence that the action of saturates in the body also depends upon which food it is eaten in – for example, hard cheese has less effect on cholesterol levels than would be assumed from its saturated fat content.

Although so far all this recent research has had little effect on official recommendations, there does seem

A word about coconut oil

In the past few years, coconut oil has grown in popularity, partly because it is often promoted as a healthy fat despite the fact that it contains 82g of saturated fat in each 100g – more than butter or lard by a long way.

Unlike most foods high in saturates, it contains a high proportion of medium-chain fatty acids, which appear to raise the metabolic rate and thus, at least in theory, might help weight loss by helping us to burn more calories. It also contains lauric acid, which seems to boost 'good' HDL blood cholesterol. While past research has concluded the oil raises LDL cholesterol, one recent major UK study found this did not happen – and in trials, it raised HDL by 15% compared with just 5% for butter. Coconut oil is also very stable when used for cooking at high temperatures with a high smoke point (see chart page 217) and is probably better to use than high omega-6 oils such as sunflower oils and other omega-6 rich oils at least some of the time, as overconsumption of these can be a factor in inflammation, see overleaf.

Meanwhile, Heart UK, the cholesterol charity, and the British Heart Foundation's current stance is that it should be used sparingly like any other high-saturated fat food, while the American Heart Association warned in 2017 that it is no better than any other food high in saturates – and that sticking to a diet low in saturated fats could prevent 5.2 million deaths a year. Clearly, more research needs to be done.

to be a consensus now that rather than eating refined carbs to replace the calories from saturates, it is much healthier instead to replace them with unsaturated fats.

POLYUNSATURATED FAT

The largest amounts of this type of fatty acid are usually found in fats that are liquid at room temperature or cooler – vegetable oil, such as corn oil, safflower oil, sunflower oil and walnut oil are high in polyunsaturates, as are most nuts.

Polyunsaturated fats have the opposite effect to saturates by lowering LDL blood cholesterol and are one of the few rich natural sources of vitamin E. Deficiencies lead to symptoms and conditions including decreased immune function, depression, and dryness of the skin, while optimum intake may reduce the risk of cardiovascular disease, digestive problems such as ulcers, joint pain and nervous system diseases.

The two major classes of polyunsaturated fats are the omega-3 and omega-6 fatty acids.

Omega-3s (sometimes referred to as N-3s) are present in several foods in good amounts, including a variety of plant oils, nuts, seeds and fish. The

omega-3s to be concerned about in healthy eating are alpha-linolenic acid (ALA) – the major source of omega-3s in our diets – eicosapentaenoic acid (EPA), and docosahexaenoic acid (DHA). Omega-3s are vital for preserving the structure of cell membranes and they are important for cardio-vascular health and our immune and endocrine systems.

EPA and DHA are described as 'long-chain fatty acids' and the only food source of these fats is fish, shellfish and fish products, particularly oily fish (see Chart), although small amounts of EPA and DHA can be converted in the body from ALA, and algae supplements containing them can be purchased. EPA and DHA are anti-inflammatory and may also help depression, memory, and cardio-vascular problems. One to two portions of oily fish a week have been shown to be particularly beneficial in reducing the 'stickiness' of the blood and its tendency to clot, and therefore in helping to prevent CHD and stroke. These fatty acids have been used for many other health problems, too, although not all research has confirmed these anecdotal benefits.

Omega-6s (sometimes referred to as N-6s) are present in many commonly used foods including salad and cooking oils, nuts, seeds and processed foods. The major source of omega-6 in our diet is linoleic acid (LA). Omega-6s are important for brain function and normal growth and development. They help stimulate skin and hair growth, maintain bone health, regulate metabolism, and maintain the reproductive system.

Another omega-6 fat, gamma-linolenic acid (GLA), is a powerful anti-inflammatory and may also

Safflower oil	73.9
Evening primrose oil	68.4
Grapeseed oil	67.8
Sunflower oil	63.2
Walnut oil	58.4
Hemp seed oil	57
Soya oil	51.5
Corn oil	50.4
Sesame oil	43.1
Margarine, soft polyunsaturated	33.8
Sunflower seeds	32.8
Groundnut oil	31
Walnuts	29.5
Sesame seeds	25.3
Pine nuts	24.9
Brazil nuts	22.9
Rapeseed oil	19.7
Pumpkin seeds	19.3
Linseed oil	15
Almonds	9.8
Cashew nuts	8.1
Olive oil	7.5
Pistachio nuts	7.1
Linseeds	5.7
Fat spread, 40% not polyunsaturated	5.1
Oatcakes	4.7
Fat spread, 20-25% not polyunsaturated	4.1
Soya flour, full-fat	3.6

help pre-menstrual and menopausal symptoms. LA can be converted to GLA in the body, and it is also present in evening primrose oil, borage oil and blackcurrant seed oil.

Our bodies can make most of the fat we need for health, but neither ALA nor LA can be made in our bodies and so they are described as 'essential fatty acids', meaning we need to get them through food.

Nevertheless, it is widely believed by researchers that high intake of omega-6 polyunsaturated fats may not be a good idea, especially used in cooking, because they may be easily oxidized in the body, producing free radicals which can damage body cells and may promote cancers, other diseases and inflammation. (For more on cooking oils for health, see Section Five.)

For that reason, around 6-10% of your daily calories as polyunsaturates is a reasonable average based on current UK and EU guidelines.

Experts advise that intake of omega-6 and omega-3 should be balanced. Most of us tend to have a lot of linoleic acid containing foods and few of the ALA containing foods. Some experts feel that a AL/ALA ratio of 4:1 would be ideal, but the ratio in many people's diets is often nearer 20:1 as foods high in linoleic acid are much more prevalent in the average diet than are high alpha-linolenic acid foods. A diet high in natural unprocessed foods and including foods on the ALA list (below) will help redress the balance.

Raising EPA and DHA intake may be even more important than reducing omega-6s. Recommendations on the amount of EPA and DHA to consume daily for full benefit vary from 500mg

Best sources of Alpha-Linolenic Acid (g/100g)	
Linseed oil	53.1
Hemp seed oil	19
Linseeds	14
Walnut oil	11.5
Rapeseed oil	9.6
Evening primrose oil	8.2
Soya oil	7.3
Walnuts	5.6
Margarine, soft polyunsaturated	2.1
Soya flour, full-fat	1.7
Fat spread, 40% not polyunsaturated	1.3
Butter, unsalted	1.2
Rabbit, raw	1.0
Corn oil	0.9
Butter, slightly salted	0.9
Tuna, canned in oil, drained	0.9
Pine nuts	0.8
Groundnut oil	0.8
Fat spread, 20-25% not polyunsaturated	0.7
Olive oil	0.7
Cream, double	0.7
Lard	0.6
Sardines, canned in oil, drained	0.4
Grapeseed oil	0.4
Ghee, vegetable	0.3
Kipper	0.3
Sesame oil	0.3
Salmon	0.2

Good sources of DHA and EPA per 100g edible portion *All values for fresh or frozen fish unless stated otherwise*

	DHA (g)	EPA (g)
Salmon, farmed	1.5	0.7
Mackerel	1.4	0.9
Salmon, wild	1.4	0.4
Anchovies, canned in oil	1.3	0.8
Herring	0.9	0.7
Anchovies	0.9	0.5
Tuna, bluefin	0.9	0.3
Tuna, canned in water	0.6	0.2
Sardines, canned in oil	0.5	0.5
Trout, brown	0.5	0.2
Trout, rainbow, farmed	0.5	0.2
Trout, rainbow, wild	0.4	0.2

Source: USDA

(for the two fatty acids combined) up to 4g. For people at risk of, or with, CVD the higher level may be prudent according to the American Heart Association. For most people, 1–2g a day would be a reasonable goal.

TRANS FATS

These are fats which are naturally present in small quantities in some foods, such as some meat and dairy produce, and which for many years were present in many manufactured foods such as biscuits, spreads and sweets. Artificial trans fats (or trans fatty acids), as they are called, are created in an industrial process that adds hydrogen to liquid vegetable oils to make them more solid and are listed on food labels as partially hydrogenated fats or oils.

This process was regularly used in the production of margarine, for example, to make oils become hard and spreadable as well as sometimes being used for texture and taste. Once hardened, these trans fats then become more like saturated fats in the way they act in our bodies.

We now know that trans fats can actually be more damaging than saturates. For instance, trans fats not only raise levels of LDL blood cholesterol but also lower levels of HDL ('good') cholesterol, unlike saturated fats such as butter, which can raise HDL levels. Trans fats can predispose us to heart disease and stroke as well as diabetes and weight gain around the waist.

As a result of scientific research and studies, in 2013 the USA Food and Drug Administration (FDA) declared that partially hydrogenated fats are no longer generally recognized as safe in human food and should be banned.

In New York and eleven surrounding counties, trans fats have been banned since 2007 and this has resulted in a 6% decline in heart attacks and strokes in the area, and a similar result has happened in Denmark after their use was drastically reduced.

The EU was set to restrict the amount of trans fats in food throughout its member states by 2018. The UK Government withdrew plans to ban them in processed foods in 2016 but nevertheless, many food companies have chosen to remove or drastically reduce the levels of trans fats in their products. The result is that in the UK our average daily intake is well within the UK guideline of no more than 2% of total calories and is estimated at around 0.5%.

To avoid trans fats, avoid products that list 'partially hydrogenated fats' in the ingredients list. They are banned in organic food production.

MONOUNSATURATED FAT

This, the last of the types of fat, is also usually liquid at room temperature but may solidify when cooled (say, in the fridge), and is found in greatest quantities in olive, rapeseed and groundnut oils, as well as in olives themselves and many nuts and in avocados, but it is also present in fairly reasonable quantities in most table and cooking fats and oils, most dairy produce, eggs, fish, meat and many other foods.

Monounsaturated fats are generally very healthy fats to eat regularly. They have a better overall effect than polyunsaturated fats on blood cholesterol, not only lowering LDL cholesterol but maintaining or even slightly raising the levels of the HDL cholesterol.

There is also evidence that a diet rich in monounsaturates – the typical Mediterranean diet – is linked with lower heart disease rates and also with increased longevity and lower risk of some cancers. Oils high in monounsaturates are also often rich sources of the antioxidant vitamin E.

The DoH recommends that the remainder of the fatty acids in our diet not eaten as saturated or polyunsaturated fats should be eaten as monounsaturated. However, for the sake of your circulation, your heart and your health, it would be wise to replace more of the saturated (and trans) fats in the diet with

SELECTED RICH SOURCES OF MONOUNSATURATED FATTY ACIDS (MFAS) (all per 100g weight)		
	Monounsaturated fatty acids (g)	Total fat (g)
Olive oil	73	100
Macadamia nuts (shelled)	61	78
Rapeseed oil	59	100
Hazelnuts (shelled)	50.5	64
Lard	44	100
Groundnut oil	44	100
Sesame oil	38	100
Blended vegetable oil	36	100
Almonds, shelled	35	56
Olive oil margarine (60% fat)	32.5	60
Corn oil	30	100
Brazil nuts (shelled)	26	68
Duck, roast, with skin	19	38
Bacon, fried, lean and fat	18.5	41
Hummus	18	29
Low-fat spread, typical	17.5	40
Double cream	14	48
Avocado	12	19.5
Mackerel fillet	8	16
Beef, minced	7	16

monounsaturates. So if, for example, your total fat intake is 35% of your total calorie intake, perhaps 5-10% would be saturates, 10% would be polyunsaturates and 15-20% would be monounsaturates.

To do this would mean eating more plant-based foods and much less animal-based and commercially produced foods (the advice given on pages 52–75 will help you to do this with ease).

CHOLESTEROL

Cholesterol is present in many foods of animal origin, including meat and dairy produce, eggs, fish (especially shellfish) and many fatty manufactured products.

In the body, cholesterol is carried in your blood by proteins, and when the two combine they're called lipoproteins. There are two main types – low-density lipoprotein (LDL) and high-density lipoprotein (HDL).

A surplus of LDL in the blood is, say most experts, a major factor in the 'furring' of arteries and formation of the plaques that lead to atherosclerosis, heart disease and stroke. High levels of blood fats – triglycerides – combined with a poor blood cholesterol profile increases the risk of these conditions. HDL – often called 'good' cholesterol – actually helps to remove cholesterol from the tissues and delivers it to the liver for excretion.

A certain amount of cholesterol is necessary for various body processes, including making hormones, vitamin D synthesis and digestive enzymes, and about threequarters of what we need is manufactured in the body, while one-quarter comes from the diet.

Dietary cholesterol has only a small effect on blood cholesterol levels, and thus the latest dietary guidelines in the USA and from the UK's National Health

Service no longer give a recommended daily upper limit on intake, but for people with CHD or risk factors (see Cardiovascular Disease, page 132), it may be wise to avoid cholesterol-rich foods especially those also high in saturated fat, such as double cream and fatty cuts of red meat. Cholesterol-lowering margarines can help, but these may reduce the absorption of antioxidants by the system.

The consensus now seems to be that it is more important to keep saturated fats, trans fat, refined carbohydrate and alcohol consumption low in order to keep or get a healthy blood lipids profile. See the Food Charts on pages 262–331 for the cholesterol content of around 300 common foods.

Interestingly, some studies in the past few years have concluded that cholesterol levels have little link with incidence of, and/or deaths from, cardiovascular disease and stroke. Others have found that HDL isn't perhaps as much of a 'goodie' as was thought. As one research team recently concluded, 'Good cholesterol is complex, with various particle sizes and subspecies floating around in the body.'

However, these results and their interpretation remain controversial until further work is done and if we follow the current guidelines to restrict saturates, trans and some carbs, this has many health benefits in any event.

PROTEIN

Most of us think of protein as the nutrient we need to eat to build us up and keep us strong – and it is true. Adequate protein is essential for our bodies and its main role is to build muscle, as well as being vital for growth and development in children, and for cell maintenance and repair. It also helps protect us from viral and bacterial infections and boosts the immune system; acts as a co-ordinator between various body processes, helps with body movement, and transports atoms and molecules around the body. Surplus protein can also be converted into energy (calories). It is a clever nutrient!

The nine essential amino acids, what they do, and good sources

Isoleucine: Helps produce haemoglobin for healthy blood; aids muscle recovery after exercise.
Good sources: Soya, beef, pork, tuna.

Leucine: Promotes growth and healing.
Good sources: As isoleucine.

Lysine: For a healthy nervous system and hormonal balance.
Good sources: Pork, chicken, cod, sardines.

Methionine: Important for fat metabolism, muscle and cartilage maintenance; anti-inflammatory.
Good sources: Tuna, salmon, hard cheese, nuts.

Phenylalanine: Can help prevent depression and maintain memory; controls satiety.
Good sources: Beef, fish, shellfish, cheese, milk, nuts, soya.

Threonine: Boosts the immune system, helps build collagen for good skin.
Good sources: Turkey, eggs, soya.

Tryptophan: Helps promote good sleep, helps prevent migraines and depression.
Good sources: Turkey, chicken, shellfish, milk, yogurt, nuts, seeds, pulses.

Valine: Essential for muscle development.
Good sources: Turkey, chicken, dairy produce, soya, lentils, black beans.

Histidine: For growth and development, production of blood cells and circulation.
Good sources: Beef, Parmesan, soya, poultry, oily fish, seeds.

WHAT IS PROTEIN?

Protein is a component of very many foods, but it doesn't always take the same form. It mainly consists of amino acids, like building blocks. Proteins from different food sources contain different combinations and amounts of the amino acids. Twenty of these amino acids are used in the body.

They can be divided into two broad types – non-essential amino acids and essential amino acids. Non-essential amino acids can be made from an excess of other amino acids in the diet, while essential ones cannot and so must be provided in what we eat. There are nine essential amino acids and each of these has its own role to play in keeping the body and mind healthy (see box on page 25). Individual foods that contain all of the essential amino acids are called 'complete proteins' but many foods contain just some of them.

Animal sources such as meat, dairy and eggs are complete proteins, while most plant sources are not. The complete protein foods used to be called 'first class' proteins, and non-complete protein foods 'second class', but those terms are no longer used as in a normal varied diet; all the amino acids will be provided by a selection of different foods.

HOW MUCH PROTEIN DO WE NEED?

Our total protein needs may alter according to our circumstances. Body weight is perhaps the most important factor – the Department of Health says adults need around 0.75g of protein a day per kg weight (see table for examples). Pregnant and breast-feeding women also need more protein than average, while factors such as our age and activity levels may alter our optimum intake. Recommended daily amounts of nutrients were originally developed to represent the minimum amount of a nutrient we need at a basic level. Protein intakes considerably higher than the minimum may, for active young adults, for example, be much more sensible.

The UK Department of Health suggests 10-15% of total calories eaten as protein is adequate for most people and in the USA their latest guidelines suggest 10-35%. Most people in Western countries eat more than the UK guidelines – the last full UK Diet and Nutrition survey of the population published in 2014 found we were eating nearer 20%. And with the popularity of low-carb eating in recent years, it is likely that that figure may even have increased. Although there is a growing interest in eating less meat and more plant foods for health and weight control, our main source of protein in the UK is meat, contributing nearly 40% of protein intake in people over the age of 3.

CAN WE EAT TOO MUCH PROTEIN FOR HEALTH?

As we've seen, protein is an important nutrient. In recent years there has been much new research on its many benefits. Here are some:

For weight control/loss: Protein seems to help by boosting the body's ability to burn its own fat; by increasing the metabolic rate and by increasing satiety and preventing hunger. It can also prevent muscle loss in dieters.

To control blood pressure: Some studies have shown that intake of around 100g a day reduces the risk of getting high blood pressure and may lower it in sufferers – but one

22-year study finds very high protein intake may increase the risk of heart failure in older men.

To control blood sugars: Several studies have found that meals high in protein reduce blood glucose spikes and offer optimum blood sugar control.

There is no exact answer to the question, 'What is too much protein?' as your optimum intake depends on many factors including your age, sex, activity levels and type, and other factors. There is some evidence that a high protein diet may put a strain on the kidneys and may demineralize the bones, but it is fairly flimsy. And in the USA and UK, there is no official safe 'upper limit' on protein intake at all, as there is with, say, saturated fat or salt.

Finding the best *types* of high-protein food for health may be more important than setting an arbitrary upper limit on protein from any source. But this is not an easy task. There have been many conflicting studies carried out recently on the health benefits or otherwise of the various different high-protein foods. Even the scientists agree that much more work needs to be done to find definitive answers. About the only thing they can agree on is that regularly eating processed meat such as bacon, ham and frankfurters probably increases the

Examples of protein RNI* for adults, UK**	
Bodyweight	**g/protein a day**
8 stones/51kg	38
9 stones/57kg	43
10 stones/63.5kg	48
11 stones/70kg	52
12 stones/76.5kg	57
13 stones/83kg	62
14 stones/89kg	67
15 stones/95.5kg	72
16 stones/102kg	77

* Reference Nutrient Intake

** Recommendations vary somewhat throughout the world

risk of bowel cancer.

Despite the confusion, dietary guidelines both in the USA and UK suggest that we eat less red meat and more proteins from other sources and this seems to be based on the need to cut down our saturated fat intake, rather than our protein intake.

So my advice is – don't just rely on meat protein. A diet high in protein-rich sources such as pulses, nuts, fish and eggs is very unlikely to cause health problems and has many positives. Plant protein sources such as lentils and beans also contain high levels of healthy carbohydrates, fibre and plant compounds that have many proven health benefits. Lastly, mixing your protein sources will make sure you get all the essential amino acids.

WHAT ARE GOOD SOURCES OF PROTEIN?

The charts below show some selected good animal and vegetable sources of protein, and you'll find more information on the protein content of common foods in the Food Charts.

Bear in mind that many foods high in carbohydrate are also quite good sources of protein – good examples are wholemeal bread, which has about 5.5g protein in 60g, and wholewheat pasta, which has about 6.7g, while one medium baked potato will give you around 8.7g.

Selected good sources of animal protein	
Food	**Protein (g)**
Chicken breast portion without skin	42
Ostrich, 100g	39
Beef, roast, lean, 100g	32
Cod, 175g	31.5
Venison, 100g	22
Beefburger, quarter-pounder	21
Salmon fillet, 100g	20
Prawns, peeled, 75g	17
Cheddar, half-fat, 50g	16
Eggs, 2 medium	14.2
Cottage cheese, 100g	14
Pork pie, 150g individual	14
Cheddar, full-fat, 50g	13
Stilton, 50g	11
Bacon, lean back, 2 small rashers (50g)	9.5
Natural fromage frais, 0% fat, 100g	7.7
Milk, skimmed, 200ml	6.6
Natural low-fat yoghurt, 100g	5

Selected good sources of plant protein	
Food	**Protein (g)**
Soya beans, 50g dry weight	18
Peanuts, fresh, 50g	13
Quorn chunks, 100g	12
Black-eye beans, 50g dry weight	12
Lentils, 50g dry weight	12
Red kidney beans, 50g dry weight	11
Cashews, 50g	8.9
Baked potato, 225g cooked weight	8.7
Vegetable burger, one 50g	8.3
Tofu, 100g	8
Pasta, wholemeal, 50g dry weight	6.7
Pasta, white, 50g dry weight	6
Soya milk, 200ml	6
Peas, frozen, 100g	5.6
Wholemeal bread, 60g (2 average slices)	5.5
Pot barley, 50g dry weight	5.3
Couscous, 50g dry weight	5.3

A FEW WORDS ABOUT CHEESE ...

If you're trying to cut down on meat, or are vegetarian, most dairy produce and eggs are good protein sources and, again, offer plenty of other health benefits. For example, cheese is often demonised as a high saturated fat food, and yet we now know this is not the whole picture. Scientists examined all the evidence in 2017 and found that full fat dairy products don't increase the risk of cardiovascular disease, and cheese has several health benefits. For example, including hard cheese in a weight loss plan results in more belly fat lost; cheese protects against tooth decay, osteoporosis and lowers the risk of diabetes and high blood pressure. Aged blue cheeses contain probiotics which improve gut health.

VITAL VITAMINS

Vitamins are the 'unseen' components of a healthy diet – the tiny particles without which we wouldn't survive. We are discovering more information about their importance in the diet all the time. Vitamins are organic substances which are indispensable for the everyday functioning of our bodies, for our good health and proper development.

Each has a different role to play, and most have to be provided in what we eat and drink. We need only very small amounts of the vitamins – normally just a few milligrams (1,000mg=1 gram) or even micrograms, written as mcg or sometimes ug (1,000 micrograms=1 milligram) a day.

Vitamins A, D, E and K are fat-soluble vitamins and thus can be stored in the body. Vitamins C and the B group are water-soluble vitamins and can't be stored. Excess is excreted in the urine, so they need to be consumed on a regular basis. Each of the eleven vitamins is discussed separately in the pages ahead.

Recommended amounts are given for each vitamin (and mineral) for adults (normally aged 19-50). The UK's Department of Health offers Reference Nutrient Intakes (RNIs) which were set back in 1991, apart from vitamin D, the RNI for which was altered in 2016. These intake values, say the DoH, are enough for 97% of people in any group. For comparison, we include the EC's Nutrient Reference Values (NRV) which are used in EC countries on food labels, and the USA's DV (Daily Values) which were set in 2016, also for food labelling. Recommended amounts for children, in pregnancy and the elderly appear in Section Three.

A short explanation of the role of each vitamin is given, followed by general sources, symptoms of deficiency and excess. Best sources charts list selected top sources for each per 100g of food item. Other items may provide more of the vitamins per 100g but may not normally be eaten in large enough quantities to make a real contribution. For example, parsley contains 673mcg vitamin A (retinol equivalent) per 100g but a normal portion is only about 2-5 g.

If you want to know whether a particular food which isn't listed here contains a certain vitamin in good quantity, check the Food Charts at the back of the book.

Many people use vitamin supplements, perhaps to try to boost a poor diet or feeling that if enough is good, more is even better. However, the use of supplements to boost vitamin intake is controversial – this is discussed in detail in Section Two on page 169.

VITAMIN A
RETINOL AND RETINOL ACTIVITY EQUIVALENTS
UK RNI 600mcg (female), 700mcg (male)
EC NRV 800mcg, USA DV (daily values) 900mcg

Vitamin A (retinol) is essential for healthy vision, eyes, skin and growth. Symptoms of deficiency include poor night vision, gradual loss of sight and reduced resistance to infection.

Excess vitamin A is stored in the liver and can be poisonous, causing liver and bone damage, headache, double vision and other side-effects. Excess retinol consumption is linked with certain birth defects and foods

Selected best sources of Vitamin A retinol (mcg per 100g)

Lamb's liver	17,300
Chicken livers	9,700
Liver pate	7,400
Cod liver oil	1,800
Butter	887
Double cream	654
Stilton cheese, blue	386
Cheddar cheese	363
Brie	320
Eggs	190

high in retinol, such as liver, should be avoided if you are pregnant (see Pregnancy section on page 187–190). The DoH recommends that regular intakes shouldn't exceed 7,500mcg in women and 9,000mcg in men.

Retinol is found only in foods from animal sources, such as liver, milk, butter, cheese, eggs and oily fish, but the body can convert carotenoids – particularly beta-carotene, the pigment found in greatest quantities in orange-fleshed and dark green vegetables and fruits – into retinol. The measurement used is a 'retinol activity equivalent' or pro-vitamin A.

Carotenoids are also important in their own right (see page 47). The carotenoid list here is not comprehensive – for more good sources, see the Food Charts at the end of the book. Carotene is not toxic, although fairly high intakes of over 30mg a day may make the skin orange-tinged, and high doses of supplements rather than foods may increase the risk of cancers and can interfere with the action of statins in the body.

Selected best sources of carotenoids (mcg per 100g)

Retinol activity equivalents (RAEs)

Carrots, old	1,353
Sweet potato (orange-fleshed), baked	855
Swiss chard	766
Chilli peppers	685
Red peppers (capsicum)	640
Spinach	640
Butternut squash	545
Curly kale	524
Spring greens	438
Frozen mixed vegetables	420
Cantaloupe melon	333
Mango	300
Tomato purée	217
Savoy cabbage	165
Dark-leaved lettuce, e.g. butterhead	151
Tomatoes	107
Broccoli	96

VITAMIN D

CHOLECALCIFEROL (D3) AND ERGOCALCIFEROL (D2)

UK RNI 10mcg, EC RNV 5 mcg, USA DV 20 mcg.

Vitamin D intake is important for the absorption of calcium and phosphorous in the body, helping to form bones and carry out other mineralization.

Deficiency can lead to soft bones and lack of growth in children, and weakness and pain in adults. Adequate intake may help prevent osteoarthritis and/or slow its progression, according to the Arthritis Foundation. It lowers the risk of colds, flu and pneumonia and some recent research shows that it can help prevent cancer – people with high levels in their blood are 20% less likely to get the disease. It can also help reduce high blood pressure as well as chronic backache and pain from fibromyalgia and menstruation.

Vitamin D is the only vitamin which we don't always need to take in via the diet. It can be manufactured by the action of sunlight on the skin, and the 2016 SACN report into the vitamin says that from April to September (UK) skin synthesis is the main source of the vitamin for most people, though older people and people with dark skin may be less able to synthesize vitamin D through the skin.

There are not many rich food sources of Vitamin D. Dietary sources are mostly from foods of animal origin such as dairy produce, oily fish and eggs, as well as fortified margarines and breakfast cereals.

It is estimated that up to ten million people in the UK, many of them children, are deficient in vitamin D. Supplements are well tolerated but the upper safe limit needs to be carefully followed.

That is because, in excess, vitamin D can produce kidney and other organ damage by causing calcium to be deposited in the organs. Levels of 50mcg a day have been known to have this effect so once again, while enough is important, taking more than enough is not a good idea. The European Food Safety Authority has set an upper safe limit for healthy people over the age of 11 of 100mcg a day, 50mcg for children aged 1–10 and 25mcg for infants.

VITAMIN E
TOCOPHEROLS AND TOCOTRIENOLS
EC RNV 12mg, USA DV 15mg

The UK has no RNI for vitamin E, but the Department of Health has set 'safe intakes', which are over 3mg a day for women and over 4mg a day for men, and they say that you can get all you need from food, and deficiencies in adults are rare. It is a fat-soluble vitamin and needs fat in the diet so it can be absorbed.

Vitamin E – actually a group of nine different compounds - has several roles in human health – it protects cell membranes, helps maintain healthy skin and eyes, and strengthens the immune system, helping to protect against illness and infection. It is anti-oxidant and as such may help to protect from cardio-vascular disease by helping to prevent hardening of the arteries and build-up of blood cholesterol and lipids.

The vitamin may also help with skin healing, male fertility and the incidence of cataracts.

It is present in many foods, including plant oils, nuts, seeds, avocados, leafy greens, cereals and seafood, and the chart shows selected best sources.

The tolerable upper intake level at which no adverse effects are observed during long-term use from supplements is 540mg (around 800IU). However, in the EU, a safety factor was used to establish an upper safe level of 300mg (450IU) per day from supplements.

People using anti-coagulant drugs such as Warfarin should avoid very high intakes as vitamin E also acts to thin the blood. The higher the diet is in polyunsaturated fats, which are vulnerable to oxidation in the body, the more vitamin E the diet should contain. Luckily, foods that are rich in PUFAs also tend to be rich in E.

VITAMIN K

EC NRV 75mcg, USA DV 120mcg.

Vitamin K is a group of fat-soluble compounds essential for the normal clotting of blood. It is widespread in food in small quantities, but the best sources are dark green leafy vegetables and the skins of fruit and vegetables.

It can also be synthesized in the intestines so deficiency in adults is extremely rare. Some new-born babies are deficient and so vitamin K may then be given as a supplement.

The UK Government's Expert Group on Vitamins and Minerals says that recommendations on intake haven't been established and there is insufficient data to establish a safe upper limit which is why no RNI appears here for the UK. However, the EGVM do say that 'for guidance purposes, a daily supplementary intake of 1mg/day would be unlikely to result in adverse effects'.

Selected best sources of vitamin E (mg per 100g)	
Wheatgerm oil	136
Sunflower oil	41
Safflower oil	41
Sunflower seeds	38
Hazelnuts, shelled	25
Sun-dried tomatoes	24
Almonds	24
Rapeseed oil	22
Cod liver oil	20
Mayonnaise	19
Corn oil	17
Soya oil	16
Groundnut oil	15
Olive oil	14.4
Pine nuts	13.5
Popcorn, plain	11
Peanuts, plain	11
Brazil nuts, shelled	7
Sweet potato, baked	6
Tomato puree	5.4
Prawns, shelled	2.2
Spinach	2
Avocado	2
Broccoli	1.5
Asparagus	1.1

VITAMIN C
ASCORBIC ACID

UK DRV 40mg, EC NRV 80mg,
USA DV 90mg.

Vitamin C is probably the best-known vitamin, with a protective role for the body, helping to maintain a healthy immune system. It is necessary for building connective tissue, bones and teeth, and helps the healing of wounds and fractures. It also helps us to absorb iron. The vitamin is water-soluble, meaning it can't be stored in the body and so we need to have it every day in our diet.

Extra vitamin C may be needed at certain times, for example when the body is under stress such as illness or high workload, and for certain people, for example smokers, heavy drinkers, and people working in polluted atmospheres.

Adequate vitamin C intake can help protect your health. It appears to lower the risk of cardiovascular disease for example. Low levels are associated both with high blood pressure and with increased risk of heart attack.

However, as with many nutrients, while enough is important, too much can have adverse effects, so the USA has set an upper limit for adults of 2g a day and the UK Department of Health puts the limit at 1g for taking supplements. High dose supplements don't offer any further protection than that from adequate intake in the diet and could even be harmful.

Much research has been done on whether or not vitamin C levels can alter the outcome of colds. The consensus seems to be that it may reduce the length and severity of some colds at a daily intake of up to 200mg.

A deficiency of the vitamin can

Antioxidants – how healthy are they really?

WHEN THE FIRST and second editions of this book were published, antioxidants were perhaps THE big story of the time. Scientists had decided that ageing and various forms of disease were brought about because of 'free radicals' in our bodies (the by-product of energy production). Excess free radicals could cause cell damage, it was decided, and caused oxidation which could, for example, cause arteries to harden.

The answer, it seemed to be, was for us all to get more antioxidants into our diets. These antioxidants, such as vitamins C and E, beta-carotene, selenium, would, we were told, 'mop up' the free radicals or neutralize them and thus stop them damaging our bodies.

We could increase antioxidants in our diet quite easily by eating more fruit and vegetables and the other foods rich in these antioxidants. But over the years, many people have chosen to get their antioxidants by taking them in the form of supplements.

And that has seen a conundrum emerge. Several large trials and meta-analyses of past trials have found that taking antioxidant supplements does nothing at all to help us live longer. Some have even found the reverse.

It now seems that free radicals are not the 100% baddies they have been made out to be but actually have important roles to play in our bodies – fighting infection and even cancers.

In any case, a healthy body synthesizes its own natural forms of antioxidants. Flooding the body with antioxidant supplements may mean that it doesn't get the chance to trigger this process, and so in the long term, the response disappears.

However – these studies looked at antioxidants taken in supplement form. As far as we know, if you eat a diet moderately high in natural antioxidants in food, they may be of benefit. But scientists are still undecided whether antioxidants in foods are actually what helps people to be healthier or live longer – some think it could be other factors in the food, or a combination of antioxidants and other factors.

The message right now seems to be – unless you have been advised by your doctor or specialist to take anti-oxidants in the form of supplements, stick with normal food – healthy fruits, vegetables, grains, pulses and so on will provide you with the compounds you need for health with minimal chance of negative effects. ■

result in poor wound healing, bleeding gums, lowered resistance to infection and long-term can result in scurvy, symptoms of which include muscle pain and tiredness, although this is rarely seen today.

An excess of the vitamin may have a laxative effect including diarrhoea and gastric upset.

Vitamin C is found mainly in fruits and vegetables, and is easily lost in storage, processing, preparation and cooking. For example, fresh peas contain 24mg vitamin C per 100g; canned peas only 1mg. The only plants that contain no vitamin C are unsprouted grains and dried pulses. The Food Charts at the back of the book give more information on foods with a good content of vitamin C.

Selected best sources of vitamin C (mg per 100g)	
Rosehip syrup	295
Guava	230
Chilli peppers, red	225
Sweet red peppers	140
Blackcurrants	130
Sweet peppers, yellow	130
Chilli peppers, green	120
Spring greens, steamed	77
Strawberries	77
Kale, steamed	71
Papaya	60
Brussels sprouts, steamed	60
Kiwifruit	59
Cabbage, red	55
Mangetout peas	54
Oranges	54
Broccoli, steamed	44
Sweetcorn, baby, steamed	39
Nectarines	37
Mangos	37
Grapefruit	36
Green leaf salad	36

THE B VITAMINS

There are many different types of B vitamin, but six are perhaps of most importance for humans and they are described in detail here. They are water-soluble vitamins, meaning the body can't store them and so you need to get them in your diet every day.

They are synergistic, working together in the body to promote healthy growth, the development and maintenance of the nervous system, for body maintenance and food digestion and for a healthy metabolism. Each, however, also has its own role to play.

The vitamins in the B group, like vitamin C, are depleted through the storage, processing, preparation and cooking of food (see page 92–111 for notes on how best to retain these water-soluble vitamins in food). And certain people will need more of the B group than others – for example, people who smoke, who are ill or stressed, who drink alcohol.

In general, it isn't advisable to take supplements of just one of the B vitamins as they do work together.

VITAMIN B1 (THIAMIN)

UK RNI 0.8mg (females) 1.0mg (males), EC NRV 1.1mg, USA DV 1.2mg

Needed to help release the energy from carbohydrate foods, vitamin B1 also helps to ensure that the brain and nerves have adequate glucose for their needs. A lack of B1 can lead to the deficiency disease beriberi. Heavy drinkers of alcohol may be short of B1. An excess isn't harmful as it is excreted in the urine. B1 is found in a variety of foods especially pork, bacon and nuts.

VITAMIN B2 (RIBOFLAVIN)

UK RNI 1.1mg (females) 1.3mg (males),
EC NRV 1.4mg, USA DV 1.3mg

This B vitamin is involved in the release of energy too, but more from fat and protein than carbohydrate. Adequate vitamin B2 is needed to maintain healthy skin and mucous membrane (for example, in the mouth) and if deficiency occurs symptoms may include a sore mouth. Excess B2 is excreted, so there is no safe upper limit. B2 is found in many foods, particularly rich sources are offal, dairy produce and fortified breakfast cereals.

VITAMIN B3 (NIACIN)

UK RNI 13mg (females) 17mg (males), EC
NRV 16mg, USA DV 16mg.

Vitamin B3 is also involved in the release of energy from food and can be manufactured from the amino acid tryptophan within the body, but the UK DoH has still offered RNIs to ensure adequate intake. A deficiency results in the disease pellagra, which initially affects the skin and can be very serious if left untreated. Excess B3 (over 3g a day) can cause liver and kidney damage, and dilation of the blood vessels. B3 is found in meat, fish and fortified breakfast cereals, as well as a variety of other foods.

VITAMIN B6 (PYRIDOXINE)

UK RNI 1.2 mg (females) 1.4mg (males),
EC NRV 1.4mg, USA DV 1.3mg

Vitamin B6 is important for the metabolism protein and carbohydrates and is also involved in the production of B3 from tryptophan. It is necessary for healthy blood as it helps to form haemoglobin, the substance that carries oxygen around the body. There is anecdotal evidence that B6 may help ease pre-menstrual symptoms, but the DoH in the UK says that 'you should be able to get the vitamin B6 you need by eating a varied and balanced diet. If you take vitamin B6 supplements, don't take too much as this could be harmful.'

B6 sources include meat, eggs, fish and whole grains.

VITAMIN B12

UK RNI 1.5 mcg, EC NRV 1.4mg, USA
DV 1.3mg

Vitamin B12 is necessary for the formation of blood cells and nerves, and a deficiency leads to vitamin B12 deficiency anaemia – a type of anaemia that causes the body to produce abnormally large red blood cells that can't function properly. Lack of B12 can also cause other health problems including tiredness, lack of energy, a sore and red tongue, mouth ulcers, muscle weakness, disturbed vision, depression and problems with memory. B12 is only found naturally in animal produce and seaweed but a little can be synthesized in the body by gut bacteria. Excellent sources of B12 are offal and meat, while dairy produce also contains some.

SELECTED BEST SOURCES OF B VITAMINS

Vitamin B1 (mg per 100g)

Quorn chunks	36.6
Yeast extract	4.1
Vegeburger, grilled	2.4
Vegetable pate	2.1
Ready Brek, prepared	1.8
Sunflower seeds	1.6
Special K	1.3
Bacon, back, grilled	1.2
Peanuts, plain	1.1
Pork fillet	1.0
Bran Flakes	1.0
Wholewheat spaghetti (dry weight)	1.0

Vitamin B2 (mg per 100g)

Yeast extract	11.9
Lambs' liver	4.6
Shreddies	2.2
Special K	1.8
Grapenuts	1.5
Weetabix	1.5
Nori seaweed, dried	1.3
Bran/oatbran flakes,	1.3
Vegetable pâté	1.3
Liver pâté	1.2
Venison, roast	0.7
Goats milk cheese	0.6
Cheddar cheese	0.5
Eggs	0.5
Tomato sauce for pasta	0.5

Vitamin B3 (mg per 100g)

Yeast extract	73
Start cereal	24
Special K	23
Chicken breast, no skin	22
Lambs' liver	21
Tuna canned in oil	21
Grapenuts	20
Turkey, light meat, roast	20
Peanuts, plain	19
Pork fillet, lean	18
Fruit 'n Fibre	17
Ovaltine powder	17
Tuna, fresh	17
Shiitake mushrooms, dried	15
Swordfish, grilled	14
Mackerel, grilled	13

Vitamin B6 (mg per 100g)

Wheatgerm	3.3
Turbot, grilled	2.5
Fruit 'n Fibre	1.8
All Bran	1.3
Lentils, dry	0.9
Salmon, grilled	0.8
Turkey, light meat	0.8
Squid	0.7
Walnuts, shelled	0.7
Beef steak, lean	0.7
Chicken breast, no skin, grilled	0.6
Hazelnuts, shelled	0.6
Swordfish, grilled	0.6
Baked potato	0.5

Vitamin B12 (mcg per 100g)

Lambs' liver	54
Seaweed, nori, dried	27.5
Mussels, shelled weigh	22
Oysters, shelled weigh	17
Sardines, canned in oil	15
Herring, grilled	15
Anchovies, canned, drained	11
Rabbit meat	10
Scallops, steamed	9
Prawns, cooked	8
Skate, grilled	8
Salmon, steamed	6
Tuna, canned in oil	5
Eggs	2.5
Lean beef	2
Cheddar cheese	1.1

FOLATE

UK RNI 200mcg, EC NRV 200mcg,
USA DV 400mcg

Also known as folic acid (which in fact is not the natural form of folate) or in recent years as vitamin B9, folate is necessary for the formation of blood cells and for proper development in infants. It's routinely given in pregnancy to help prevent birth defects such as spina bifida. Deficiency can lead to a type of anaemia called folate deficiency anaemia and can also contribute to high levels of the amino acid homocysteine in the body, which has been linked to heart disease. In the USA, flour is fortified with the vitamin mandatorily, and is due to be fortified in the UK in 2019. Folate is found in offal, leafy greens, whole grains, nuts, pulses and fortified breakfast cereals.

Folate (mcg per 100g)	
Yeast extract	1150
Chicken livers	995
Black-eyed beans, dry	630
Soya beans, dry	370
Grapenuts	350
Soya flour	345
Wheatgerm	331
Special K	330
Cornflakes	250
Lamb's liver	205
Chickpeas, dry	180
Asparagus, steamed	155
Baby sweetcorn, steamed	152
Purple broccoli, steamed	140
Swiss-style muesli	140
Red kidney beans, dry	130
Brussels sprouts, steamed	110

MINERALS

Minerals are inorganic substances, and various vital body processes as well as normal development are reliant on adequate intakes of them. Altogether, 15 minerals have been classed as essential in the diet. The major minerals, needed in larger quantities, are calcium, magnesium, potassium, sodium and phosphorus. Iron and zinc, although needed in milligrams rather than grams (1,000mg=1g), are also usually classed as major minerals.

The 'trace elements' needed in much smaller (but equally essential) quantities are selenium, copper, fluoride, iodine, manganese, chromium and cobalt.

In general, the three main functions of minerals are as constituents of bones and teeth (particularly calcium, magnesium and phosphorus); as salts regulating body fluids (sodium, potassium and chloride); and as components of enzymes and hormones, regulating or helping all the functions of the body, including the nervous system, blood supply and energy release (most minerals).

A deficiency of certain minerals may result in all kinds of health problems, such as anaemia (iron), osteoporosis (calcium) and weak immune system (zinc). Research over the last few years is also finding strong evidence that optimum intake of certain minerals can help to prevent heart disease, for example, calcium, magnesium and the antioxidant mineral selenium.

Minerals are present in most foods

Selected best sources of calcium (mg per 100 g)	
Poppy seeds	1580
Parmesan cheese	1200
Gruyère cheese	950
Kombu seaweed, dried	900
Whitebait in flour, fried	860
Cheddar, reduced-fat	840
Edam	770
Cheddar, full-fat	740
Sesame seeds	670
Mozzarella, full-fat	590
Sardines canned in brine, drained, including bones	540
Brie	540
Tofu, steamed	510
Danish blue	500
Sardines, canned in oil, drained, including bones	500
Nori seaweed, dried	430
Feta cheese	360
White chocolate	270
Almonds, shelled	240
Soya beans, dry weight	240
Figs, ready-to-eat	230
Milk chocolate	220
Muesli	200
Low-fat natural yoghurt	190
Goats'-milk soft cheese	190
Haricot beans, dry weight	180
Spinach	170
Brazil nuts, shelled	170
Chickpeas, dry weight	160
Naan bread	160
Kale, steamed	150
Greek yoghurt, sheep's	150
White bread, French	130
Dairy vanilla ice-cream	130
Semi-skimmed milk	120
Skimmed milk	120
Tilapia fish	120
White bread	120
Whole milk	115
Prawns, cooked and shelled	110
Purple sprouting broccoli, steamed	110
Spring greens, steamed	75
White cabbage	49
Broccoli, steamed	40

and drinks, in varying quantities. A healthy diet, providing adequate calories, should ensure intake is at least the minimum recommended, but minerals are not always easily absorbed by the body (calcium needs vitamin D, for example, and absorption of several minerals can be hindered by certain acids in other foods). Also, we may need more than the minimum recommended levels at certain times; for example, women with heavy periods may need extra iron, and so on. In the pages ahead, we look at the main minerals that may be lacking in our diet.

For more information on the body's requirements of minerals throughout every stage of life, see Section Three. For notes on recommended daily amounts and the pitfalls of supplementation, see page 29. The Food Charts at the back of the book give information on the mineral content of many common foods.

CALCIUM

UK RNI 700mg, EC NRV 800mg, USA DV 1,300mg

Calcium, as the major constituent of bone and tooth mineral, is the mineral needed in greatest quantities. The average human body contains about 1kg of calcium and around a gram a day is needed to maintain that level.

Adequate calcium intake is vital throughout life. In infants and through to adulthood, it is vital to ensure peak bone mass is reached. In women it is important to help prevent osteoporosis in later life. Calcium is also important for the smooth functioning of the muscles, including the heart, for blood clotting, for nerve function and other activities.

There is some evidence that low calcium levels may be linked with CHD, as hardness of tap water is related to lower CHD. Symptoms of deficiency include muscle cramps and weakness. Rickets is a disease caused by calcium (or calcium absorption) deficiency. Only about 40% of the calcium that we eat is absorbed. Adequate vitamin D is needed for this process (see Vitamins, page 30) and absorption can also be affected by certain foods. Essential fatty acids may help absorption, and exercise helps maintain bone mass.

Foods high in insoluble fibre, such as wheat bran and whole grains, can hinder absorption (if taken at the same time), due to the phytates they contain (although this effect may be temporary), and so can oxalates, found in spinach, rhubarb, chard, chocolate and beetroot, and the tannin in tea and coffee. If you drink tea or coffee, leave a gap between your meal and your drink. A diet containing very high levels of protein (120 g a day or more) may cause bone demineralization and calcium to be excreted in the urine.

Calcium works closely in the body with magnesium, and a high calcium intake may require additional magnesium. Calcium needs of special groups of people (e.g. pregnant women, children and the elderly) are discussed in Section Three. Calcium in a vegetarian diet is discussed on page 84. Rich sources of calcium include cheese, yoghurt and milk, dark green leafy vegetables, white bread and flour (fortified). Canned fish (such as sardines and salmon) can be a rich source, but only if the bones are eaten.

IRON

UK RNI 14.8mg (females 19-50) 8.7mg (males, and females 50-64), EC NRV 14mg, USA DV 18mg

Iron's main function is to carry oxygen from the lungs to all the cells of the body. Half the body 's store is used to make haemoglobin, which acts as the carrier. Iron can also increase resistance to infection and help the healing process. Lack of adequate iron (or iron absorption) leads to anaemia, with symptoms including tiredness, pallor, weakness and lack of energy.

Women, in particular, need to ensure their diet is high enough in iron as it is lost in the blood through menstruation. It is thought that many women are iron-deficient. However, caution needs to be taken if using supplements – excess iron can cause stomach upsets, constipation and kidney damage and very high doses can be fatal, and the DoH says more than 20mg a day is too much.

Iron is supplied in the diet by both animal foods and plants. Iron from meat sources is better absorbed than that from plant sources, but if body stores of iron are depleted, or when needs are great, then absorption from plants increases.

Absorption is affected by other factors, including intake of phytates, oxalates and tannins (see Calcium) and also by calcium itself, which can bind with iron.

Vitamin C helps iron absorption, and certain foods, such as dark leafy greens, contain both iron and vitamin C in good amounts and thus are particularly useful. Other iron-rich foods should be eaten when possible with foods rich in vitamin C. Some examples of this are cabbage and

Selected best sources of iron (mg per 100g)

Curry powder	58.3
Ground ginger	46.3
Nori seaweed, dried	19.6
Special K	13.3
Ready Brek	13.2
Black pudding	12.3
All Bran	12.0
Lentils, green or brown, dry weight	11.1
Cocoa powder	10.5
Sesame seeds	10.4
Pumpkin seeds	10.0
Soya beans, dry weight	9.7
Chicken liver	9.2
Soya mince (TVP)	9.0
Lentils, red, dry weight	7.6
Lambs' liver	7.5
Liver pâté	7.4
Weetabix	7.4
Peaches, dried, no-soak	6.8
Haricot beans, dry weight	6.7
Fruit 'n Fibre, plus most other commercial cereals	6.7
Red kidney beans, dry weight	6.4
Cashew nuts, plain	6.2
Pot barley, dry weight	6.0
Couscous, dry weight	5.0
Bulgar wheat, dry weight	4.9
Apricots, dried, no-soak	3.4
Beef, lean	2.1
Kale, lightly boiled	2.0
Eggs	1.9
Lamb, lean	1.6
Bacon, lean grilled	1.6
Brown rice, dry weight	1.4
Baked beans in tomato sauce	1.4
Spring greens, lightly boiled	1.4
Broccoli, lightly boiled	1.0

lentil soup, a snack of an orange and a handful of cashew nuts, omelette with peas and grilled tomatoes, and steak with broccoli.

Good iron sources are offal and red meats, dark green vegetables, pulses and whole grains, nuts and seeds, and fortified breakfast cereals. Many dried herbs are excellent sources but are not used in great enough quantities to make much contribution to your diet. Ground spices can do so, though – for example, a teaspoon of ground ginger gives nearly 1mg, and curry powder slightly more.

ZINC

UK RNI 7mg (females) 9.5mg (males), EC 10mg, USA DV 11mg.

Zinc is present in all our body tissue and helps the activities of a wide variety of enzymes. It is essential for normal growth and development; for a healthy reproductive system and fertility, and for healthy foetal development. It helps to keep skin healthy, helps wound healing, regulates the sense of taste and is important for immune system strength. A recent study found that taking zinc acetate tablets can significantly reduce the length of common colds when taken in high doses of up to 92mg a day. At levels this high, zinc may hinder copper and possibly iron absorption, but the participants in a Finnish study showed no adverse side-effects.

A deficiency of zinc during pregnancy and infancy can cause retarded growth and sexual development. A deficiency in adulthood can cause increased risk of infections, skin and hair problems, slow wound healing, impaired sense of taste and smell, low sperm count, night blindness and other problems. There is also some evidence that low zinc coupled with high copper levels is linked to violent behaviour. Zinc levels may be affected by smoking and alcohol. It is found in greatest quantities in meat and dairy produce. It is also found in good amounts in whole-grain cereals and pulses, but

like calcium and iron its absorption may be hindered by eating foods rich in phytates, oxalates and tannins (see page 39).

Both calcium and iron can also interfere with zinc absorption, though it is thought that this is only of relevance at doses supplied in supplements. People at risk from zinc deficiency may then be smokers and heavy drinkers, some vegetarians, people with long-term illness, and anyone who eats a poor or meagre diet.

SELENIUM

UK RNI 60mcg (females) 75 mcg (males), EC NRV 55mcg, USA DV 55 mcg

Selected best sources of zinc (mg per 100g)	
Wheatgerm	17.0
Calves' liver	14.2
Poppy seeds	8.5
Oysters, raw, weight including shells	8.3
Quorn	7.5
Cocoa powder	6.9
All Bran	6.7
Pumpkin seeds	6.6
Pine nuts	6.5
Seaweed, nori, dried	6.4
Beefsteak	6.0
Cashew nuts, plain	5.9
Crab, canned in brine, drained	5.7
Corned beef	5.5
Fresh crab, meat only	5.5
Sesame seeds	5.3
Parmesan cheese	5.3
Pecan nuts, shelled	5.3
Lamb leg, roasted, lean	5.2
Sunflower seeds	5.1

Selenium is an important trace element – it is an antioxidant (see page 33) and, as such, may help to protect us from heart disease and premature ageing. In one large American study, selenium supplementation at 200mcg per day was associated with a 50% drop in deaths from cancers of the lung, prostate and colon but other studies have been inconclusive, and selenium also seems to increase the risk of non-melanoma skin cancer.

Working with vitamin E, selenium helps control the production of hormone-like substances called prostaglandins, and is important for normal growth, fertility, thyroid action, healthy skin and hair, and more. One study showed that women with low levels of selenium had increased risk of miscarriage and other tests show that selenium levels are often low in people with Crohn's disease and HIV.

Because selenium comes from plants or plant-eating animals, the amount we eat relates to that in the soil – some areas, including the UK, have

Selected best sources of selenium (mcg per 100g)

Brazil nuts, shelled	1917
Mixed nuts and raisins	170
Lambs' kidneys,	160
Dried mushrooms	110
Lentils, green or brown, dry weight	105
Tuna, canned in oil, drained	90
Tuna, canned in brine, drained	78
Squid	66
Lemon sole	60
Tuna, fresh	57
Mullet, red, grilled	54
Wheat flour, wholemeal	53
Sardines, canned in oil, drained	49
Sunflower seeds	49
Swordfish	45
Mussels, cooked	43
Sardines, grilled	38
Wholemeal bread	35
Cod	33
Salmon	31
Pork, fillet, raw	31
Cashew nuts, plain	29
Prawns, cooked	23
Walnuts, shelled	19

Selenium is, however, toxic in excess, producing nerve disorders and hair and nail loss. The UK Department of Health says that we should be able to get all the selenium we need by eating a balanced diet, but that taking supplements up to 350mcg a day is unlikely to cause you any harm. In the USA, the safe upper limit for selenium is 400 micrograms a day in adults, with levels above that considered an overdose. This is equivalent to little more than four Brazil nuts a day as one Brazil contains about 96mcg selenium.

MAGNESIUM

UK RNI 270mg (females) 300mg (males), EC NRV 375mg, USA DV 420mg

Magnesium is present throughout our bodies and has many roles to play. It works with calcium to maintain healthy bones, it helps release energy

Selected best sources of magnesium (mg per 100g)

Cocoa powder	520
Brazil nuts, shelled	410
Sunflower seeds	390
Sesame seeds	370
Instant coffee (dry weight)	330
Pine nuts	270
Cashew nuts, plain	270
Soya mince granules	270
Soya beans, dry weight	250
Liquorice	170
Hazelnuts and walnuts, shelled	160
Shredded Wheat	130

low levels; the USA level is high. One recent study found that UK intake is an average of only 34mcg per day – about half that required.

Unlike other minerals, the amounts in the food we eat can't be guaranteed (as this depends on where it comes from), but brazil nuts are a very rich source and fish, seeds and offal should all be good sources. Levels listed here are a guide only.

and to absorb nutrients, as well as regulating temperature, nerves and muscle function. It is important for the secretion of hormones as well as supporting our immune system. Adequate levels are important to maintain a healthy heart and blood pressure. Lower levels of CHD have been noted in hard-water (calcium- and magnesium-rich) areas.

Magnesium helps to regulate blood sugars, there is evidence it can help relieve PMS and may be involved in preventing osteoporosis. If magnesium is deficient, symptoms include muscle weakness and abnormal heart rhythms, tiredness, appetite loss and cramps. Absorption can be hindered by heavy alcohol consumption.

Magnesium-rich foods include whole grains, nuts and seeds, and green vegetables. Tap water can also be a good source if you live in a hard-water area.

PHOSPHORUS
UK RNI 550mg, EC NRV 700mg, USA DV 1250mg

About 1kg of bodyweight in every adult is phosphorus and most is in the skeleton. It is an essential part of all body cells, helping in the release of energy and regulating protein activity. As it is a major constituent of all plant and animal cells and added to many processed foods, deficiency in the diet is not likely and, on average, we eat about twice the UK RNI.

High intakes without adequate calcium may upset the body's phosphorus/calcium balance and cause bone demineralization, and so may be a factor in osteoporosis. Luckily, many foods high in phosphorus are also high in calcium – milk and cheese, for example.

Other foods rich in phosphorus include meats, fish and eggs. For women with risk factors for osteoporosis it may be wise to keep a watch on phosphorus intake, but not by cutting back on a nutritious natural diet.

POTASSIUM
UK RNI 3,500mg, EC NRV 2,000mg, USA DV 4,700mg

Potassium works with sodium to regulate body fluids and is essential for correct functioning of the cells. It regulates nerves, heart-beat and blood pressure. If the diet is high in sodium, more potassium will be needed to help prevent fluid retention. In trials, young men who had a low potassium intake (390mg per day) were less able to excrete excess sodium and their blood pressure was higher than when they took the RNI. High blood pressure can be lowered by a diet low in sodium and high in potassium.

Potassium is found in a wide range of foods, and clinical deficiency is unusual, but diets low in fresh fruit and vegetables, which are good sources, and high in salt may create

an imbalance. Also, people taking diuretics or laxatives, or on some types of drugs, e.g. steroids, may excrete too much potassium.

Severe deficiency can result in serious heart problems – even heart attack. Excess is unlikely in a normal diet, but very high levels of supplementation would be toxic. Low-sodium, potassium-rich foods include dried fruits, pulses, nuts, potatoes, bananas, garlic, onions and many other fruits and vegetables.

SODIUM

UK RNI 1,600mg, EC NRV not set, WHO (less than) 2,000mg, USA DV 2,400mg

The UK reference nutrient intake for adults for sodium is 1,600mg, which represents 4g of salt a day (as salt contains 40% sodium and 60% chloride). This is a target salt intake – it doesn't represent ideal or optimum consumption level, but an achievable goal. That is because on average we (adults) still consume too much sodium/salt in our diets – around 8g of salt, or double the RNI, and the consensus for many decades has been that this is too much. The National Health Service says that the upper safe limit is 6g of salt a day (2,400mg sodium). The recommended maximums for children appear on page 179.

In recent decades, a high salt diet has been consistently linked with increased risk of high blood pressure and cardiovascular disease which is why health departments across the world have set goals for reducing salt consumption and why governments have taken measures to reduce the sodium content of processed foods.

However, in the past few years, doubt has been thrown on the idea that we should reduce our salt intake as much as possible for health protection. For example, in 2016 one very large global analysis of approximately 130,000 people found that low salt intake – under 3g of salt or 1,200mg sodium a day- was strongly linked with an increased risk of strokes, heart attacks and death in people with normal blood pressure.

The conclusion was that while lowering sodium intake in people with high blood pressure who are currently eating a high sodium diet (about 10% of adults) is still important to help prevent CVD, that in people with normal or low blood pressure, a low salt diet is not ideal.

This is why heart experts writing in the *European Heart Journal* in 2017 pointed out that there is little evidence supporting tough sodium intake guidelines recommended by the American Heart Association who say reducing sodium intake to 1,500mg is desirable (to lower BP further than what will be achieved at a level of 2,400mg a day).

A moderate salt intake, then, may be the compromise for most of us without existing high BP – somewhere between the RNI of 4g salt (1,600mg sodium) up to the UK Government's stated maximum for adults of 6g salt (2,400mg sodium), as part of a healthy diet containing plenty of fresh fruit and vegetables to help promote the sodium potassium balance.

Sodium is unlike all other minerals necessary to humans in that it is the only one we recognise as having its own taste (as part of salt). So we add it to foods to enhance their flavour, for example. Sodium also occurs

naturally, in low or fairly low amounts, in foods such as meat, fish, shellfish, vegetables and even fruit.

Sodium helps regulate the body's fluid balance along with potassium, and is present in all body fluids, especially outside the cells. Sodium is also necessary for nerve and muscle activity but excess sodium in the diet is linked with fluid retention and kidney stones, and a diet high in sodium increases the need for potassium.

Sodium deficiency in a healthy person is not common, but may happen during heavy or prolonged exercise especially in high temperatures when it is lost through perspiration and the urine. Signs of sodium deficiency are cramps, weakness, fatigue, nausea and thirst.

Main sources of sodium in the diet are salt used in cooking and at the table (approximately 20% of the sodium we eat), and many manufactured products including stock cubes, bottled sauces, cured and smoked foods, pickles, savoury snacks, canned vegetables and cereals. That said, the levels of salt in many of these foods are constantly being reduced and there are also many 'low' or 'reduced' salt versions of favourite foods in the shops.

As an example of how you would reach your UK RNI of 4g salt a day, you would eat, for example, a 30g bowl of corn flakes with milk, an average Cheddar cheese (30g) sandwich on two slices of brown bread with 10g butter and 10g sweet pickle, a 25g pack of plain salted crisps, and a vegetable and chicken stir-fry with 10ml soya sauce, which in total contain over 4g salt.

For people who want or need to cut down their salt intake, the easiest way

Selected Foods and their sodium/salt content* (per 100g)

	Sodium (mg)	Salt (g)
Chicken stock cubes	16,300	40.7
Soya sauce	7,120	17.8
Bacon rashers, back, grilled	2,700	6.7
Parma ham	2,000	5
Smoked salmon	1,880	4.7
Pretzels	1,720	4.3
Danish blue cheese	1,286	3.2
Tomato ketchup	940	2.3
Sweet pickle	811	2
Corn flakes	729	1.8
Cheddar cheese	653	1.6
Butter, salted	643	1.6
Prawns, shelled	566	1.4
Potato crisps, salted	527	1.3

* All values approximate and do not refer to manufactured 'low or lower salt' versions

NOTE: Health departments across the world often quote sodium, rather than salt levels, while food labels usually quote only salt amounts in a product. To convert the amount of sodium in a food to salt, simply multiply it by 2.5. E.g. – 100g prawns contain 566mg sodium, so they contain (566 x 2.5) 1415mg salt or, for the amount in grams, approx 1.4g salt (as there are 1000mg in 1 gram).

is to reduce the amount of processed foods and added salt they eat and get a natural diet high in vegetables, salads, fruit, pulses, nuts and seeds.

OTHER MINERALS

Fluoride: A deficiency will encourage tooth decay, but symptoms are rare as most of our dietary fluoride comes from fluoridated tap water and toothpaste, as well as in tea.

Iodine: Found most abundantly in dairy milk and seafood. Required for thyroid gland functioning, and deficiency can cause goitre, but in the UK, intakes are well above the RNI of 140mcg a day though this may be declining in recent years as non-dairy milks become more popular.

Chromium: Important for helping to control blood glucose levels and insulin function and may help to control blood cholesterol. There is no RNI, but safe levels have been concluded to be up to 25mcg a day. Meat, offal, eggs, seafood, cheese and whole grains are good sources. Some people take chromium supplements to help minimise hunger and help burn fat when trying to lose weight, but the claims for the supplements are not fully supported by science and taking them may have dangerous side effects.

Copper, sulphur, manganese: Deficiencies of these trace elements are rare, although a diet very high in zinc may inhibit absorption of copper.

PLANT CHEMICALS – WHAT THEY ARE AND WHAT THEY DO

Many food scientists now believe that for your health's sake, it may well be even more important to eat a diet rich in vegetables and other plant foods than it is to cut down on saturated fat and 'junk food'. Here we look at the fascinating world of phytochemicals in food, and how they can protect your health.

Phytochemicals are compounds that occur naturally in plant foods such as fruits, vegetables, grains, pulses, nuts and seeds. Phyto is the Greek word for plant, hence phytochemicals. These tend to be compounds which aren't nutrients as such but have been described as 'biologically active non-nutrients'.

There are literally thousands of different phytochemicals and they can be present in plants in quite high amounts. They include the substances responsible for giving the plant its colour, flavour, odour and other traits – its particular unique characteristics, you could say. A plant can contain more than one type.

They are nature's way of protecting the plant from disease, and much research has been carried out over the past 20 years or so to discover how they can help humans too. It seems they have much to offer. For example, they can stimulate the immune system, reduce inflammation, slow the growth rate of cancer cells, regulate hormones, help kill damaged cells in the body, fight carcinogenic substances in our food and in the air and prevent DNA damage.

To get the widest array of benefits, eating a variety of plant foods is important. Also, phytochemicals seem to work best in combination with one another and within their original plant host. This means that supplements containing extracted versions of them may not work nearly so well to provide benefits, or may not even work at all.

So when it comes to phytochemicals, the most clever way to get them is in a diet rich with a variety of plants. Here we look at some of the most researched phytochemical groups and see what they may do for you. See also Antioxidants on page 33. The 'special notes' column in the Food Charts at the end of the book gives information on phytochemicals in individual foods.

CAROTENES

There are hundreds of different carotenes, also called carotenoids.

Lycopene is the red pigment found in, for instance, tomatoes, and it may reduce the incidence of heart attacks by up to 50%, may lower LDL blood cholesterol and protect against various types of cancers including those of the prostate, lung and stomach.

Beta carotene is the orange pigment found, for instance, in carrots and butternut squash. Adequate intake has been linked with a lowered risk of certain cancers and may help slow cognitive decline and retain healthy lungs in older people and smokers, though the evidence for these benefits has not been consistent.

Lutein, found in dark green leafy vegetables, may also protect against cancers and protect eye health, as may *beta-cryptoxanthin*, found in mangoes, and *canthazanthin*, in mushrooms.

Zeaxanthin works with lutein to help eye health.

SULPHIDES

Onions, garlic, leeks and chives contain *allyl sulphides* (the chemicals that make your eyes water!), which seem to stimulate the immune system and may slow down the growth of cancers and ulcers. They may also fight cardio-vascular disease by, for example, favourably altering blood lipids and helping to prevent blood clots. They also seem to have a strong antibiotic and antiviral effect.

GLUCOSINOLATES

This group of phytochemicals acts as a natural pesticide for plants and is found mainly in green vegetables such as broccoli, Brussels sprouts, cabbage, kale and cauliflower. The stronger the taste, the higher the potency, research indicates.

Broccoli is a particularly rich source of glucosinolates which break down into *sulphoraphane* that stimulates our natural defences against disease. *Sinigrin* is found in large quantities in sprouts and it appears to suppress the growth of pre-cancerous cells. Watercress is rich in *isothiocyanate* which can break down and render harmless one of the main cancer-causing agents in tobacco smoke.

PHYTOESTROGENS

These are a group of phytochemicals with a structure similar to oestrogen, the female hormone that protects against heart disease and osteoporosis. There are two main types in our

diet – *isoflavones*, which belong to the flavonoid group and are found in pulses, particularly soya beans, for example, and *lignans*, present in high amounts in flax seeds, and in rye, barley and other cereals, as well as in lesser amounts in many fruits and vegetables. Both isoflavones and lignans have been shown in research studies to have the potential to reduce breast cancer risk. Several studies have found that eating soya beans can decrease the risk or recurrence of breast cancer and another long-term study found over 50% decrease in endometrial cancer in women who ate a diet high in plant oestrogens.

FLAVONOIDS

There are thousands of members of the bioflavonoid group! Some of the most researched include *catechins*, found in tea for example, which may help prevent certain types of cancer. *Hesperidin* is found in citrus fruits, and works to reduce inflammation in the body and help prevent chronic diseases.

Quercetin, found in black tea, red wine, berries, kale, onions and apples for example, has been shown to help prevent asthma and may reduce the risk of heart disease and some cancers.

PHYTOSTEROLS

Beta-sitosterol, campesterol, and *stigmasterol* are the main phytosterols found in plants. They have been shown to reduce plasma cholesterol levels and have anti-inflammatory, antidiabetic, and anticancer properties as well as showing promise in treating fatty liver disease. They are found in good quantities in unrefined vegetable oils, nuts, seeds, beans and whole grains, for example.

ALCOHOL

In 2015, the last year statistics have been available, 86% of men and 79% of women in England said they drank alcohol and the amount we are drinking has barely changed in recent years. According to the Department of Health, 31% of men and 16% of women drink over safe limits.

Most people drink because it makes them feel happy and relaxed by releasing endorphins to calm the brain. However, alcohol is a drug and an intoxicant with the power to kill – around ¾ of a bottle of whisky

(24 units of alcohol) consumed rapidly would produce coma and death in many people. Alcohol is also a source of energy, containing 7 calories a gram and, in the UK, it is estimated that between 6 and 9% of a drinker's calorie intake comes from alcohol.

While some alcoholic drinks do contain a few nutrients, (for example, beer contains some B vitamins, red wine contains some iron) alcohol is a non-essential energy provider.

At high intake levels it has many drawbacks, both major and minor. The short-term effects of intoxication can include a detrimental effect on brain power, decision making, sight, safety and so on which is why drink-driving laws are in place. Regular high alcohol intake can induce dependence and a host of health problems including weight gain, irregular heartbeat, increased risk of some cancers including cancers of the mouth, throat, liver, colon, bowel and breast, as well as fatty liver and diminished brain power. Binge drinking is linked to later life diabetes in young women. Alcohol abuse remains one of the major causes of ill health and premature death throughout the world.

However, at intakes below the safe limit, alcohol doesn't appear to pose health problems for most people, and there is some evidence that moderate drinkers have less incidence of cardiovascular disease than people who don't drink at all. This benefit may be linked partly with the plant chemicals found in alcohol, for example, flavonoids in red wine and in beer – but it could also be connected with alcohol's ethanol content.

That said, scientists studied data from nearly a million people and found that one drink a day increased the risk of atrial fibrillation (abnormal heart rhythm) by 8%, and two drinks by 16%, and so on. And a recent (2017) large review of over 100 studies from the World Cancer Research Fund found that just one glass of wine a day raised the risk of pre-menopausal breast cancer by 5% and post-menopausal by 9%.

More research needs to be done – and I'll drink to that …. but it may be a glass of low-alcohol wine. Many brands of alcohol-free or very low alcohol wines are now available and can make a good alternative to standard wines if you are trying to cut down alcohol

intake or even give up. Otherwise, a glass of decent red grape juice can be a good substitute, with all the health benefits of red wine and none of the drawbacks.

SO WHAT ARE SAFE LIMITS FOR ALCOHOL INTAKE?

To keep health risks from alcohol to a low level if you drink most weeks, in the UK, both men and women are advised not to drink more than 14 units a week, not to binge drink all the units in one evening, and to have at least one or two days alcohol free a week. (During pregnancy, see opposite.)

To that, I would add, taking your drink with a meal may confer optimum benefit and reduce any risks even further. Spread your weekly drink units out evenly through the week and avoid binge drinking (such as taking all your alcohol units for a week in one evening session).

One unit of alcohol is 8g or 10ml of pure alcohol, about the amount an adult can process in an hour. Fourteen units is equivalent to 6 pints of average-strength beer or ten small glasses of low-strength wine. For more information on what a unit is, see Box.

CALCULATING UNITS

With wine, and to a lesser extent with beer, there can be problems in working out exactly how many units you are getting. Many people think they are drinking one unit when they have a glass of wine, or reckon that half a bottle is three units, but sadly this is not often the case.

A glass of wine can easily be 1½, 2 units or even more, and half a bottle of wine can be 6 units or more. Why? Well, what is a 'glass' of wine? A

standard glass is 125ml, the kind pubs usually use. It is quite small, and you get six glasses to the 75cl bottle of wine. Restaurants and private homes usually use much bigger glasses, so a glass then might easily be two or more units.

The bigger problem is that the standard wine unit is based on a wine strength of only 8% alcohol by volume. This is a very low level for a modern wine. Average alcohol by volume today is nearer 12%. Some wines can go as high as 14-15% ABV.

A 125ml glass of 12% wine – 50% stronger than 8% wine – will, then, represent 1½ units, not 1, and a 12% bottle of wine will be 9 units, not 6. If you're drinking out of a bigger glass than standard, and having high-strength wine, you can see how easy it would be actually to be drinking twice as many units as you might think you are.

Beers also vary tremendously in alcohol by volume. One unit of beer is based on alcohol by volume of 3-4%. Some strong beers go up to 10%. Half a pint of such beer would be over 2 units.

HOW TO CALCULATE ACCURATELY HOW MANY UNITS YOU ARE DRINKING

Luckily there is an easy formula you can use to work out what you are drinking.

1. Find out the alcohol by volume (ABV) of what you are drinking – it will be printed on the bottle or can. This is a measure of the amount of pure alcohol as a percentage of the total volume of liquid in a drink.

2. Multiply the total volume of the drink in ml by the ABV. E.g. the drink is 500ml and the ABV is 10%, so the answer is (500 x 10) 5,000.

3. Now divide this result by 1,000. So the answer is (5,000 divided by 1,000) 5.

4. If you drink all the drink you will have consumed five units (source NHS UK).

Alternatively, if you go to Alcohol Concern's website they provide a calculator table – you just key in what you are drinking and how much, and it tells you how many units.

FACTORS THAT MAY EFFECT YOUR ALCOHOL TOLERANCE

✳ Women used to be given a lower safe alcohol limit than men before the new DoH advice was issued in 2016. This was said to be because women generally have a smaller liver (which processes the alcohol) than men and less of the alcohol-processing enzyme ADH in their stomachs so it was assumed they would metabolize alcohol less well than men. This probably still applies to at least some women, especially those who may be smaller than average.

✳ Drinking alcohol when you have not had anything to eat for several hours or more means it will affect you more quickly and more strongly.

✳ Alcohol with bubbles such as champagne will affect you more quickly as the air bubbles take the alcohol into the bloodstream more quickly.

✳ If you are run down, tired, stressed, weak or ill, your alcohol tolerance is likely to be diminished.

PREGNANCY

Alcohol affects female fertility and is associated with increased risk of miscarriage or preterm birth.

WHAT IS A UNIT OF ALCOHOL?

1 UNIT IS:

✳ 1 x 125ml glass 8% alcohol by volume wine.

✳ 300 ml (1⁄2 pint) standard beer or lager or stout (3-4% alcohol by volume).

✳ 300 ml (1⁄2 pint) standard medium cider.

✳ 1 single measure (25 ml) any spirit.

✳ 1 single measure (25 ml) port or sherry (20% alcohol by volume).

1½ UNITS IS:

✳ 1 x 125ml glass 12% alcohol by volume wine.

✳ 1 x 125ml glass champagne.

2 UNITS IS:

✳ 300 ml (1⁄2 pint) special strong lager (7% alcohol by volume).

✳ 600 ml (1 pint) ordinary beer or lager or stout (3-4%).

✳ typical home-poured measure of spirits (a double – 50ml).

Drinking alcohol during pregnancy, especially in the first trimester, can affect the foetus and foetal health and growth. Children exposed to alcohol in the uterus may suffer from serious cognitive effects and behavioural problems.

According to new (2016) guidelines from the UK's Chief Medical Officer:

• If you are pregnant or planning a pregnancy, the safest approach is not to drink alcohol at all, to keep risks to your baby to a minimum

• Drinking in pregnancy can lead to long-term harm to the baby, with the more you drink the greater the risk. ■

Putting it All Together

SO – HOW DO you turn all the theory and official advice about healthy eating into an actual, enjoyable daily diet for yourself? If you're feeling a bit daunted – don't be.

There is no real need to worry about the exact nutritional content of every morsel of food you eat— trying to count grams of fat or the protein or carbohydrate in every meal, for example, would not only be time-consuming but almost impossible.

Instead, I show you how to make choices for meals and snacks that will naturally give you all the nutrients you require and a few of those that you don't. We look at different meal opportunities, your preferences, and give you more information on the good choices to make when you go shopping.

Here you'll find hundreds of ideas, sample diets and plenty of inspiration.

YOUR HEALTHY EATING SUMMARY

CARBOHYDRATES

To get your 50% or so of carbohydrates you need to ensure that at every meal you have a good portion of minimally-refined or unrefined food/s such as any wholegrain cereal, wholemeal pasta, potatoes/sweet potatoes with skins on, wholegrain bread, or pulses for example. Veg and fruit will also add good carbs to the diet.

PROTEINS

Adding one or two protein–rich foods into most meals will mean you easily reach your target protein allowance. 'Protein rich' means choosing fish, game, poultry, pulses, eggs, hard cheese and lean meats. Portions of these can be quite small, especially for cheese and meats. Remember, if you

choose pulses, they also have an excellent starch content and will count towards your carbohydrate intake. Yogurt and milk are two other good sources of protein as are nuts, seeds and vegetable protein products such as Quorn and tofu. The Eatwell Guide illustration (see page 13) from Public Health England in 2016 has milk and dairy produce recommended intake at 8% of total calories, which represents about half the total protein needs of an adult.

FATS

As fat is present in a great many foods including the 'protein' foods we've just discussed, as well as many 'carbohydrate' foods and pulses, you don't really have to try that hard to reach your recommended levels of fat in the diet – about 30-35%. What you do need to do is choose foods that will provide you with the healthier fats such as olive or rapeseed oil, nuts, seeds, avocados and oily fish rather than choosing too many of the foods high in saturates. If you look at the Food Charts at the back of the book you'll be able to see the fat content of the foods that you enjoy.

VEGETABLES AND FRUIT

At most meals you also need about two portions of vegetables in good-sized portions as described overleaf – and make sure you get around two portions of fruit a day, too. The pages that follow offer many ideas for incorporating your veg and fruit into tasty meals and help you decide how many portions a day you really need.

DRINKS

Use what you drink as another chance to get nutrients — vitamin C from smoothies, calcium from milk or fortified soya milk, even phytochemicals

from tea — but don't forget that one of the best drinks of all is water; which will add no calories to your diet and can even help boost your metabolic rate. Try not to drink too much fruit juice which is stripped of most of its fibre. It's better to drink water and have a whole piece of fruit. Try to avoid all fizzy drinks and sweet squashes because these either contain added sugar – linked to obesity (see page 14) and tooth decay – or artificial sweeteners, which are also linked to obesity and may harm your gut bacteria as well as other negative side-effects (see right).

SNACKS

If you need a snack, look upon it as a chance to get some great nutrition into your body. Fresh fruit, nuts, seeds or a small piece of hard cheese or a slice of cooked chicken or tofu would be great. For larger snacks, add in good bread. If you only snack when you are hungry (which is a good idea) then you should always get some protein and fat in your snack, as these keep hunger at bay for longer and have a minimal effect on your blood sugar level.

SUGARS AND ALCOHOL

As by far the largest part of your daily calorie needs have now been taken up, you will only have a little room left for the sugars and for alcohol... add these to your diet in moderation, if at all. As a general guideline, take a maximum of 10% of your total day's food intake in the form of sugary, fatty or alcoholic extras and treats that add little in the way of important nutrients to your diet. Is it a good idea to replace sugar in your diet with artificial sweeteners? The short answer is that they don't perhaps have as much benefit as you might think as much research shows they do little to reduce a sweet tooth and may have other negative side-effects.

THE IMPORTANCE OF VARIETY

Balancing most of your meals this way forms the basis of a healthy diet for life. There is, however, one other very important tip, which will also ensure that most people will get adequate amounts of all the necessary vitamins, minerals, healthy bacteria and phytochemicals. The message is 'variety'. Eat as wide a variety of foods as you can – different sources of carbohydrate, varying types

Superfoods, food fads and fashion

The last guideline for good nutrition is this; try not to be gullible. There are a lot of food fads that come and go, new diets that ask you to cut out this food group or eat that food every day to stay healthy. Indeed, the latest figures show that one in ten of us cut a whole food group out of our diets.

Some products come into fashion and are hyped as the new 'superfood', but you can bet that you could get a similar nutrition profile from a food much easier to get, very much less expensive – and probably nicer tasting! Later in this section I'll be looking at some of these fads and ideas and analysing them for actual usefulness (see Restricted Eating page 88).

Variety and balance are perhaps the most important requirement for a healthy diet, and within this framework there can be room for all kinds of food. Don't cut nutritious foods from your diet or restrict yourself unnecessarily unless you know you have a particular health complaint which needs you to do so (see Section Two).

of protein, lots of different vegetables, salads and fruits. This is because even foods of the same group are not all good sources of the same things. For example, protein-rich cod is a good source of some B vitamins and selenium but contains little calcium, while protein-rich hard cheese is a good calcium source – and so on.

FIVE – OR TEN A DAY? INTERPRETING THE FRUIT AND VEGETABLE GUIDELINES

Departments of health throughout the Western world are advising us to eat at least five portions a day of fruits and vegetables for good health. Most are brilliant sources of fibre, vitamin C, plant chemicals and can help keep our microbiome (gut bacteria) thriving. But there is strong research that seems to show more would be better – indeed, some experts are suggesting ten portions as the ideal amount.

The American Heart Association suggests 8-10 portions a day for people on a 2,000 calories a day diet, and a large review of 95 world studies into the link between vegetable/fruit intake and health, published in 2017 in the *International Journal of Epidemiology*, found that an intake of 800g a day, rather than the 400g that five portions represents, had a significant effect in reducing the risk of cardiovascular disease and cancers and would reduce deaths by up to 20%.

At the moment in the UK, the official advice from Public Health England is still to go for at least five portions but going for more will have no negative effects long-term, probably has many benefits, and could be the way for health-conscious people to go.

WHAT COUNTS AS A PORTION?

The total weight of all five portions should usually be at least 400g of edible fruit or vegetable so that is an average of 80g per portion. Sometimes different weights count – e.g. in the case of dried fruit, 30g is a portion because after drying, fruit is much more energy dense as the water content has decreased considerably. The chart on page 57 shows what a portion is for a variety of fruits and vegetables.

Potatoes, sweet potatoes and yams are excluded as they are starchy carbohydrates and should be counted towards the day's complex carbohydrate intake. However, other root vegetables such as swede, turnip,

A 2017 survey by Diabetes UK found that two-thirds of people eat three or fewer portions of fruit/veg a day despite being aware of the 'five a day' mantra. Here are some examples of how easy it is to incorporate vegetables and fruit into your menus:

≫ **1** ≪

- Portion of berries on your breakfast cereal
- Handful of dried fruits mid-morning
- Large bowlful of mixed salad with bread and cheese at lunch-time
- Portion of carrots, portion of spinach and portion of peas with roast chicken in the evening.

(6 portions)

≫ **2** ≪

- Chopped apple and banana with breakfast yogurt
- 1 small avocado on toast at lunch-time followed by orange
- Double serving of mixed stir-fried Mediterranean vegetables (200 g/7 oz) in evening with baked fish.

(6 portions)

≫ **3** ≪

- 1 nectarine and a portion of melon chopped over breakfast muesli
- Large portion of home-made mixed vegetable soup for lunch (counts as 2 portions)
- Large bowlful of salad leaves and two grilled tomatoes with steak for supper.

(6 portions)

parsnip and carrot can be included in the five a day.

Pulses like kidney beans, lentils and soya beans can be included (and that includes baked beans in cans), but as they are also a protein source and contain good amounts of starchy carbohydrate, the Food Standards Agency says that, however much you eat, pulses can only count as one portion a day. Unlike most other vegetables, pulses also contain no vitamin C unless sprouted.

Fruit and vegetable juice or smoothies can be included, but however much you drink over 150ml, it only counts as one portion a day, as the fibre is lost in juices, and the fruit sugars in both juices and smoothies juice are more likely to produce tooth decay so overconsumption should be avoided. Fruit juice is best freshly squeezed rather than bought long-life. Fruit squashes are excluded.

Dried fruit can be counted, but only as one portion a day. Although dried fruit is usually high in fibre and can contain useful minerals and vitamins, it contains no vitamin C, is energy-dense and high in sugar.

Frozen and canned fruits and vegetables are included. Frozen items have a similar nutritional profile to their fresh counterparts – and sometimes can actually contain more vitamin C if picked and frozen immediately (see Food from Farm to Table, page 92). Canned produce contains less vitamin C than very fresh or frozen vegetables and fruit. If you do buy tins, produce canned without sugar or salt is the best option – and should perhaps be regarded as an occasional replacement for fresh or frozen rather than a regular buy.

Vegetables and fruits in ready meals and composite dishes can be included as long as they include enough fruit or vegetables to constitute a portion (see the box). A home-made apple pie will probably count, as will the vegetables in a casserole or pie. Mixed fruits or vegetables reaching the required weight for one portion will count as one portion. Many processed foods are unlikely to meet the portion size requirement. Items such as packet pasta sauces and soups should not count. Commercially made salads, such as coleslaw, will count if portion size is met.

All other fruits and vegetables not mentioned above will count as long as portion size guidelines opposite are followed.

Items can be cooked, and there is research to show that cooking vegetables in a little oil, or eating them with an oily salad dressing, actually helps their plant chemicals to be better absorbed, though raw vegetables tend to retain more of their vitamin C.

Selections should be as varied as possible. Different fruits and vegetables have differing nutritional qualities – e.g.

avocados are high in healthy fat and vitamin E, while carrots are high in beta-carotene and low in fat. So try to eat (at least) five different fruits and vegetables each day – a good rule of thumb is to get as many different colours as you can.

PORTION SIZES AND WHY THEY VARY

Portion size of your 'five a day' is important. A couple of lettuce leaves or two or three slices of tomato in a sandwich won't be enough to count – most salad items eaten raw weigh very little because of their high water content and you need a really good bowlful of them. All the portion sizes are minimums – larger portions may be preferable, depending on your size, age, appetite and own needs.

The table below gives portion size guidelines per person, and throughout this book; unless otherwise stated, 'a portion' is as listed here.

Food	Portion Size	Example
Very large fruits:	One good slice (80 g)	Melon
Large fruits:	One fruit	Orange, apple, banana
Small to medium fruit:	Two fruits	Kiwis, plums, tomatoes
Very small fruits:	1 cupful or 80 g	Berries, cherries
Cooked fruits/fruit salads:	3 heaped tablespoons/80 g	Stewed apples, fresh fruit salad
Dried fruits*:	1 heaped tablespoon/30 g	Apricots, raisins
Fruit or vegetable juice:	150ml	Orange juice, tomato juice, smoothie
Green leafy vegetables:	4 heaped tablespoons/80 g	Cabbage, broccoli
Root vegetables:	3 heaped tablespoons/80 g	Carrots, swede
Small vegetables:	3 heaped tablespoons/80 g	Peas, sweetcorn
Other vegetables:	3 heaped tablespoons/80 g	Onions, courgettes, tomatoes
Pulses:	3 heaped tablespoons (cooked)/80 g	Baked beans, lentils
Salad:	1 dessert bowlful	Mixed lettuce, tomato, cucumber

(*dry ready-to-eat weight—stewed dried fruits count as cooked fruits)

BREAKFAST

When the first edition of *The Food Bible* was published, breakfast seemed to be the one sacred meal of the day – a very important meal indeed. Indeed, in the UK, NHS advice on their website is still that people shouldn't skip breakfast. But, because much research has been done in the past few years, it's worth taking a new look at whether or not you really do need to 'breakfast like a king' – and if so, what is the best breakfast food? The answers might surprise you.

WHY DO I NEED BREAKFAST?

It sounds like a no-brainer. You've had nothing to eat for up to 12 hours, so when you get up in the morning, your body needs food. You must break your fast. Around 80% of us have a meal within an hour or so of waking, feeling it is the right thing to do, even if we're not particularly hungry. We've heard breakfast helps brainpower, is needed to increase our blood sugar levels and energize us and stops us eating too much later in the day.

But after a decade of huge interest from nutritional scientists in finding out whether all this is actually true, we still don't have definitive answers to the big breakfast questions. For example, a 2014 study comparing non-breakfast eaters with eaters found no difference in their metabolism, fat, or health at the end of the trial. In 2017 it was claimed that skipping is much better for the blood glucose levels of people with diabetes than eating. But in 2013 and 2014, three other studies found breakfast lowered the risk of diabetes in children and women, and the risk of heart disease in men.

For weight control, the evidence is tipping in favour of not eating breakfast – more studies seem to find that breakfast eaters take in more calories overall than non-breakfast-eaters.

Having read all the evidence, it seems to me that for most of us in good health, nothing dreadful will happen to you if you prefer to skip breakfast and either have a mid-morning snack or wait to eat until lunch. It seems also to be the case that, if you do take breakfast, it doesn't have to be big – a small one is fine. But if you are about to spend the morning doing heavy physical activity it would be wise to get a breakfast in, and perhaps make it a bit larger.

What may matter most to affect your health or wellbeing is what you have for breakfast. Few of the trials and studies conducted in recent years analysed the meal content to see what effect the different choices have on our bodies. Nevertheless, we do know it's beneficial to incorporate certain items into breakfast to make it a worthwhile meal, and that there are other items we can happily ignore.

WHAT IS THE BEST BREAKFAST?

Many people want a breakfast that is quick to prepare and quick to eat, which may be why a bowl of cereal and/or a slice of toast is still a very popular breakfast. But, as you will see below, it is lacking in many of the nutrients that I would expect to find in a healthy breakfast, and not very likely to keep you feeling full all morning.

The second breakfast here is just as quick and easy to prepare, and many people would say looks and tastes more attractive, but it has a really good range of nutrients both for health and for keeping hunger at bay until lunchtime. Why is it so much better? Well it contains most of the things you want in a balanced meal, and few of the less desirable ones, as explained in its caption. But of course, it is by no means the only sort of breakfast you can eat that is healthy.

If you want cooked, then eggs are brilliant. They are no longer in the doghouse either (until recently they were demonised because of salmonella and their cholesterol content, both of which are now resolved). They are enjoying their rightful time in the sun because of their high protein, mineral and vitamin content – and if you buy organic you will get omega-3s too. They have a great balance of fat and protein and, served with wholegrain bread and one or two pieces of fruit, make a good start to the day.

In truth, you can eat anything at breakfast time that you would eat at other times. Fish, avocado, beans, cheese, sugar-free nut butters are all good, as are minimally processed whole grain foods. Just try to get some fresh fruit or veg into the meal, some good fats and some protein and you won't go far wrong. Small amounts of dried fruits are alright too – go for those with extra benefits, e.g. dried apricots and figs are rich in iron. Judge your portion size according to how hungry you are in the morning and how physical you're going to be in the next few hours.

A TYPICAL QUICK BREAKFAST, BUT NOT IDEAL

30g cornflakes, 125ml skimmed milk, 30g slice of white toast with 5g margarine and 2tsp marmalade.

283 calories, 4.6g total fat, 1.3g saturated fat, 9.4g protein, 54g carbohydrate, 1.6g fibre.

This breakfast of cereal and toast is the kind that millions of people eat every day and one which most people would consider healthy. Yes, it is low in fat and saturated fat, not high in added sugar, and contains a good amount of calcium (and some other vitamins and minerals, because cornflakes are fortified) and plenty of carbohydrate. Yet it has several drawbacks.

Because the cereals are refined and the bread white, it is very short on fibre, containing only 1.6g in the whole breakfast, or little more than 5% of an adult's daily recommended intake. It is very low on healthy fats. There is only a trace of vitamin C in the meal (in the marmalade) and virtually no plant chemicals. Most importantly, it is low in protein and low in total fats. Both these two factors coupled with the low fibre and fairly low calorie content mean that someone eating this breakfast would suffer a spike in blood sugars soon after eating and probably feel hungry again before long.

JUST AS QUICK, AND A BETTER BET FOR MOST PEOPLE

This breakfast is much better than the first. It contains a reasonable amount of total fat which will slow the conversion to sugar in the blood and keep hunger at bay (as will the higher protein content and the fact that the banana is high in resistant starch). The saturated fat content is within the DoH guidelines as it represents around 9% of the calories in the meal. It is mostly in the yogurt, which means this offers the important vitamin D, which isn't present in skimmed milk or fat-free yogurt. Also, because the yogurt is organic and thus from cows raised on a natural diet, it also contains healthy fats including, for example, omega-3s.

The nuts and seeds are very good sources of essential fats as well as protein and phytochemicals. The oats are minimally processed, low GI and heart-friendly. The breakfast gives two portions of fruit towards the day's fruit and veg intake and contains over half a day's RNI for vitamin C as well as providing calcium, iron and vitamin E, plus over half of an adult's recommended fibre intake for the day.

40g plain rolled oats, 80g fresh raspberries, 1 slightly underripe small banana, sliced, 125ml full fat organic natural yogurt, 1 tbsp skin-on almonds, chopped, ½ tbsp milled flaxseed, ½ tbsp pumpkin seeds.

502 calories, 20.3g total fat, 5.4g saturated fat, 19.1g protein, 67g carbohydrate, 15.3g fibre.

Breakfast on the go

If you want or need to have breakfast after you've left home, maybe the best option is to take a packed breakfast if you can – a yogurt, cereal and fruit bowlful in an insulated container would be ideal. Otherwise, an egg or avocado and tomato sandwich on rye, or even a bag containing nuts, seeds and a piece of fruit would be better than much of what you can get in shops or cafes.

If you do need to buy your breakfast, be careful about buying a cereal bar as they can be high in added sugars (check the label) and sometimes their protein and healthy fat content is low. Some chains such as Pret offer good healthy breakfasts and breakfast smoothies to take away. Their websites have nutrition details.

SO WHAT ABOUT THE BACON?

Can you still eat a traditional British breakfast – the eggs, but with bacon too?

We are advised by the DoH to cut right back on highly processed meats in our diet because they can increase the risk of bowel cancer. Processed meat refers to meat that has been preserved by smoking, curing, salting or adding preservatives. This includes sausages, bacon and ham. And cooking bacon until it is crisp may compound the problem – burnt particles create chemicals also linked with increased risk of cancer. So having a daily full British seems to be off the menu – but once a week or so, it is probably OK, especially if you add plenty of healthy fresh items such as tomatoes and mushrooms. Cancer Research UK has produced statistics to show the risk is not that great when compared with other lifestyle choices that can cause cancer such as smoking or being obese. For more information on processed meats and cancer, see page 128.

A NEW LOOK AT LUNCH

Whether or not you've had breakfast, most people function better if they have a lunch, even if it is something small. If you skip, you may find that around 4-5pm you're are so hungry you'll grab the nearest snack to hand, which may be a cupcake or a pack of biscuits – in other words, something high in fat and sugar.

Hunger isn't the only consideration, though. For most of us, lunch needs to be something quick and easy – even when we're not working, there's usually little time to spare. But it doesn't HAVE to be a boring sandwich every day.

Lunch-time is an ideal time to pack in some powerful nutrients to help you to health. It's a good time to get your quota of fish (canned is fine) or pulses (nothing wrong with beans on toast); to eat plenty of salad; to get ahead on your vegetable intake with big bowls of soup. Like breakfast, your lunch should be a sensible balance of

carbohydrates, proteins and fat.

Because your evening meal is going to be higher in carbohydrate and lower in protein (see overleaf), your lunch can contain a large proportion of your day's protein intake. Research shows that a high-protein lunch is better for afternoon brainpower than a high-carb one. It will also keep hunger pangs at bay for longer, a consideration if you have to have your supper late.

Talking of which – do you know what you're going to have to eat this evening? Try to pick something completely different for lunch. Meat tonight? Why not go veggie for lunch? Pasta tonight? Even more reason to have a lower-carb lunch, perhaps.

When choosing a lunch for speed, beware of the possible nutritional pitfalls. Quite a lot of takeaways and ready meals (even savoury ones) are high in sugar/salt/saturates and may not provide enough vegetables/fruit towards your daily intake.

Anything in pastry is probably very high in fat, saturated fat and calories, so limit items like pasties, pork pies and sausage rolls to very occasional use. A good alternative now and then would be a 'crustless' quiche – with

most, there is a little pastry on the base but not on the sides.

We all need to grab a take-out sandwich now and then. But very few have a good lunchtime carbohydrate to protein ratio – usually they are mostly carbs, a fair amount of fat, and very little protein squashed in between the bread. Better options may be a wrap, which has room for much more filling which is often a good mix of protein and vegetables, or a ready-made salad in a bowl. Today supermarket shelves are filled with options that include quinoa, the higher-protein grain, and plenty of pulses instead of rice or pasta, mixed in great combinations with vegetables, fruits, spices and so on.

If you do find yourself with no option but an old-fashioned bread sandwich, you will almost always want to add a piece of fruit, or a fruit bowl, as sandwiches really rarely offer even one portion of your day's vegetables. Using the nutrition details on your sandwich pack, try to pick one not too high in sugar/salt/saturates.

There is nothing wrong with white bread now and then, but choose sourdough if you can, as it is high in immune-boosting bacteria and a lower GI bread than most. Wholemeal will boost your day's fibre intake and to avoid blood sugar spikes, try dark rye bread, or breads with added nuts and seeds.

Home-packed lunches to take to work can be a healthy alternative to a lunch-time cafeteria meal or takeaway, but even so, it is all too easy to put together a packed meal that's very high in salt, fat and sugar, and low in fibre and vitamins. They can also get boring, so if you eat – or could eat – a packed lunch regularly, invest in suitable plastic containers and vacuum flasks for salads, desserts and soups. Dressings and utensils can usually be kept at work. Plan ahead for these home-packed lunches – when you make a winter soup, for example, make treble the quantity and freeze in single portions.

Eating lunch at home? This is the ideal time to load your plate with lots and lots of fresh salad items with many different colours. Then add some protein – chicken, tuna, prawns,

REWORKED LUNCH TO GO

BEFORE

Cheese ploughman's, apple and cola

This is a typical lunch-box or takeout meal. The contents are 2 slices white bread spread with 2 tsp margarine-type spread and filled with 40g Cheddar cheese, 2 tsp sweet pickle, 2 tsp mayonnaise, half a sliced tomato and 2-3 leaves iceberg lettuce; 1 small apple and a small bottle of diet cola.

This contains: 529 calories, 27.6g fat, 10.4g saturates, 15.9g protein, 58g carbs and 4.6g fibre.

Despite the 'diet' cola, and the addition of an apple, the lunch is not all that well balanced. It is high in total fat (at 47% of the meal's calories) saturates (18% – nearly double recommendations), and salt (at around half the day's maximum intake). Protein at 12% is low for a lunch, and there's only 15% of your day's fibre target in here, and just 1¼ portions toward your day's fruit and vegetable goal. Diet drinks don't help with weight control or loss (see page 54). Plus points? The cheese and white bread are good sources of calcium (and cheese may offer other health benefits, see page 28) and the apple is a good source of flavonoids.

AFTER

Cheese and roast butternut squash salad

Here's a lunch with a similar amount of cheese and carbs but its profile is much better. The contents are 30g of feta cheese, 80g ready cooked Puy lentils, 30g each baby kale and red onion, 100g left-over roasted butternut squash, 50g cooked quinoa, 10ml extra virgin rapeseed oil, 2 tsp apple cider vinegar, 1 apple, 200ml coffee.

This contains: 443 calories, 17.7g fat, 5.8g saturates, 17.3g protein, 55.5g carbs and 13.7g fibre.

The meal is within guidelines on fat and protein intake at 35% for total fat, 11% for saturates and 16% for protein. Feta, like Cheddar, is rich in calcium and protein and should contain some healthy omega-3 fats if it is a proper goat's/sheep's milk variety. Lentils give protein and a range of vitamins, minerals and plant chemicals, as well as healthy carbs and fibre. The lunch contains 3 portions towards your fruit and vegetable intake and the virgin rapeseed oil is a very healthy fat. Coffee gives a caffeine hit like cola, but we now know it is a very healthy drink (see page 71), is great for day-long brainpower, and can even lower the risk of heart disease.

hard cheese, egg, tofu, cooked pulses perhaps – and some carb (the ready-cooked pulses and grains in 2-minute bags are ideal quick additions), and finally decide on your dressing. Olive or rapeseed oil, balsamic or wine vinegar or a juice for sharpness, some mustard, black pepper and a little salt and you have a great dressing that will help the plant chemicals in your salad to be better absorbed. A soup could follow the same principles – just sauté some vegetables in the oil, add some cooked protein, and serve with rye or sourdough.

SOME SUGGESTIONS FOR HEALTHY QUICK LUNCHES

Tip – pre-cook ingredients when you're cooking something else or use up leftovers such as roast vegetables or cooked grains. Store in fridge for a day or two (see guidance on storing, page 108–109).

* Easy hummus (see recipe page 219), crudités, falafel.

* Salad of roast beetroot, goat's cheese, pecans, red onion, Puy lentils.

* A wrap filled with roasted sweet potato, cooked black beans, red pepper, spring onions.

* Baby leaf spinach, avocado and cannellini bean mash on sourdough toast.

* Homemade coleslaw with walnuts and chicken (see recipe page 230) with cooked chicken fillet.

* Seared tuna (can be served hot or cold), avocado, tomato and quinoa salad.

* Artichoke, auburgene and spelt warm salad (see recipe page 245).

EVENING EATING

Most of us look forward to our evening meal and treat it as the main food event of the day when there's often more time to prepare food, and it's time to relax and savour what we eat, perhaps for the first time in the day with family or friends. Here we look at what makes a delicious and healthy meal to end the day – and whether desserts, snacks and so on can fit into your eating plan without you having to feel guilty …

Evening is the best time of the day to go to town with carbohydrates. These have a calming effect because they appear to stimulate the production of serotonin, the 'good mood' compound, in the brain, and may help the brain 'slow down', to relax and get a good night's sleep. The carbs should be complex and preferably not too high on the glycaemic index so that they sustain you through until morning – wholegrains and pulses are ideal.

To that you need to add some higher protein foods and some that contain good fats – just like at breakfast and lunch. These will also sustain you through the night and offer a range of other nutrients and health benefits.

And of course, to that you will add vegetables/fruit so that your daily tally

EVENING MEAL TIPS

✳ Try to eat your supper no later than two hours before you go to bed, so that your digestive system has time to get to work on the meal and won't disrupt your sleep.

✳ Try to have meat-free meals at least twice a week; one vegan and one vegetarian would be a good idea.

✳ Have a fish supper twice a week if you can – one of them oily fish.

meets the recommended amount, which is a minimum of five portions – and up to ten may be even better (see page 55).

As well as carbohydrates, there are other nutrients that can help you relax and get a good night's sleep. These include calcium, found in good amounts in dairy produce, nuts and seeds, magnesium, also found in nuts and seeds as well as cocoa powder, and tryptophan. This is an amino acid found in protein foods which converts to serotonin. Tryptophan rich foods include eggs, cheese, milk, tofu, nuts, seeds and turkey.

ROUND UP

So – we're nearly at the end of the day, and how did we get on with eating a nutritious day's food, and how nearly in line were we with the recommended levels of all the nutrients? Here's how

MEAL MAKEOVER

BEFORE

Classic steak supper

225g sirloin steak, 75ml ready-made peppercorn sauce, 2 chestnut mushrooms, sliced and fried in 2tsp olive oil, 150g ready-made oven French fries, salad of lettuce, cucumber, tomato, rocket to fill a standard dessert dish, dressed with 2 tsp ready-made French dressing.

This contains: 854 calories, 43.8g fat, 12.9g saturates, 76.8g protein, 52.8g carbs and 5.8g fibre.

Here you have plenty of protein (in fact for an adult woman this is a whole day's recommended amount at nearly 15% of your ideal calorie intake!), plenty of calories and a dish high in iron and B vitamins,

but, bearing in mind that an evening meal is good if it contains a high proportion of fibre-rich carbohydrate, the 23% carbs it contains (mostly refined, from the chips) is about half what we're looking for. At first glance it seems there are plenty of vegetables because of the salad – but a dessert bowlful will weigh only about 50-60g as items such as salad leaves weigh very little, so you have less than one portion of vegetables here, and the mushrooms – about 40g – will push it to just over one portion. Fibre's quite low (if you ate this meal, and the 'before' breakfast and lunches on previous pages, you would be getting only 12g fibre altogether, which is less than half the recommended 30g) and, assuming a thin band of fat is left on the sirloin steak to cook, the fat content is high at 46% of the calories in this dish, as is the saturated fat content at 13.6% of the calories.

our 'After' breakfast, lunch and supper together look when all added together, in nutritional terms:

Calories: 1509, which is 72% of a day's recommended intake of 2103 calories for an adult female (2103) which means there are 594 left to 'spend'.

Fat: 62.6g, which is just over 36% of total calories (eaten in the 3 meals), and that is almost perfect, but we don't want to go much higher as we're around the limit of 35% already.

Saturates: 15.8g, which is 9.4% of total calories (eaten in the 3 meals), and is within the 10% limit recommended, but we don't want to go much higher.

Protein: 64.1g, which is 17% of total calories (eaten in the 3 meals) and is absolutely fine – but most people would be fine eating more.

AFTER

Classic stir-fry supper

100g tofu OR turkey slices, stir-fried with 1 small red pepper, 50g broccoli, 30g mangetout, ½ head pak choi (all chopped as necessary), 1 tsp each fresh finely-chopped chilli, ginger and garlic, 2 tsp soya sauce, and served with 125g egg-fried rice (made with 150g cooked weight brown rice, 1 egg, 2 tsp groundnut oil, 50g beansprouts, ½ tsp Chinese five spice, 1 tbsp flaked almonds).

This contains*: 564 calories, 24.6g fat, 4.6g saturates, 27.7g protein, 62.3g carbs and 10.6g fibre.

* If you choose the turkey option the counts will be very slightly different.

Here you've got a variety of different vegetables and sprouts, all adding up to around 2½ portions, plus there is a great range of spices, all of which will provide various disease-preventing phytochemicals and fibre. There is also plenty of vitamin C in the stir-fry. The tofu (or turkey) is a good low fat source of protein so that total fat (at 36%) and saturated fat (at 7%) levels are just about perfect. Groundnut oil is a very good oil for stir-frying as it has a high smoke point (see page xxx) and contains healthy unsaturated fats. The almonds add more healthy fats, as will the egg if it is organic. Brown rice adds fibre and brings the dish's total carb content up to nearly the recommended 50% (of total calories in the meal) level, but we are still a little short – so see the next few paragraphs for the solution!

Carbohydrates: 129.3g, which is 46% of total calories (eaten in the 3 meals) and, going on the DoH recommendation that carbs should be around 50% of our intake, that is slightly low.

Fibre: 39.6g, which is 132% of your total recommended day's intake.

Fruit and Vegetable portions: 7½ – more than the official five a day and getting up near the 8–10 a day that some experts believe would be better.

So now, let's add some frivolity!

TIME FOR DESSERT … OR A SNACK OR DRINK?

With calories left in the bank, and some carb intake to make up – here are some ideas!

• **Add in a daily semi-skimmed milk allowance for drinks** – 200ml will be around 100 calories and will add mostly carbs and protein with just a small bit of fat.

Or perhaps you'd like a comforting hot chocolate drink to take to bed – add a tablespoon of cocoa powder and 1–2 tsp sugar to skimmed or semi skimmed milk; it will really help you sleep (see tryptophan page 66).

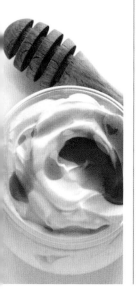

• **You want pudding? You can add in a dessert** – you have had hardly any added sugar in your diet today so there is room for a couple of spoonsful of something sweet and added!

The UK recommended amount of added sugar you should stay below is 5% of total calories, which, on 2,103 calories a day, is 28g sugar or about 6 teaspoons.

What about one of our recipe desserts? Most are low in fat but high in carbs so would fit in perfectly with your remaining nutrient profile.

The thing about desserts, snacks, cakes and so on is that while they may contain a certain amount of the nutritional 'baddies' such as sugar, and maybe salt and saturated fat, they do have scope to contain some very good things, too.

So if you are going to have a dessert or sweet thing, try to make sure it does have some positives. Depending on what you choose, it could be high in vitamin C and/or fibre, and/or plant chemicals and/or certain minerals and/or could provide some of your five a day … see the panel for my top ten desserts/cakes and why, and find some snack ideas below.

OTHER IDEAS

Or perhaps you'd rather roll over the calories and carbs you've saved, and get more in your eating plan tomorrow? Your eating plan is yours – as we said at the beginning, nobody can stick to an exact blueprint every day. So maybe tomorrow you'll fancy a handful of dried fruit to chop and sprinkle on your breakfast? Again, low in fat, high in carbs.

Or maybe you want more calories for your evening meal as you're going out, or you'd rather have a lunch 25% bigger than the one we looked at today. You might even like a glass of red wine with your evening meal sometimes or treat yourself to your favourite chocolate bar.

Or maybe you'd like an extra snack during the day. You could have, for example, a wholemeal fruit scone spread with some high-fruit conserve for around 300 calories, or a couple of oatcakes topped with crunchy peanut butter for around 200 calories, or a small slice of fruit or carrot cake for about the same. Delicious healthy smaller snack ideas include a pot of natural yogurt with a teaspoon of honey drizzled over; a round oatcake spread with sugar-free nut butter; a small piece of hard cheese with a few grapes.

Top Ten Desserts/Cakes

Mixed fresh berry salad with yogurt ice cream (vitamin C, fibre, plant chemicals, calcium, protein, contributes to 5 a day)

∽

Any of the desserts in the recipe section in this book (various health benefits)

∽

Griddled peaches topped with chopped hazelnuts and melted dark chocolate (vitamin C, fibre, plant chemicals, healthy fats, magnesium, iron, five a day)

∽

Bananas baked in their skins, split and topped with Greek yogurt and chopped almonds (fibre, potassium, calcium, five a day)

∽

Classic pancakes made with wholegrain flour and topped with berries and berry coulis, Skyr (fibre, vitamins A, B group, C, D, plant chemicals, calcium, protein, five a day)

∽

Individual summer pudding – strawberries, raspberries, red or black currants made into compote, poured over sliced brown bread, refrigerated for a few hours (fibre, vitamin C, plant chemicals, five a day)

∽

A plate of strawberries dipped in melted dark chocolate (fibre, vitamin C, plant chemicals, magnesium, iron, five a day)

∽

Cooking apple cored and filled with mixed chopped dried fig, apricot and date plus chopped nuts, baked in its skin (fibre, range of vitamins and minerals, plant chemicals, up to two of your five a day)

∽

Fresh pitted sliced cherries and blueberries layered in a glass with Skyr yogurt beaten with a little honey, toasted flaked almonds and dark chocolate flakes (fibre, vitamin C, calcium, protein, plant chemicals, healthy fats, five a day)

∽

Cashew or almond butter sandwiched between thin slices of dark chocolate, topped with a drizzle of warmed espresso coffee (fibre, plant chemicals, healthy fats, magnesium, zinc)

DRINKS FOR HEALTH

Your body is almost two-thirds water and so it is vital that it gets enough fluid to stay hydrated. If not, dehydration can cause short-term symptoms such as headache, tiredness and lack of concentration, and severe dehydration can cause other problems too such as low blood pressure, rapid heartbeat and mental confusion.

HOW MUCH IS ENOUGH?

The amount of fluid you need depends on several considerations. In general, factors including the weather, the temperature, and humidity in your indoor environment can influence it, and also your individual profile, such as how much physical activity you do, and your age. But on average the UK DoH suggest 6-8 glasses of fluid per day plus the fluid that you get when you eat (which provides around 20% of your daily fluid intake). One easy way to tell if you are drinking enough is to check the colour and amount of your urine – if it is a very pale straw colour you are drinking enough; if it is dark yellow, you are probably not.

WHAT FLUIDS COUNT TOWARDS THE TOTAL?

Fluid includes not only water but also other drinks that are made with water or naturally contain water, such as tea, coffee, milk, fruit juices and soft drinks. We look at the pros and cons of the most popular drinks here.

WATER

Perhaps the ideal drink as it is free (tap water is fine and may even contain more minerals than bottled so-called mineral waters), is calorie-free and widely available.

MILK AND MILK ALTERNATIVES

Dairy milk is one of our main sources of calcium, as well as providing protein, B vitamins and iodine. Full-fat milk is somewhat high in saturated fat but contains vitamin D; semi-skimmed and fully skimmed are alternatives lower in fat and saturates but with little or no vitamin D. Milk taken as a late-night hot drink can help sleep (see Insomnia, page 156). Probiotic kefir is another good alternative, while goat's and sheep's milk are two alternatives to cow's milk and are rising in popularity. For people with a lactose intolerance or vegans, there are plenty of milk alternatives based on plants, such as soya milk, rice milk, coconut milk and almond milk. These usually contain fewer calories than milk, which may be useful for people watching their weight, as well as less fat, saturates and nutrients, but some are fortified with vitamins and minerals such as calcium. Read the label before making a decision based on your own preferences.

FRUIT AND VEGETABLE JUICES AND SMOOTHIES

Juices may be good sources of vitamin C, but are often high in acid and sugar

and thus can contribute to tooth decay. They are higher in calories than most people realise (80-85 for a 200ml orange juice for instance) and high in sugar (16g in 200ml juice). They've also lost almost all their fibre and plant chemicals. Smoothies are also high in calories and, usually sugar, unless you make a green vegetable smoothie, but they retain the original plant's fibre and much of the plant chemicals and are lower on the glycaemic index than juice so are better for general health. Most experts say that it would be best to eat the whole fruit and drink water with it, rather than drink juice, smoothies or squashes.

TEA

Teas (from the plant camellia sinensis, which is the tea most of us drink) of all colours – black, green, white – contains useful plant chemicals in the flavonoid group (see page 48) that can protect your health (even if you add milk). They also contain caffeine which can help brain alertness and physical capacity and endurance, and are virtually calorie-free. They are mildly diuretic, but not enough to counteract their hydrating effects.

HERBAL AND OTHER TEAS

Dried teas based on herbs may each have mild health properties – for example, lemon balm and chamomile can be calming, ginger may help joint pain, and so on. Each is as hydrating as water, virtually calorie-free and a good choice for a natural, low-sugar drink. Kombucha is a refreshing fermented tea containing probiotics usually served cold. Matcha is a ground Japanese green tea more potent in flavonoids than green tea leaves as drinks made with it will have you consume the grounds. Redbush

(rooibos) tea from Africa is caffeine-free, low in tannins and a good source of cardiovascular system protective polyphenols, with a mild flavour and calming properties.

COFFEE

Recent research has changed coffee's reputation as a rather unhealthy choice – now it seems that it actually has very many useful health properties. Coffee, including decaff, is packed with plant chemicals such as coumarins, catechins, phenols, tannins, terpines and quinones and more, which have various properties such as being antioxidant, antibacterial, antiviral, anti-inflammatory and thus help protect against most of the major diseases including CVD, cancer and

diabetes, and can also help your body burn fat while its caffeine content boosts endurance. Two to five cups a day seems to be an optimal amount, and best consumed during the day rather than in the evening. Limit to two cups a day if pregnant.

HOT CHOCOLATE

Ready-made commercial hot chocolate drinks usually contain high levels of added sugars so are best kept for very occasional use, but plain cocoa powder mixed with your choice of hot milk is a good drink as the cocoa bean, like coffee, has many beneficial effects, being rich in chemicals, fibre and magnesium, all of which can help cardiovascular health, for example.

SQUASHES AND CARBONATED DRINKS

These are usually sources of many additives and are often very sweet and high in calories. High intake is associated with obesity. They contain few nutrients unless they are added by the manufacturer. Low-calorie

versions are similar, but with added artificial sweeteners (see page 54) which may have disadvantages of their own; for example, they may raise the risk of diabetes. Energy drinks, promoted as increasing physical and/ or mental energy, such as carbonated canned drinks containing caffeine, sugar, vitamins and a variety of other ingredients depending on the brand, are usually high in calories and sugar and should be consumed with caution – the WHO for instance recently said they could pose a danger to public health.

More information on individual drinks can be found in the Food Charts and elsewhere throughout the book.

A BASIC HEALTHY DIET

The sample seven-day diet plan on page 74, shows how an adult in normal health could put together all the preceding information into a delicious healthy everyday diet. The portion sizes when given are suitable for an average adult not needing to lose weight and will average at about 2,000 calories a day. For young, active or tall people larger portions may be needed to maintain weight, for older and sedentary or shorter people smaller portions may be needed, and in general males tend to need more calories than do females. Get in touch with your appetite and be sensible about portion sizes. Eating more than you need will result in weight gain, even if your diet is healthy.

For people with particular medical conditions, see Section Two; for people in different life stages or circumstances (e.g. pregnant or elderly) or with particular food preferences, see Section Three, and for people who need to lose weight see Section Four. ∎

TO SUMMARIZE THE HEALTHY EATING GUIDELINES APPROPRIATE FOR MOST ADULTS:

Eat around half of your diet as complex carbohydrates – wholegrains (including bread, and pasta) potatoes and pulses. Carbs low on the Glycaemic Index (page 210) may keep you feeling full for longer and regulate blood sugar levels.

✳ Include vegetables/salad/fruit at every meal and eat some raw, some cooked. Aim for around five portions.

✳ Include good sources of protein at every meal – often plant-based sources such as pulses.

✳ Eat a good balance of fats – including the non- or minimally-processed plant fats. Most of your fat intake should come from foods naturally high in fats rather than foods with added fats. These include oily fish, seeds, nuts, fruits and their oils.

✳ So go easy on bought foods high in fat, such as pastries, cakes, pies, cream and full-fat cheese and fatty cuts of meat.

✳ Eat less sugary foods and added sugar. For sweetness go for naturally sweet items like whole fresh fruit or small amounts of dried fruit.

✳ Keep an eye on your salt intake.

✳ Eat more plant-based meals.

✳ Get as wide a variety of foods as possible into your diet.

✳ Eat the best quality foods that you can – fresh, wholesome, unadulterated, and for meats, dairy foods and eggs, produce from animals that led a natural life often has a better nutrient profile.

✳ Drink plenty of fluids – water is best and tea and coffee in moderate amounts are good for most people, too.

✳ Most importantly – relax and enjoy your food. Make some time to plan your meals ahead and enjoy the pleasures of preparing food.

The Basic Health Diet

Items in italics represent recipes in Section Four.

DAY ONE

Breakfast
125g natural yogurt topped with 2tsp each pumpkin and sunflower seeds and 1 chopped orange
1 large slice of dark rye bread spread with sugar-free peanut butter

Lunch
Chilli Lentils with Greens
150g cooked weight brown rice
1 apple

Evening
Potato and Mediterranean Vegetable Bake
Large bowlful of mixed salad leaves with a little olive oil and lemon dressing

Snack
2 round oatcakes topped with 25g extra mature hard cheese

DAY TWO

Breakfast
Mixed fruit salad of chopped plum, raspberries or blackberries and apple
150ml natural full fat yogurt
1tbsp chopped walnuts

Lunch
5 ready-made chickpea falafel balls
1½tbsp *Beetroot Hummus*
1 mini wholemeal pitta
Radish and onion side salad with balsamic vinegar dressing

Evening
Speedy Herbed Swordfish
Green beans, broccoli
Boiled new potatoes drizzled with cold pressed extra virgin rapeseed oil
1 banana

Snack
Apple Flapjack

DAY THREE

Breakfast
75g no-added-sugar oat-based muesli high in nuts and seeds
125ml semi-skimmed dairy, soya or coconut milk
1 orange

Lunch
Squash and Sweet Potato Soup
1 slice artisan sourdough bread
1 nectarine or peach

Evening
Chipotle Lime Chicken
Corn on the cob, parboiled, tossed in rapeseed oil, baked
Green salad

Snack
1 small handful skin-on almonds

Breakfast
2 poached eggs
1 grilled tomato
1 large slice wholewheat bread, toasted, with butter to spread

Lunch
Warm Winter Coleslaw with Walnuts and Chicken
2tbsp cooked wholewheat pasta
10 large red or black grapes

Evening
Almond, Chickpea and Raisin Pilaf
Rocket and watercress salad

Snack
2tbsp natural fromage frais with 2tsp honey

Breakfast
1 ripe avocado, mashed with olive oil and balsamic vinegar
1 slice dark rye bread, lightly toasted
1 orange

Lunch
Mushroom and Red Pepper Skewers with added cubes of halloumi or tofu
2tbsp ready cooked brown rice
Mixed lettuce salad with olive oil and white wine vinegar dressing

Evening
Lamb Tagine
150g cooked bulgar wheat
Mango Filo Tart

Snack
1tbsp unsalted cashew nuts

Breakfast
150g Greek yogurt with chopped apple, pumpkin seeds and pistachio nuts

Lunch
Spiced Lentil and Vegetable Soup
1 slice Oat Bread with butter to spread

Evening
Miso Marinated Salmon
Stir-fried pak choi
Beansprouts

Snack
2 semi-dried apricots, 1 semi-dried or fresh fig

Breakfast
50g no-added-sugar oat-based muesli high in nuts and seeds
80g fresh raspberries and blueberries
100ml semi-skimmed dairy, soya or coconut milk

Lunch
Sweet Potato Hash with Poached Eggs
1 apple

Evening
Pasta with sauteed Broccoli florets and *Anchoiade*

Snack
1 round oatcake topped with sugar-free cashew butter

Choosing a Diet to Suit Your Lifestyle

SO WE'VE SEEN what the ideal diet is like – but how can you translate that into the way YOU live? In the next few pages we look at how healthy eating can fit into any lifestyle, from those on a tight budget, people who entertain a lot, and people who prefer ready meals, takeaways or eating out through to those with particular eating preferences.

FAST FOOD

Today because of our busy, busy lives, the popularity of fast food has never been greater. A quarter of all the calories we eat and drink now come from food produced outside the home. The majority of us have a takeaway meal at least once a week and the figure is rising, according to research from Public Health England in 2017. The last National Food Survey found consumption of takeaways has doubled since 1974 and we spend around £30 billion a year on them in the UK. Burgers, pizza, chicken, chips and kebabs are the most popular items.

Takeaways are frequently blamed for the rise in obesity in the UK and in other countries. This is probably a combination of factors – they tend

to be high in calories and fat. One big survey found that up to 60% of the calories in takeaway meals may be fat calories, when the recommended limit in the UK is 35%.

Meals can also be high in salt and low in vegetables/salad/fruit and fibre so, if eaten regularly, could be an unhealthy choice. However, most of the popular chains do offer a choice today of more healthy items.

CHOOSING TAKEAWAYS

At most burger and chicken chains you can choose salads, vegetarian options and lower-calorie options, while at the pizza bars there are usually pizzas with thinner bases and healthier toppings on sale.

Similar sounding choices can vary enormously in their nutrient and calorie count. For example, a chicken burger can be less than 400 calories or around 600, and fat content can vary from about 30g down to about 8g with saturates from 5g down to 1g.

Because menus change fairly quickly it isn't possible here to give exact details to compare – but all the larger popular chains do provide nutrition details on their websites, or at the shops if asked.

In general, perhaps you are more likely to be hard-pushed to get healthy options if you visit a traditional British fish and chip shop, and at independent Indian and Thai takeaways. Such meals are most likely to have a very high fat content – that, plus the fact that many are served in large portions, will push the calories up.

Takeaways – what to watch

✳ Many seemingly vegetarian takeaways contain animal fat (e.g. chips fried in lard) so if you're vegetarian you need to ask.

✳ Take care if you suffer from allergic reactions – some takeaways contain, for instance, dyes, (pilau rice, perhaps fish batter, even chips), flavour enhancers such as monosodium glutamate (Chinese meals) and soya products (batters, burgers, pasties) and other additives.

✳ If your takeaway is lacking in vegetables, it only takes a few minutes to add your own (see ready meals).

READY MEALS

The simplest alternative to a takeaway meal is a ready meal – and sales of these are booming, too. Britons spent £3 billion on ready meals in 2016, *The Grocer* magazine says, more than any of our neighbouring countries. People in the UK consume, on average, at least one ready meal a week, with curries and Chinese dishes being the most popular.

Most supermarkets have a 'healthier' range of ready meals, but even if they don't, over the past few years the standard of ready meals has improved greatly regarding their healthy balance of ingredients. Many now make an effort to include more vegetables in the meal, for instance. Of course, not all are healthy platefuls – but it is easy to check the labels (see page 105 for more on interpreting labelling) and choose something that matches your own healthy eating criteria/fits in with what else you are eating today.

And if the meal you want to buy

doesn't have much in the way of veggies, it is easy to add them using a ready-prepped pack or some salad.

VERY QUICK AND EASY DO IT YOURSELF IDEAS

Instead of a takeaway or a ready meal, you can produce a home cooked meal for yourself in minutes. Here are a few ideas for home-made fast food:

✳ Omelette and bagged mixed salad. For carbs add a banana for dessert.

✳ Dry-fried salmon fillet on bed of ready-cooked 2-minute lentils, salad.

✳ Ready-cooked 2-minute brown rice stirred with cooked prawns, ready-made Balti curry sauce paste and chopped tomatoes for a quick biryani.

✳ Chicken breast fillet pieces skewered with baby mushrooms and brushed with olive oil, grilled, salad, ready-cooked 2-minute quinoa.

✳ Marinated tofu mixed with half a pack of stir-fry vegetables cooked to instructions, ready cooked wholewheat noodles.

EATING OUT AND ENTERTAINING

Almost one in five meals in the UK are now eaten in establishments outside the home, according to Public Health England. There is such a vast choice of where to eat when you decide to go to a restaurant or pub for lunch or supper, and then a large choice on the menu, that there should not be any problem about picking a healthier meal. However, several factors may stop you from doing so.

You want to treat yourself – you don't go out that often, so when you do, you want to go where you want and pick what you want. Well, my advice is – go ahead. If you rarely eat out, then in the scheme of things, whatever you pick is not going to have a great influence on your health or your size. I'd say if you eat out once a month or so, just have a good time.

You don't know what ingredients are in that meal – some cuisines are designed to confuse you somewhat about what, exactly, it is you are going to be eating. It might be a cuisine with which you're not that familiar, or

maybe the dishes have a vague name but don't explain much. If you are not sure, you should ask the waiter to tell you the details. And it is always worth asking if something can be slightly tailored to your own liking – for example, can the cream be left out or the butter omitted.

It's a sharing meal – you're in a group and there is a collective decision about what will be ordered, be it tapas or a collection of Chinese dishes for example. This sounds like a celebration, or something you don't do that often. Again, try your best to fork up the items that suit your health goals, but if that's not possible, don't worry too much.

Everyone else is doing it – i.e., having bread and oil to start with; having lots to drink, having starter and main and dessert. You don't want to be a spoilsport. We've all been there. But honestly, no-one is going to mind if you skip the bread, drink more slowly (or say you're driving), choose the smallest lowest-calorie thing for starter (melon? A clear soup? A prawn skewer?) and share your dessert with

your like-minded neighbour.

You picked the wrong type of restaurant – some cuisines are naturally healthier, some less so. For example, traditional northern French/Parisian cooking is high on butter, cream, cheese and bacon, while southern French/provincial cooking tends to contain healthy fats, little dairy, and plenty of vegetables. Traditional Indian restaurants may favour long-cooked spiced casseroles using fatty cuts of meat – the melted fat swimming on the top of your dish is a giveaway. Modern Indian dishes, though, tend to be low in fat, drier and fresher. The food in mid-range Chinese restaurants may be high in salt and sugar, while Japanese cuisine tends to be cleaner with lower salt and sugar content.

Some tips for healthier eating in restaurants

✳ It's always easy to find a simple healthy meal in a fish restaurant (not fish and chip shop type!) – grilled or pan-fried fresh fish of any kind is good, served with vegetables.

✳ If in doubt, go for something plain – a smallest-size steak and salad, for example, or a grilled chicken dish with vegetables.

✳ Pasta dishes, unless wholegrain pasta is specified, are likely to be high in simple carbs and high in calories and, unless you have a tomato-based sauce, likely to be low in vegetables.

✳ Vegetarian options are often higher in vegetables but may be laden with cream or creamy cheese, so go carefully.

✳ Vegan options (becoming much more widely available) are very likely to be some of the healthiest on the menu if you're looking for high-carb, high-vegetable and low saturates.

A DELICIOUS ITALIAN MEAL OUT FOR HALF THE CALORIES AND FAT

TYPICAL ITALIAN RESTAURANT MEAL
2,050 calories, 100g fat (approx).

Choose this meal – 45% of which is fat – and you will be eating all your day's calories (for most women) and more than a day's fat allowance for women OR men in one go. The meal is also low on fresh fruits and vegetables and fibre. Italian garlic flat bread, 75g (approx. 350 calories, 12g fat)

Starter: portion of calamari (fried squid), (approx 300 calories, 15g fat).

Main course: portion of Pasta Carbonara (approx 900 calories, 45g fat). This dish of pasta with a sauce made from eggs, cream and bacon is very high in fat and saturates.

Dessert: Portion of tiramisu (approx 500 calories, 30g fat). Made from eggs and mascarpone cheese, this trifle is a typically rich Italian dessert.

HEALTHIER ITALIAN MEAL
1,150 calories, 41g fat (approx).

With almost half the calories and less than half the fat and plenty of fresh fruit/salad.
Plain bread, 75g (approx. 240 calories, 5g fat)

Starter: Melon and Parma ham (approx 150 calories, 5g fat). Melon provides vitamin C and fibre, and average portion Parma ham weighs only 50g or so, so fat content is relatively low.

Main course: Spaghetti Napoletana (approx 450 calories, 10g fat).Large mixed side salad with olive oil dressing (120 calories, 10g fat). Sauces based on tomato are ideal Italian food – seafood or a little grated cheese can be added for protein. The salad provides vitamin C, and fibre. The dressing provides healthy olive oil.

Dessert: Portion zabaglione (200 calories, 11g fat). A fairly low-calorie treat.

ENTERTAINING AT HOME

Treat cooking for friends, neighbours and clients as you would going out for a meal. If you entertain rarely, it is not important to provide a meal that matches all the guidelines in 'Building Blocks of a Healthy Diet'. But if you do it very regularly, you will want perhaps to offer simple food.

Cram plenty of vegetables into the courses and serve less meat and dairy and more fish or plant protein. Rely more on flavour from herbs and spices, garlic, onions and tomatoes, for example, than from cream and cheese (though small amounts of hard cheese can be fine). There is no obligation to

produce a rich creamy dessert – most people will be happier with a small portion of, for example, a fruit sorbet, or a yogurt ice topped with strong espresso.

Use some of the recipes in the back of this book for inspiration.

BUDGET EATING

A complaint that I often hear from people is that they can't afford to eat a healthy diet – it is too expensive. Well – I have to disagree. With a few sensible tips and strategies, anyone can eat a good diet without spending a penny more than they did on whatever diet they were following before. Here's how.

Many of the healthy eating ideas and strategies you'll find in this book suggest eating in a way that should save you money. Eating less meat and more pulses, for example, should save you many pounds. Cutting back on less-healthy high-sugar items such as cakes, pastries and desserts should also save a lot. And swopping fizzy drinks for water certainly will! If you want to lose weight, rather than just eat for health, this one measure alone of reducing sugar in your diet should be enough to see weight coming off and save you money, too! Add in simply eating smaller portions, and the following ideas, and you will be pleasantly surprised how much spare cash you have.

WISE SHOPPING

Write a list before you shop so you don't fling random items in your trolley

(but be prepared to swop one or two things for similar products that are on offer, see 'be adaptable'). Shop when you are not hungry, as research shows we buy more than we need if we go round the supermarket feeling hungry. Shop alone – having other people, especially children, along makes you buy more. Don't be tempted by faddy diet plans that require you to buy super-expensive items, they are not necessary to eat healthily or to lose weight (for more on that, see Section Four). Shop at the end of the day when there will be many more items in the bargain section because they are at the end of their sell-by life.

USE YOUR FREEZER

Many healthy items can be found in the freezer sections and they are very often less expensive than their fresh counterparts – and are equally nutritious. A large 400g pack of, for example, green beans, might cost £2 while the fresh beans may be £2 for 150g. Berries are almost always considerably cheaper frozen.

You should also buy items you will use frequently – perhaps chicken breast fillets, salmon portions – either in bulk or when on special

Fruit and veg money-saving tips

❋ Remember that unfashionable veg and fruits (spring greens, blackcurrants) are usually just as good sources of plant chemicals and vitamins as are the more trendy and more expensive ones (kale, blueberries).

❋ Canned fruits and vegetables in water can be good standbys, especially in winter (they still count towards your five a day although their vitamin C will be somewhat diminished compared with fresh).

❋ If you find bargain price fresh vegetables when shopping, remember you can cut, blanch and freeze nearly all of them successfully.

❋ Fresh fruits bought in bulk can either be frozen as they are (e.g. berries, cherries) or chopped and microwaved for a minute or two then bagged (e.g. apples, plums, pears).

❋ Fruits nearing the end of their happy life in your fruit bowl can be pureed and frozen, or bananas with skins going brown can be frozen whole, then used to make banana ice cream.

❋ Fruit will keep its vitamin C content and remain fresh for longer if stored in the fridge rather than a warm room.

offer, and freeze them in individual portions. Similarly, you can buy a large wholegrain loaf even if you live alone, cut it into slices and freeze them individually so there is no waste. And if you're making meals yourself, make double or more and freeze the extras in single portions.

USE YOUR CUPBOARD

Very many store cupboard items are ultra-healthy and, very often, some of the least expensive foods you can buy. Think cans of pulses and tomatoes, dried pulses, dried wholegrains. And you're saving money by storing foods at ambient temperature.

USE YOUR LEFTOVERS

Avoid waste by making the most of your leftovers. Leftover veg can be turned into soups, added to stews, frozen for making curries and casseroles another time. Leftover meal portions such as curries and stews can be frozen. Make leftover scraps of cooked meat into a Chinese stir-fry or finely chop and add beans for a chilli.

Be adaptable – choose what's less expensive (e.g. swap one veg for another) if it will make little difference to your meal plan. Look in the bargains section at the supermarket, swap brands, maybe even swap shops to save money. Remember it can often be cheaper (and can be quicker if you're waiting for a home delivery) to make your own supper than rely on takeaways or ready meals.

VEGETARIAN AND VEGAN EATING

When I first wrote *The Food Bible* 20 years ago, vegetarianism was still thought of by many people in our staunchly meat-eating country as a rather weird idea. Now, how things have changed! It's estimated that up to 6% of the UK population, or 4 million people, are vegetarian.

This has meant that the choices available to vegetarians have expanded so that eating out, shopping for ingredients and ready meals, eating while travelling and general levels of choice have all become so much better, and that is true across the world.

If we haven't become 100% vegetarian, most of us now know that eating less meat is a healthy and planet-friendly thing to do, so we may eat more vegetarian meals, take one or two days out a week to eat vegetarian (e.g. 'meat-free Mondays') and generally have less of a close relationship with meat in our diets – so-called 'flexitarian' eating. On many levels, this is a good and positive step.

A VEGETARIAN DIET AND HEALTH

The vegetarian diet is perceived by most as a healthy one, and although there are a few potential pitfalls, this is, for the most part, true. Research has also shown that vegetarians and vegans tend to lead more generally healthy lives than non-vegetarians, for example, drinking less alcohol and taking more exercise.

Statistically, if you choose to go vegetarian – eating no meat, poultry, fish or flesh of any kind – you are choosing an option that should boost your chances of living a long and healthy life. Large research studies agree that, compared to non-vegetarians, vegetarians have up to 30% less heart disease, up to 40% less cancer, 20% less premature mortality, less obesity, lower blood pressure and less occurrence of several other disorders.

The health-giving properties of a typical vegetarian diet may also not simply be due to it containing no flesh. The benefits may be, for example, from eating more plant foods, such as fresh fruits and vegetables, grains and pulses, thus bringing the diet more in line with the healthy blueprint outlined in the previous pages of this section – more carbohydrate, more fibre, more vitamin C, more phytochemicals, for example.

Vegetarians, on average, have a lower body weight than non-vegetarians, and lower calorie intake itself has also been linked with longer lifespan. The vegetarian diet will also probably be higher in unsaturated fats (though this isn't always the case) and higher in essential fatty acids than that of a meat eater.

However, other statistics back up the theory that it isn't just giving up meat that procures the health benefits for the vegetarian. For example, health benefits similar to the vegetarian diet have been found in non-vegetarians who tend to eat high amounts of fruit and vegetables and little dairy produce. The population of the Greek island of Crete has extremely low rates of heart disease, cancer, obesity and early death, while eating meat in moderation and above average amounts of fish.

There are also unknown numbers of vegetarians who eat little fresh fruit and vegetables and exist on a vegetarian version of a junk diet. Teenage vegetarians seem particularly prone to eating an unbalanced and/or unvaried diet (see the Teenage Section, page 184–186).

The moral here appears to be that a healthy diet – whether vegetarian or non-vegetarian – is one high in natural plant foods (fresh fruits and vegetables, grains, nuts, seeds, pulses), low-saturated fat and non-animal fat sources of protein, and natural oils. If a vegetarian diet fits in with this blueprint, then it will be healthy.

THE THINGS TO WATCH OUT FOR WHEN STARTING A VEGETARIAN DIET ARE:

✳ Don't just give up meat and not replace it with other sources of the important nutrients that meat contains, particularly protein, selenium, iron and B vitamins.

✳ Don't just use dairy produce as your only meat replacement — if you do, you are likely to be eating too much saturated fat. However, there is plenty of research to show that hard cheeses and full-fat natural yogurts have several health benefits, so they can be incorporated into your regular diet. Low- or moderate-fat dairy products, such as skimmed milk, also have their place, providing calcium as well as protein.

✳ Eggs are a good source of iron and vitamins, and also provide protein. They do contain some saturated fat (but organic eggs will contain less saturates and more healthy fats) and we know now that their cholesterol content does not have a detrimental effect on cardiovascular health for the vast majority of people.

✳ Do eat plenty of plant sources of protein, such as pulses of all kinds and soya-based products, such as tofu, and, if you like it, textured vegetable protein (TVP). Quorn is a protein food made from a commercially manufactured mycoprotein similar to the protein to be found in mushrooms.

✳ Do take care to eat plenty of vegetarian sources of iron, selenium, and calcium (see box). Red meat is rich in easily-absorbed iron (haem iron); the iron from plant sources (non-haem iron) is less well absorbed, but with care a vegetarian diet can provide enough. In a recent survey, selenium levels have been found to be low in vegetarians

Vegetarian sources of:

Iron – curry powder, cast-iron cooking utensils, ground ginger, seaweed, fortified breakfast cereals, lentils, cocoa powder, sesame seeds, pumpkin seeds, soya beans, soya mince, dried peaches, haricot beans, red kidney beans, cashew nuts, pot barley, couscous, bulgar wheat, dried apricots, dark green leafy vegetables, eggs, brown rice, baked beans in tomato sauce, broccoli.

Selenium – Brazil nuts, lentils, sunflower seeds, wholemeal bread, cashew nuts, walnuts.

Calcium – poppy seeds, Parmesan cheese, Gruyère cheese, Cheddar cheese, Edam, sesame seeds, mozzarella, Brie, tofu, Danish blue cheese, feta cheese, white chocolate, almonds, soya beans, figs, milk chocolate, yoghurt, haricot beans, spinach, brazil nuts, chickpeas, kale, white bread, milk, prawns, broccoli, spring greens, white cabbage.

and vegans, but this varies from area to area – see toxicity advice on page 42. Vegetarians cutting down on dairy produce should eat plenty of seeds, tofu, pulses, nuts and leafy vegetables for their calcium content.

✻ Do get plenty of the foods rich in essential fatty acids, such as nuts, seeds and plant oils. If you don't eat fish you will be missing out on the omega-3 fatty acids EPA and DHA, but these can be converted in the body from alpha-linolenic acid, and linseeds (flaxseeds), linseed oil, hemp seeds and hemp seed oil, and walnuts are some of the best sources.

✻ The healthiest vegetarian diets are those that follow the general principles for healthy eating as outlined in this section and contain a wide variety of fresh, natural and whole foods, vegetables and fruits.

✻ For plenty of ideas on vegetarian meals, desserts and snacks, see our recipe section starting on page 215. Vegetarian and vegan recipes are marked with symbols (see page 217).

PLANT PROTEIN VERSUS ANIMAL PROTEIN

Animal sources of protein such as meat, dairy produce and eggs are what is termed 'complete' proteins, meaning that they contain all of the essential amino acids (see page 25), while most plant sources of protein may be termed 'incomplete' proteins, as they don't. The exceptions to this are soya and quinoa, both of which contain complete protein.

Until fairly recently it was thought that vegetarians should combine different protein sources at each meal to obtain all eight amino acids to provide 'complete' protein. This idea is now outdated, and researchers now

DIFFERENT TYPES OF MEAT-FREE, VEGETARIAN AND VEGAN EATING

Demi-vegetarian: Usually eats everything except red meat. Sometimes poultry is also excluded, but fish is included, though may be eaten only infrequently.

Pescatarian: Eats no meat or poultry but eats fish. May or may not eat eggs and dairy.

Lacto-ovo-vegetarian: Eats all dairy produce and eggs, but no flesh of any kind.

Lacto-vegetarian: Eats all dairy produce, but no eggs or flesh of any kind.

Vegan: Eats only plant foods—no dairy products, eggs or flesh, and no honey.

Fruitarian: Eats only fruits (at least 75% of diet), uncooked vegetables (mostly leafy vegetables), raw nuts, seeds and beansprouts.

Sproutarian: Eats mostly sprouted seeds, grains, pulses and rice.

Macrobiotic: Excludes all meat, poultry, dairy produce and eggs, but at initial levels may eat fish. Diet may progressively become more and more restricted, with the final level being a diet of brown rice only.

Raw foodism: Some vegans, fruitarians and sproutarians, as well as other people, choose to eat only raw food.

know that a varied diet on a daily basis, containing a wide range of vegetarian protein foods, is sufficient, without worrying about providing 'complete' protein at every meal.

THE LONE VEGETARIAN IN THE FAMILY

Catering for a sole vegetarian may seem daunting and can be time-consuming if you need to make separate meals for family members. Often the sole vegetarian may be a teenager. Here are some ideas to make catering easier:

✳ Gradually introduce more non-meat meals into the whole family's menus – many of the recipes at the back of the book should inspire you. Meat lovers will appreciate the robust flavours and textures of brown or green lentils and several of the pulses, especially Egyptian brown beans, borlotti beans and black beans.

✳ Make full use of wholemeal pasta – you can cook pasta with a vegetarian sauce based on tomatoes or pesto, for example, freezing the surplus sauce in batches, and serve a sauce with added meat for the rest of the family. Again, vegetarian pasta dishes make an excellent dish for meat eaters anyway.

✳ Some vegetarian dishes are easy to cook ahead and freeze. Things like bean casseroles, curries based on potatoes, aubergines, squash (freeze undercooked), nut and bean burgers and loaves all freeze successfully.

✳ Make main-course salads for the whole family and substitute non-vegetarian items for the lone veggie, e.g. salad Niçoise for the family, but use silken tofu instead of tuna for the vegetarian.

✳ For lunches or suppers, make chunky soups which are basically vegetarian and committed meat eaters can add chunks of chicken, ham, prawns, etc.

✳ Pizzas please everyone – and, again, you can add small amounts of shellfish or meat topping as required.

✳ Pulses are an important nutritional source for vegetarians — canned, precooked beans are fine, and widely available, but if you do soak and boil your own pulses you can freeze leftovers in individual bags for another occasion.

✳ There is now a wide range of healthy non-meat and non-dairy burgers, rashers, sausages and patties available in the supermarkets. It is important to find out just what the person you're catering for will and won't eat before cooking anything for him or her.

NON-VEGETARIAN OR VEGAN INGREDIENTS TO WATCH OUT FOR

Rennet: This enzyme from the stomach of animals is used in the production of some hard cheeses (as a curdling agent) and, therefore, these cheeses are unsuitable for most vegetarians. If a hard cheese isn't labelled 'vegetarian', it probably does contain rennet. However, many hard cheeses are now being produced without rennet, using plant curdling agents, and these are widely available.

Gelatine: Derived from the bones of animals (often cows) and therefore obviously unacceptable to most vegetarians. Can be present in any commercial dessert or product requiring a setting agent—e.g. mousses, moulds, jellies, even fruit yoghurts. The vegetarian alternative is agar-agar, derived from seaweed and fairly easy to obtain.

Worcestershire sauce: Usually contains anchovies, but some brands don't, so read the label.

Stock cubes: Vegetable stock cubes are usually free of animal produce, but it is worth reading the label.

Margarine: May contain fish oils. Read the label.

Honey: Some vegetarians, and vegans, won't eat honey because it comes from bees.

When catering for any type of vegetarian it is best to talk to them to discover just exactly how strict they are. Some vegetarians also eat only organic produce and/or whole foods.

VEGAN EATING

Vegan eating has risen in the UK by 360% in the past decade, and it is estimated that there are over 500,000 vegans. There is also a large number of people who include vegan meals

Vegan sources of:

Calcium: Fortified soya and other fortified plant milks, white bread, baked beans, dried figs, leafy green vegetables, tofu, nuts, muesli, pulses.

Selenium: Brazil nuts, lentils, sunflower seeds, wholemeal bread, cashew nuts.

Iodine: Seaweed, Vecon, kelp supplements.

Vitamin B12: fortified breakfast cereals, fortified soya milk and other fortified plant milks, Marmite, Vecon, fortified bread, vegan B12 supplements.

Vitamin D: Fortified vegetarian margarines, fortified breakfast cereals, fortified soya milk and other fortified plant milks, sunlight.

Riboflavin: fortified breakfast cereal, soya milk, fortified soya and other fortified plant milks, Marmite, Vecon.

in their flexitarian diet – and the availability of imaginative, delicious vegan ready meals, takeaways, ingredients and treats is testimony to that.

Vegans eat no dairy produce of any kind, or eggs, or anything from an animal, including honey. Calorie consumption is consistently lower in vegans than in non-vegetarians and in vegetarians, because the diet contains more high-bulk/low calorie foods like fruits and vegetables, and protein intake is about 75% of average.

The vegetarian and vegan store cupboard

Here is a list of items you will find invaluable in your store if catering for a non-meat eater, or converting yourself. Remember even store cupboard items deteriorate with time, so don't buy large packs for one person, as they may not be eaten soon enough.

✳ Dried pulses of several kinds, including various lentils and an assortment of differently coloured and textured beans, plus chickpeas.

✳ Canned beans, chickpeas and lentils as above; especially good if you are busy. Chickpeas are an ideal standby for a quick snack – puréed with olive oil and garlic, they make a quick and tasty hummus.

✳ Shelled and unshelled unsalted fresh nuts and seeds, such as almonds, hazelnuts, walnuts, Brazils, pumpkin seeds, sunflower seeds, sesame seeds. Need to be stored in a cool dark dry cupboard. Chopped and ground nuts are best stored in the fridge.

✳ Grains which don't take long to prepare, such as quick-cook brown rice, quinoa and bulgar.

✳ Other grains, such as barley and millet, which are useful for casseroles – or you can buy packs of mixed grains.

✳ Selection of pastas and noodles (best wholegrain), and some quick-cook polenta.

✳ Breakfast oats and no-added sugar muesli.

✳ Flours of various kinds, including high-protein types such as chickpea and soya.

✳ Dried fruits, such as apricots, prunes, figs, dates, sultanas.

✳ Cans of tomatoes and other vegetables which are good in cans, such as sweet peppers and artichoke hearts, black and green olives.

✳ Cans of ready-made hummus, pasta and pizza sauces, chilli sauce, soya sauce, black bean sauce.

✳ Dried spices and herbs.

✳ Jars or tubes of tomato paste, passata, pesto.

✳ Vegetarian stock cubes and vegetarian Worcestershire-type sauce.

✳ A good selection of extra virgin oils, which need to be stored in a dark, cool cupboard.

✳ Vinegars, perhaps including white and red wine, cider, balsamic.

✳ Honey (not for vegans – maple syrup would be a suitable substitute), molasses, unrefined sugars.

However, the average vegan diet provides MORE than the national average of vitamin C, magnesium, copper, folate, beta-carotene and essential fatty acids. Total fat intake is about 25% lower than average and saturates intake is 50% lower, while carbohydrate intake is nearly 55% of total calories consumed, and fibre intake is higher than the national average and higher, indeed, than in vegetarian diets.

Nutrients that are most likely to be in shortfall if care isn't taken are calcium, selenium, iodine, vitamin D, vitamin B12 and possibly riboflavin.

RESTRICTED EATING

Since I wrote the first edition of *The Food Bible* there has been a huge increase in the number of people who follow what are often termed faddy and/or restricted diets. For example, I have a friend whose diet excludes dairy, wheat, gluten and 'white' (refined) carbs, while another avoids red meat, all processed foods and sugar, and eats only what she considers to be 'clean' food. We all know someone who swears by their 'superfood' diet of hard to get berries, super-expensive seeds and flours made from coconut and teff - anything except wheat. Indeed – you may be that person. But is restricted eating really benefitting you? I take a look at the pros and cons.

It's important to be clear that there are some medical conditions which mean the sufferer needs to exclude certain foods. Some of the most common include lactose intolerance, which mean lactose-containing foods such as milk and other dairy products need to be excluded or severely restricted; coeliac disease, which is an allergy to gluten, found in wheat, rye, and barley (and a similar compound found in oats is also often avoided). And there are some foods – such as peanuts, shellfish, and eggs – that can cause a severe allergic reaction in a minority of people, who must scrupulously avoid even a tiny amount of them.

For these people, the avoidance of the trigger food/s is, of course, the only sensible and medically-approved action. Special diets for diagnosed health conditions are discussed in Section Two.

And we can't include vegetarians/ vegans in this list of people who practise food avoidance as not only have veganism and vegetarianism been recognised as a way of life for communities and people across the world back into history, they also tend to be the result of social, environmental or faith beliefs. And, as we've seen earlier, by and large these diets promote good health.

But hundreds of thousands of people – maybe more – who haven't received a medical diagnosis, and are not simply vegetarian, nevertheless avoid certain foods that they believe make them unwell or overweight or sometimes simply less attractive. Some experts call food avoidance like this a form of eating disorder, while the 'gurus' of the various restricted eating regimes will promote the opposite view.

FREE FROM DIETS

Gluten-free has perhaps gained the biggest following of all the free-from diets in the past ten years or so, rising worldwide over 12% in 2016 and many followers are aware that they are not gluten intolerant although many believe that they are.

Going gluten free, which means giving up all foods that contain wheat, rye, barley (and sometimes oats) as well as a myriad of gluten-containing processed foods, is not easy. The pros are that giving up all those processed foods may be beneficial as a more natural diet is likely to be healthier. Giving up the most popular grains, particularly wholegrains, is less beneficial unless you replace them with healthy gluten-free grains like buckwheat, brown rice and quinoa.

Interestingly, recent wide-ranging research at Harvard University has found that people following a gluten-free diet are more likely to develop diabetes and heart disease and that there is no evidence that reducing gluten consumption provides long-term health benefits for people who are not coeliac. Processed gluten-free foods can be higher in fats and sugar than their gluten-containing counterparts.

Dairy-free diets can increase the risk of osteoporosis because dairy is the main source of calcium in our diets so again, care needs to be taken. And the health benefits of avoiding dairy are currently being hotly disputed as it seems previously persecuted items such as hard cheese, dairy milk and

yogurt may actually be beneficial for most of us.

Sugar-free diets are perhaps the most sensible free-from to take on board. Free sugars have no health benefits, little or nothing in the way of nutrients other than calories and contribute to weight problems, dental caries and the obesity epidemic in the young.

The main problem with many sugar-free 'gurus' is that if you look at their recipe books and websites, in fact they often advocate sugar alternatives which are – sugar. Honey, maple syrup, date syrup, agave nectar, for example. They are all basically sugar and have a similar effect in our bodies. Eat too much – you'll probably get fat. We discuss sugar and alternatives more in Section Four.

Clean eating diets: The rise of the clean-eating gurus has been recent but powerful. People – usually young and beautiful people – telling us to 'eat clean'. Of course, we don't want to 'eat dirty' so it sounds like a good idea. But what is it?

Basically it is usually about eating whole foods, or 'real' foods – those that are processed as little as possible, unrefined, natural. Perhaps organic, local, as well; may be meat-free, sugar-free, dairy-free, alkaline, or a combination of any of those, too.

There are some good points to the promotion of clean eating. A whole and natural diet should be a healthy and happy thing. But the negative may be that it is just a bit too obsessive; too restrictive.

Life is busy and complicated enough, without having to follow lots of rules on exactly how and what to eat and without remembering what's forbidden. Such a regime could potentially be the springboard for orthorexia.

Most of the clean-eating regimes (and there are many variations) will reduce the calories you consume, so they could be called slimming diets by another name – another reason why I believe a lot of people begin them. You don't have to say, 'I'm on a diet' ('I'm fat, I'm old-hat') – just 'I'm eating clean' ('I'm on trend'). That said, the term 'clean eating' seems to be fading from fashion even as I write ...

Superfoods – what are they and do we need them?

A big fad of the early years of this century was the quest for a diet high in 'superfoods' – items that are often hard to find, nearly always expensive and exclusive therefore. Foods that come to mind are goji berries, wheat grass, acai berries, edamame beans, white tea, shiitake mushrooms and sprouted chickpeas (but there are plenty more).

Yes, each of these items have health benefits. But not one of them has benefits that can't be found elsewhere, and cheaper. And perhaps the alternatives will taste even nicer, too. All berries are rich sources of vitamin C, plant chemicals and fibre, for example, while black and green teas are packed with good-for-you chemicals and broad beans and peas are great alternatives to edamame beans at a quarter of the price.

Pears, apples, oranges, cabbage, sprouts, broccoli – these are perhaps the real 'superfoods' along with dozens of other 'ordinary' foods – because we eat them in reasonable quantities rather than just adding a few pricy goji berries to our cereal, for example, and because they all have a range of health-giving properties. Unsung heroes – never forget them.

If you particularly like them and can afford them, then by all means add 'superfoods' to your diet, but please don't think they are all necessary in order for you to eat healthily.

SUMMARY

Let's face it, food used to be what you could get, near where you lived. You ate what you ate to survive and because there was little choice. With our modern life of multi-choices has come the long list of restrictive eating patterns. It makes you different. It may make you stand out, get people interested in you. But will it make you well? I doubt it.

It could even make you ill. Back in the 1990s the term orthorexia (an obsession

with healthy eating) was coined by a US doctor, and the American National Eating Disorders Association says, 'Orthorexia starts out as an innocent attempt to eat more healthfully, but orthorexics become fixated on food quality and purity. They become consumed with what and how much to eat, and how to deal with "slip-ups". An iron-clad will is needed to maintain this rigid eating style. Eventually, the obsession can crowd out other activities and interests, impair relationships, and become physically dangerous.'

While eating a healthy varied diet can be a great natural pleasure, it is rarely necessary to take things a lot further than that in order to be as healthy as you can be via food. And avoiding whole food groups and/or strictly following rigid rules about what you must and mustn't eat can be detrimental to a happy and healthy life, for certain.

Most of us have foods we like, foods we like less, and a very few foods that we really dislike. Most of us have so much food choice around us that avoiding those few disliked foods isn't a problem – the nutrients they contain can easily be found elsewhere.

But if you do, or are considering, restricting yourself by avoiding large food groups such as dairy or grains, or avoiding one of the macronutrients – fat, or carbs for example – it's worth asking yourself a few questions first. Who are the people telling me to eat this way? What is their knowledge? What do the scientists say are the pros and cons of avoiding these foods? Do your research. And if you decide to go ahead, make sure you know what nutrients you may be missing out on by following the restricted diet, and make sure you know how to replace those nutrients in your diet. ■

Food From Farm to Table

FOOD SUSTAINABILITY, food availability, food ethics and food safety – these are all legitimate concerns for most people today, just as much as is food and health. In this section I look at the choices to be made all along the food chain, and how to deal with them.

FOOD PRODUCTION

Modern intensive farming is the result of our international quest for cheap and plentiful foods, in the face of a growing population. However, it has brought all kinds of problems which governments have been working to solve in recent years.

CROPS

After the Second World War, the use of chemicals in the production of our food crops – everything from grains to vegetables, fruits and salads, from field to orchard to greenhouse, which account for around 33% of our UK

total spend on food – quickly became standard procedure. It seemed nothing but a good idea to use pesticides to kill insects and other creatures that were damaging crops, herbicides to kill weeds that were choking them and fungicides to cure diseases, as well as applying artificial fertilisers to help maintain the fertility of the new-style large-scale farms where, with the help of modern mechanization, food production could be vastly increased by growing just one type of crop on the same land, year after year.

Within a decade or two we had – almost miraculously – food that was plentiful, cheap and widely available. And as our fruit and veg appeared clean they no longer needed scrubbing before use...

As the agri-industry took off, farms became vast and specialized; hedges, woods, ponds and wildlife disappeared and, by the end of the twentieth century, hundreds of different chemicals, which often lingered on our food, were being used.

Nowadays, many crops are also treated after being harvested with preservatives and inhibitors to prolong their life for transportation, storage (sometimes for months or even years) and shelf-life.

But by the early years of this century, the drawbacks of intensive farming were beginning to become apparent. Many common pests and diseases were becoming resistant to the chemicals used. Fertilizers, too, often needed to be used in larger and larger quantities to achieve the required results, and artificially fertilized soils were sometimes found to be deficient in vital nutrients such as selenium. And many people began to realise they did not enjoy the idea of intensive farming methods – not only for personal health reasons (for example, unwittingly eating pesticide residues on their food), but also for the environment's sake.

Minimising residues on food

Wash all fruits and vegetables thoroughly before eating.

* The most effective way is to peel vegetables and fruits where appropriate – apples and carrots are particularly likely to carry residues on their skins.
* For items that can't be peeled, wash in a mild organic liquid soap and rinse very thoroughly.
* Discard outer leaves of leafy greens and salads.
* Buy organic.

Thus, the past ten years has seen governments, official bodies and food production companies working ever harder to find solutions on how to feed the world sustainably, while eliminating the intensive farming practices that can cause the most damage. The EU recently banned several insecticides because of their impact on bee population for example, and strict rules are in place for the use of herbicides and pesticides on our farmland and foods are regularly tested for residue levels, and maximum levels set for safety. Modern farmers must increasingly justify and assess the impact of their activities on the environment with hefty penalties and fines if they do not adhere to the rules.

The work to date has produced some results, such as the decline of use of nitrogen and phosphorus fertilisers in recent years; estimated agricultural emissions of nitrous oxide have fallen by 10%, of ammonia by 12%, and of methane by 11%.

The concepts of Integrated Crop/

GENETIC MODIFICATION AND FOOD

The world – with a population estimated to be nine billion within 20-30 years – needs to create up to twice as much food in the next few decades, while at the same time facing challenges to preserve the environment and tackle climate change (which mean that food sources need to be more resilient to extreme conditions). The need for higher food yields from land will be paramount, it seems.

While the public, especially in the UK, has been vehement in its dislike of the idea of genetically modified or engineered food, the subject can't be ignored. Indeed, many leading experts believe that genetic technology may be the main solution to our future food security, not only by giving us higher-yield crops but also by engineering crops that contain better nutrient levels, and that are resistant to disease, drought, and so on.

Despite much protest, the fact that half the countries of the EU ban cultivation of GM foods, and they are not grown commercially in the UK (while the UK is currently reviewing its legislation) and GM ingredients are by and large shunned in all UK supermarkets, the world has experienced a big increase in the amount of GM crops grown in the past two decades, and it seems genetic engineering of our food is not going to go away anytime soon.

But are GM foods safe for human consumption or not? The majority of scientific research says – yes, it's safe. Twenty years of large and thorough studies haven't found significant risk to health, or to the environment.

If however you don't want to buy any foods with GM elements in them, then the labels must say if a food does contain or consist of 'genetically modified organisms' according to current EU regulations. For GM products sold 'loose', similar information must be displayed next to the food. However, products from animals fed on GM material do not have to be labelled, and neither do, for example, products produced with GM technology, for example, cheese made using GM enzymes. Organic food production is GM free.

Pest Management are encouraging producers to use natural methods of pest control such as nematodes and mulches, and by choosing naturally disease-resistant varieties of crops to grow, and while chemicals are still used in certain circumstances, preventative spraying is discouraged.

MEAT FARMING

Price is the single biggest factor in consumers' food purchasing decisions, according to a Defra survey reported in 2016 – and perhaps the item that we want to save most money on is meat, as it can be one of the most expensive items in the shopping trolley.

Low-cost meat, in general, means farming animals that grow quickly and take up as little space, food and labour as possible in so doing. In order for this to happen, intensive farming may take on board several practices with which many people find they are becoming disenchanted.

To keep feeding costs low, animals once routinely put out to graze on grass, which is not a fast way of adding weight, are now often kept indoors in small spaces and fed on manufactured foods, such as pellets made from the ground-up remains of other animals. This saves on land and labour costs.

Unfortunately, the animals don't get enough exercise, so they become weak, and in crowded conditions are more likely to become unhealthy and more prone to infections, which can quickly spread through a farm. This means antibiotics need to be used almost constantly. Forty per cent of all antibiotics in the UK are given to farm animals.

Antibiotic residues can last through the food chain until our meat and dairy food is on the plate and it is thought that this widespread use of antibiotics is a main reason why the medications no longer work well on humans – the bugs in our bodies have largely become resistant

Animals that do graze on 'natural' pasture may be eating food that has been sprayed with chemical weed-killers and fertilizers, which may show up later in the meat and milk (see below).

For people who don't like the sound of buying meat farmed in this way, there are alternatives. Labels such as 'grass fed' 'outdoor reared' are good to buy, and see our section on organics, too. Yes, these are more expensive – but as we are urged to eat less red meat for our health's sake, this may be a good place to say – buy smaller amounts, eat less.

Another tip is to buy lean meat, as residues tend to accumulate in the fat of animals. Think perhaps of buying game birds from your local butcher rather than factory farmed meat. In any case, it always helps ensure better quality meat if you buy from a source who can tell you where it came from.

DAIRY PRODUCE

Cow's milk and dairy products such as butter, cheese and yoghurt represent about 10% of what we spend on food

in the UK, and they are enjoying a renaissance in popularity as we are told of their health benefits. As with meat production, the pressure is on dairies and producers to keep costs low and output high, and this is partly because the supermarkets pay so little to dairy farmers for their produce. Thus, many of the dairy herds in the UK are kept in sheds rather than out in fields and given pre-produced feed.

Like other farm foods, milk and dairy goods may contain small amounts of any pollutants or medications that the animal has eaten. Dairy cows, for example, are at high risk of succumbing to mastitis – an infection of the udder that affects 30% of dairy cows and is routinely treated with antibiotics. Dairy is regularly monitored by the government and most of the dairy food and milk consumed in the UK is pasteurized, which is a heating process that destroys most of any potential harmful bacteria present.

Unpasteurized (raw) milk is available to buy direct from some farm shops, farms and markets, and fans of it say it tastes better than pasteurized milk and contains beneficial bacteria which are destroyed in the heating process, as well as more of the vitamin B group, which is destroyed at high temperatures. It is, they say, also more easily digested.

However, raw milk may contain bacteria such as salmonella, E. coli, and listeria, all of which can cause severe illness. In recent years, this fact has been somewhat underplayed, but in 2017 a US report from the US Centre for Disease Control and Prevention stated that those who drink raw milk are 840 times more likely to become ill. Children, people who are unwell, pregnant women and older people are particularly vulnerable to food poisoning and shouldn't have unpasteurised milk or cream, or some dairy products made with unpasteurised milk.

EGGS

Eggs are probably more popular in the UK than they have been for 30 years or more, because producers have managed to all but eradicate salmonella from them and they are nutritious and healthy. The consumer has a large choice of which type of egg to buy, regarding how it has been produced.

Eggs sold in the UK must be stamped with the method of production: 0 is organic, 1 is free-range, 2 is barn, and 3 is caged and the method should also be on the carton. The British Lion symbol tells you that the eggs are British-laid and the hens have been vaccinated against salmonella. All this said, production standards vary even within each category. Hens which produce the eggs carrying the Freedom Foods logo however do receive regular inspections to ensure high welfare standards.

Caged

Battery cages were banned in the EU in 2012, and mass-produce hens now live in 'enriched' cages. The birds have a little more room – 13 to 14 hens per square metre – but they have their beaks trimmed off to stop the birds pecking each other. Eggs from non-EU countries and excluding the UK may have been laid by birds housed in old style battery cages. The birds are often fed with a crumb mix of items that may include wheat, maize, soya, seeds, minerals and often shell grit.

Barn eggs

Barn-living hens live in large, sometimes massive, barns and can roam within that building. They also have perches and nest boxes for laying eggs. But most barn-raised hens stay inside all their lives with up to nine hens per square metre and also have their beaks trimmed.

Free range

Free range hens may live in barns – again, sometimes mind-bogglingly massive as there is no maximum flock size specified unless the eggs are RSPCA assured, when it is 16,000 max – but which have access doors to the outside for use during daylight hours, where there should be vegetation and four square metres or more of space for each bird. At night they are kept inside the barn with perches and bedding, and nine hens a square metre. Beak trimming is commonly, but not always, practised. Eggs from free range hens have up to 30% more vitamin D than from caged birds.

Organic

Organically raised hens have less crowded living conditions indoors – up to six hens per square metre, and outdoors they have 10 square metres for Soil Association standards (4sqm EU standard). The flocks must be no more than 3,000 birds (2,000 for UK Soil Association standard) and the beaks must not be trimmed. The diet should in most circumstances be organic, must be free from GM ingredients, and antibiotics must not be used routinely.

Other categories of eggs have emerged in recent years but aren't categories with numbers like the previous four.

Pasture-raised eggs are a type of freerange egg when hens are allowed to roam free, eating plants and insects (their natural food) along with some commercial feed. Pasture-raised eggs may also be organic, but not necessarily. Eggs from hens raised by the pasture method have been shown to contain more – sometimes much more – beneficial nutrients including omega-3 fats, vitamin A and E than do non-pasture raised eggs.

Omega-3 enriched eggs have a higher proportion of the healthy fat because the hens are fed an omega-3 rich diet but may live in barns and not see pasture at all.

FISH

We are all being encouraged to eat two portions of fish a week and yet the Marine Stewardship Council has a long list of fishes that are now endangered and they advise us not to buy them – indeed, the fishing industry is tightly controlled in what it can and cannot catch, so the number of different species of fish we can buy from British waters is limited.

Also, our rivers, seas and oceans are becoming more polluted and so the fish that are allowed to be caught may be polluted by industrial waste or bacteria, or even oestrogen-mimicking chemicals released into river waters. A 2017 scare found that wild salmon may be polluted with the dangerous anisakis larvae. So farmed fish is the alternative many of us choose, with fish farming having increased as an industry from 5% of consumed fish in 1970 to over half of all the fish we buy now.

But sadly fish farmers have their problems too – in recent times outbreaks of sea lice infestations have hit supplies. Incidence of farms affected has increased from a quarter to over a half in recent years. In the UK, farmed salmon, for example, is reared in huge cages in lochs or coastal in conditions not dissimilar to intensively reared animals. And because of the nature of aquaculture, diseases and pest issues are becoming more common and harder to eradicate. The lice are killed by means of warm water wash or hydrogen peroxide. Others have been affected by AGD – which causes fish to suffocate and can transfer to wild fish – and other diseases, which are usually treated with antibiotics.

Another issue is that, as many of the species farmed are carnivorous, they are fed largely on wild-caught fish. Over 450 billion fish are caught each year for reduction to fish oil and fishmeal and much of this fish feed may be from polluted waters.

However, we still want to eat fish and if we choose wisely and accept that prices are rising because of scarcity and farm issues, we can eat fish safely.

For the best advice on fish that's safe and ethical to eat right now, visit the Marine Stewardship Council's website.

For safer fish

✳ Look for the MSC (Marine Stewardship Council) label on fish.

✳ White fish from the deeper waters, such as cod and haddock, is less likely to be affected by pollution.

✳ Scallops, crabs, lobsters and the prawn family are less likely to be affected by pollution/bacteria than shellfish that live on the shoreline, like mussels and oysters. The latter are cleaned before sale, or cultured, in which case they should be sold as such and be pollution-free naturally.

✳ Farmed organic fish, including cod, bass and other white sea fishes, is a good alternative to farmed salmon.

✳ Oily fish and fish livers are more likely to be affected as toxins such as cadmium and dioxins are stored in fat and liver.

ORGANIC FARMING

Sales of organic food in the UK are worth £2 billion annually (1.5% of the food and drink market). Organic farming can take up to 5 years to establish and only a handful of chemicals (as opposed to about 300 in standard farming) are allowed under rules laid down in the UK by the Advisory Committee on Organic Standards (ACOS), which allows 7 bodies, such as the Soil Association, to inspect and certify farms.

Methods used are based on the traditional ones of keeping crops healthy with good soil, rotation and natural fertilizers, wherever possible, and choosing suitable crops for the

Organic pros and cons

Pros:

✳ Residues of chemicals and antibiotics can be up to five times lower in organic than conventional produce.

✳ Some studies find higher level of nutrients in organic food than conventionally produced food, including some anti-oxidants and, in dairy produce, omega-3 fats.

✳ The longer growing/maturing periods, production methods and lower water content mean some people say organic food has more flavour.

✳ Organic dairy produce may protect children from eczema.

Cons:

✳ Usually around 60% more expensive.

✳ Takes more land to produce organic food.

✳ Imported organic food has travelled many airmiles, and some foreign organic standards are lower than ours.

✳ Some organics may need to be consumed quickly because of lack of preservatives.

local environment. Pests and weeds are normally controlled by natural predators and methods.

Organic producers believe that their methods are better for the environment and for the long-term health of the planet, diversity of species and food security and sustainability. However, a recent major report from the University of Columbia found that yield is 40% lower than on conventional farms, the extra land needed to produce a comparable amount of food actually adds to greenhouse gasses and water shortages and the increase in lost wild habitat across the world. But that organic farming may be better for biodiversity and soil health. In the UK in 2017, the Advertising Standards Authority banned an organic milk producer's claim that it was 'good for the land'.

FOOD PROCESSING AND PRESERVING

FRESH FOOD – BUT IS IT?

Once food is harvested or slaughtered, much of it is sold unprocessed via the shops. When you go to buy it, however, all is not necessarily as it seems. How fresh is 'fresh', for instance, and does it matter to your health? There are various ways the food industry can keep things looking fresh for weeks, months or even years. For example:

Post-harvest spraying: Many fruits, including apples, pears and grapes, and some vegetables, including potatoes, may be treated with preservative sprays (E230–233) to prolong life. There is no way of telling which have been sprayed, but a person eating a healthy diet rich in fruits and veg may be getting quite a dose. Organic food should not be sprayed.

Controlled-atmosphere storage/ climate-controlled warehouses: Most of the biggest-selling fruits in the Western world – such as oranges, pears, and lemons – are routinely harvested and then stored in a controlled atmosphere with reduced oxygen and increased nitrogen and carbon dioxide. This prevents ripening and ageing. The major commercial gas, SmartFresh, used on several fruits, contains 1-methylcyclopropene, which halts production of ethylene, the gas produced when fruits ripen. It is used for example on apples, bananas, tomatoes and pears. Today, apples can be stored this way for at least two years.

Modified-atmosphere packaging is used for many foods, particularly salad bags and fresh meat, to improve shelf-life and appearance. It means the replacement of air in a pack with a single gas or mixture of gases; for example, the amount of oxygen/carbon dioxide in the pack is manipulated. Ready salad leaves and vegetables are also often washed in water containing chlorine.

Waxing: Citrus fruits, apples and various other fruits and vegetables, including organic ones, are often wax coated with natural waxes approved for the purpose. This keeps the fruit moist and extends shelf-life. A substance sometimes used in waxing, shellac, is derived from insects so would not be vegetarian or vegan-suitable. There is no obligatory labelling, but 'unwaxed' fruits are usually labelled as such.

Genetic engineering: For more on this see page 94, but basically food scientists can now inject 'long-life'

genes into various foods, such as tomatoes, pineapples and bananas. These raw foods are not currently on sale in the UK.

Irradiation: Irradiation, described by the UK Government as 'similar to pasteurization', can be used to kill bacteria that cause food poisoning, can delay fruit ripening and help stop potatoes and onions, for example, from sprouting. It is a process that has been declared safe by the World Health Organization and others. There may be some vitamin loss, they say, but no more than would happen with normal storage. Several types of food, including herbs and spices, fruit, vegetables, cereals, fish and poultry, can be irradiated in the UK, but labelling must state 'irradiated' or 'treated with ionising radiation'.

FOOD PROCESSING

In general, the more a food is processed, the more it is likely to lose in terms of its natural nutrients, and the less 'natural' it will be. As a very simple example, strawberries are high in vitamin C and fibre, but add them to sugar and make strawberry jam in a factory and you lose almost all of the vitamin C, and some of the fibre. Highly processed food is often highly refined, and tends to lose its vitamins, plant nutrients and fibre most frequently.

Where some things are taken away, however, others are added. Processed food is notoriously rich in high-calorie, not so healthy ingredients such as sugar and saturated fat. The cream that is skimmed off milk is used in items such as desserts and sauces. And so on!

STORE CUPBOARD FOODS COMPARED

CANNED:

Pros: will store for up to several years, convenient, low cost, long life.
Cons: brine-canned foods high in salt; syrup-canned foods high in sugar. Vitamins B and C depleted because canning process uses heat. Cans are often coated with the chemical BPA linked with some cancers and other health problems. The European Food Safety Authority has declared it poses no risk, but many experts are still concerned about its safety. Some major manufacturers are looking for alternative coatings.

GLASS BOTTLES/JARS:

Pros: can store for several years; glass is a clean vessel with no chemical leaching. Re-usable.
Cons: vitamins and food quality will be depleted if stored in light. Breakable.

PLASTIC BOTTLES:

Pros: Unbreakable, easy to store.
Cons: BPA leaches into liquids, but Cancer UK says the risk to healthy is minimal; others disagree. Should not store for long periods.

UHT:

Pros: can store for up to 6 months.
Cons: vitamin loss and taste change; BPA may be present.

AMBIENT:

(processed food stored at room temperature, such as jellies)
Pros: can store up to 3 months.
Cons: generally high in chemical preservatives/E numbers.

DRIED:

Pros: convenient, can store up to a year.
Cons: Depending on the type of food dried, may lose flavour, vitamin C, texture, or become tough. Dried fruit may have sulphur dioxide added.

Processed/refined food often contains fortifying ingredients to replace lost vitamins and minerals (as in many breakfast cereals, for example, or in the case of white bread which, by law, is fortified with calcium in the UK), perhaps adding fibre and other 'healthy' things which is then sometimes termed 'functional food'!

Less welcome than these additions, though, are the ones that are put in the processing pot for other reasons.

E NUMBERS AND ADDITIVES

Processed food labels may well contain a long list of E numbers, additives and items that you wouldn't consider necessary. Yet it is estimated that each of us eats about 2.25kg (5lb) of additives a year.

✳ **Colours E100-E180:** Used to make perhaps less-than-attractive foods look better or to restore a 'natural' colour to items where colour has been lost in processing.

✳ **Preservatives E200-E285, E1105:** Used to prolong product life and prevent bacteria build-up. Even 'healthy' foods, such as dried apricots, will probably contain preservative (in the case of dried fruit, usually sulphur dioxide, a known allergen).

✳ **Antioxidants E300-E321:** Used to stop the product going rancid.

✳ **Emulsifiers, stabilisers, thickeners E322-495:** Used in products such as fat-reduced desserts, soups and sauces to enhance texture and stop separation.

✳ **Processing aids E500-E578:** Used for a variety of reasons.

✳ **Flavour-enhancers E620-E640:** Used to improve flavour in processed foods.

✳ **Glazing agents E901-E914:** Used to add glaze and shine, and attractive appearance to foods.

✳ **Flour-improvers and bleaches:** e.g. E920- E926: Used in baked goods and breads to improve texture, cooking quality and whiteness.

✳ **Sweeteners e.g. E420/421 and E953-959:** To add sweetness in place of sugars.

✳ **Miscellaneous E999-E1518.**

In addition to these, your product may also contain one or more flavourings which don't have E numbers and needn't be declared on the label. For people without known reactions, the additives are deemed safe (at normal levels of intake) by the government. However, nobody really knows what long-term effects there might be on, say, a person who eats a diet high in additives (a typical 'junk food diet') from early life on, and research indicates that some additives can cause cancer in animals.

Food additives that may cause problems

A small percentage of the population may be allergic to, or intolerant of, one or more. Those reported to cause most problems are:

✳ The coal-tar and azo dyes E102 (tartrazine), E104, E110, E122, E123, E124, E127, E128, E131, E132, E133, E142, E151, E154, E155.
✳ The colorant cochineal (E120).
✳ The colorant annatto (E160b).
✳ The preservative benzoates and sulphides (E210-E219 and E220-228).
✳ Antioxidants E310, E311, E312, E320, E321.

IN YOUR HANDS

FOOD AT THE SHOPS

Now it's over to you – the farmers and manufacturers have done all they can to bring you food. It's your turn. What will you buy? The amount of choice in the shops these days is so huge that it can be hard making the right choices.

You want food you – and for many of us, the family – will enjoy. And you want it to be healthy and safe to eat. These next few pages help you make the right choices in shopping, storing, preparing and cooking.

BEFORE YOU SHOP

Planning your meals is the ideal way to go, both to save time, money and wastage and to get yourself a balanced diet. If you can do this once a week, even better – but even if you can only manage planning a day ahead, do it!

A list is a great idea – research shows it will help you spend less money, be less tempted by extras and special offers you don't need and will save you time in the shop. When making the list, see what you've still got in the fridge and try to plan meals or snacks you can make using leftovers and items nearing the end of their useful life.

Don't forget to take a cool bag for chilled and frozen items, especially in summer – if they de-chill or de-freeze – especially poultry, meat and fish – it could be a health hazard. Cool bags are also useful to take home fresh fruit and vegetables. If you have more than a couple of minute's journey home in a hot car or walking on a hot day, their vitamin C content will diminish otherwise.

WHERE TO SHOP

Ninety per cent of us in the UK do most of our shopping in supermarkets and shopping in them does have several advantages – convenience, variety (which can be used just as easily to help you buy a healthy diet as it can cause you to overeat), often good prices and a high turnover of goods, which helps ensure freshness, and therefore maximum vitamin C content, in products such as fruit, vegetables and salads.

Smaller local shops, farm shops and markets are well worth supporting, so perhaps at least some of your food shop could be done here. Perhaps save money at the supermarket on basics and spend what you save here, on items such as handmade bread, locally grown produce, local meat, and homemade pickles from the women's market, for instance.

Be wary of produce displayed in hot windows or on benches outside during the summer months, as again, vitamin C and B content is reduced in these conditions.

LOOK FOR QUALITY

You're staring at a cabinet full of pre-packed meat cuts, or a stack of vegetables, and you pick up the first one to hand. But it does pay to use your eyes, nose, and even hands, to choose the freshest, best items? Here are some pointers:

✳ Vegetables with wilted or yellowing leaves and fruits that have lost their bloom are likely to have been around too long and will have low levels of vitamin C. A few slight blemishes on local fruit, for example, is fine.

✳ Know what vegetables and fruits are in season in the UK and try to buy them rather than out of season goods which have air miles and have probably been stored artificially for long periods (see page 100), again, losing nutrients.

✳ Meat need not look bright (often a sign it hasn't been hung long enough to be tender), but it shouldn't look grey. Don't buy. Meat and fish shouldn't smell meaty or fishy. Only game should have an aroma (unless it's sold packaged, of course). If fish has an ammonia smell, don't buy.

✳ Always check that eggs aren't cracked or broken, and that they are clean.

✳ Look for quality assurance labels, which may not mean a huge amount but are better than nothing.

✳ If the item is packaged and has a use-by date, pick the item with the date furthest away. These items will often be at the back of the shelf and/ or underneath products which have a shorter life. Supermarkets will always get their stackers to put products with these shorter dates on top and at the front so that they are sold.

✳ When buying ready meals and processed foods (anything not fresh) read the labels for nutritional quality (see next page).

PLEASE DON'T BUY TOO MUCH!

'Continued damage from over-consumption today looks set to reduce choices for today's children in their lifespans, let alone future generations. Study after study suggests rich countries such as the UK are over-consuming not just in health terms but in land use, ecosystems services and with regard to climate change. Food is a major threat to all of these.' Tim Lang, Professor of Food Policy, University of London, March 2017.

Professor Lang's words, as part of a paper he wrote titled, 'Re-fashioning food systems with sustainable diet guidelines' explain that buying and eating too much will result not just in obesity and ill health but has wider implications.

So when you shop, remember one of the best ways to save money as well as your waistline, and possibly our planet and populations, is to buy what you need to maintain a good weight, and good health, for yourself and whoever else you are shopping for. And no more.

Here are some tips on doing that easily:

✳ Shop after you have eaten – hungry shoppers almost always buy more.

✳ Shop alone. Research shows if you go along with children or friends, again, you will buy more.

✳ Stick to your list. The exception to that rule of mine is if you find an item very similar to one on your list that is on special offer (e.g. your list says mangetout but the sugar snap peas are half price, or you were going to buy haddock for tonight but there is a vastly reduced pack of salmon that goes out of date tomorrow), or that looks terrific (e.g. there's local cheese instead of the factory cheese you were going to buy) or that will replace a similar item the shop hasn't got in stock.

✳ Remember all the way around the

store or market – what you buy is in your hands. It is only by choosing the quality, healthier items and leaving the sugary, highly processed, rubbish items on the shelves that we will eventually get nothing but good food to choose from – and in the right quantities both to save our waistlines and our planet.

FOOD LABELLING – WHAT YOU NEED TO KNOW

The name and description

If you glance at the photographs on some packs, you may find that all is not as it seems. For instance, a UHT carton with a tempting photo of citrus fruits on the front, calling itself 'citrus juice drink' may contain as little as 10% real juice, the remainder being made up of water, sugar, colourings and flavourings. NOT quite so good for you. And this is legal.

Strawberry flavour yogurt may never have been near a real strawberry or even real strawberry juice or extract; it will simply use artificial flavouring. This, too, is legal. Meat in cheap 'pork' sausages and other meat products, such as burgers, can include mechanically recovered meat, a kind of slurry removed by machine from a carcass after all the other meat has been removed. 'Meat' can also include rind, skin, sinew and gristle.

Another problem is that the percentage content of what you would consider to be the main ingredients in a product may, in fact, be quite small. For instance, you may be getting only a small percentage of meat in a 'steak pie'. Yet another problem arises for those avoiding certain ingredients for health or other reasons. Say you're trying to avoid all beef products. You may be surprised to find, on reading the ingredients list, that a chicken stock cube contains beef extract. Or, you're trying to go vegetarian — only to find that many yogurts and desserts contain gelatine, which is made from beef bone. Read the small print carefully to find out what you're really buying.

Health claims

Food packaging often makes health claims for the food, such as, 'helps maintain a healthy heart', or 'helps aid digestion'. Any claims made about the nutritional and health benefits of a food must be based on science. Only claims the European Commission has approved can be used on food packaging, which may change in the UK after Brexit.

General claims about benefits to overall good health, such as 'healthy' or 'good for you', are only allowed if accompanied by an approved claim. This means that these claims must be backed up by an explanation of why the food is 'healthy'. Labels mustn't claim that food can treat, prevent or cure any disease or medical condition.

Some manufacturers' banner claims such as 'free from artificial colourings and preservatives' in their products to distract from the fact that they do contain, say, artificial sweeteners and flavourings. As another example, 'No added sugar' banners may also be misleading as many such products contain high amounts of other, similar, sweeteners, such as honey or concentrated fruit juices. Even the term 'organic' can mislead, as processed foods, containing a number of ingredients, may contain up to 5% non-organic ingredients.

Reduced- or low-calorie content may be a selling point for people watching their weight. A reduced-calorie (energy, joules) product must have 75% or less energy than a similar product for which no energy claim is made, and a low-calorie product must have a maximum of 40 calories per 100g product.

A claim that a food is low in fat may only be made where the product contains no more than 3g of fat per 100g for solids or 1.5g of fat per 100ml for liquids (1.8g of fat per 100ml for semi-skimmed milk).

To say that a food is 'light' or 'lite', it must be at least 30% lower in at least one typical value, such as calories or fat, than standard products. The label must explain exactly what has been reduced and by how much, for example 'light: 30% less fat'. However, take care with these products as often when they are reduced in say, fat, they may be high in sugar instead.

Foods labelled as 'no added sugar' may still contain sugar which is intrinsic in one or more of the ingredients – for instance, fruit.

Then there are special health or product claims – words like 'natural', 'traditional', 'farm-fresh' have very little meaning when applied to processed foods. For instance, farm-fresh eggs are usually battery eggs. Pictures of country scenes mean nothing. And neither do names such as 'Dingle Farm', used to make the buyer believe they are buying into a rural idyll, perhaps.

The Ingredients list

So if you can't tell exactly what you are buying from the banner descriptions and illustrations, you must check the ingredients list. You should find percentage quantities of at least the main ingredients listed (in accordance with the EC Quantitative Ingredient Declarations directive).

Ingredients are listed in descending order of content by weight, i.e., the ingredient contained in the greatest amount is listed first, and so on, so that the last ingredient listed is the least. Therefore, if an item such as sugar or fat that you are trying to cut back on is high up the list, you know maybe this is a food you should avoid.

E numbers must be included in this list, but may be expressed by name alone, making it hard to detect which you are eating unless you have their names handy, but additives used in an ingredient (e.g. dried fruits in a fruit cake may have been preserved using sulphur dioxide) needn't be mentioned and neither need flavourings.

Sugars come in a variety of guises, including glucose, dextrose, fructose, glucose syrup, lactose, maltose and treacle. Concentrated fruit juices used as sweeteners, honey and brown sugar are all similar to basic sucrose and no better for the teeth. Several of these items can appear in the ingredients list – add them all up and you may have a very high sugar item.

Trans fats (see page 22) will usually appear on the ingredients list as 'partially hydrogenated fats'. Look out for them in margarines, cakes, biscuits, pies and pastries, though in 2012 most supermarkets agreed to sign up to a voluntary agreement not to use artificial trans fats and they are now present in a relatively small number of processed foods.

Some ingredients need not be listed and some foods and alcohol are exempt from having to declare their ingredients.

Use by dates

After complaints that consumers are getting confused by 'Use by' 'Best Before' and 'Sell by', manufacturers are tending to simplify things. 'Best Before', which is supposed to be an indicator of the food's eating quality rather than safety, is disappearing from labels across the world – all that really need concern you is the 'Use By' date, which appears on perishable foods. Get one that's as far away as you can and try to use it, or freeze it if it is a freezable food, before that date.

Sell by dates, and display by dates are not required by law, and are for the shopkeepers and people who work in the shop rather than the consumer.

For more advice, see the feature on foods at home overleaf.

The Nutrition Panel

The main nutrition panel is usually shown on the back or side of a packaged food. As a minimum it must, under new rules, show the amount of each of energy (calories), total fat, saturated fat, carbohydrate, sugars, protein and salt per 100g or 100ml of the food, plus the amount of any nutrient for which a health claim has been made. Amounts per serving or per portion with the weight of that serving or portion may also be given but isn't mandatory.

Here is a typical nutrition panel for the UK which appears on the NHS website. It tells you the amount of all the major nutrients in both 100g of the product and in a typical portion.

The RI (Reference Intake) column, which is voluntary and so by no means always given, shows the percentage amount of a nutrient that is provided in a portion of the product. The 'RI for an average adult' column shows what your total daily intake of that nutrients should, on average, be.

The RI amounts that labels use are:
Energy: 2,000kcal
Total fat: 70g
Saturates: 20g
Carbohydrate: 260g
Total sugars: 90g
Protein: 50g
Salt: 6g

So in this instance, you can see that that one slice/portion of 44g contains, for instance, approximately 5% of the RI for calories, 1% of the RI for total fat, and 2% of the RI for sugar.

Sometimes manufacturers will also print a precis of the product's nutrient values on the front of the package too in larger type, for quick reference, and sometimes this includes red, amber and green colour codings for each of the nutrients, which say whether the food is high, medium or low in fat, saturated fat, sugars and salt. Red means high, amber means medium and green means low. In general, the more green on a label the 'healthier' the product is, and the more red, the less healthy it is.

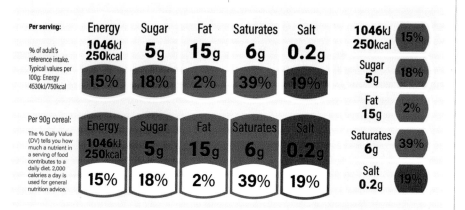

FOOD AT HOME

Food is one of our major household expenses so once you get it home, you want to make sure that you deal with it to keep it as fresh as possible (retaining nutrients, avoiding food poisoning and avoiding waste) for as long as possible, or in the case of longer-life foods, store it in the best possible place. You also want to prepare and cook it so you're getting the most enjoyment from your food as well as the maximum amount of healthy nutrients possible. Our tips on this page will help you to do all this.

STORING FOODS

Fruits, most vegetables and salad items: Most should ideally be kept in the fridge until needed, and only brought into room temperature a short while before using. Cool storage keeps the vitamin C content high and prolongs life. Most items can be stored in airtight containers or bags, the crisper compartment or for items such as mushrooms, berries and tomatoes, in an open card container with some vent holes in the base to prevent mushiness.

Bananas are best kept in cool conditions outside the fridge. Potatoes should be kept in cool (but not frosted) dark conditions. Fruits you've bought to 'ripen at home' will only ripen if stored at room temperature. Once ripe you can then put them in the fridge.

Even in a fridge, fruits and vegetables will gradually deteriorate, so use up items on a rota basis and discard any that are wrinkled, browned, dry, yellowing, woody or mouldy. Don't wash, if necessary, until you want to eat them – damp items will deteriorate more quickly.

Frozen foods: These should be transferred immediately to the freezer. If an item has unavoidably begun to defrost a little it is usually safe to refreeze – but don't refreeze completely thawed items unless the label says you can do so, or part-

defrosted meat and fish items.

Food to be frozen: These should be blanched (in the case of vegetables) or otherwise prepared/cooled if necessary, and frozen in containers or heavy-duty plastic bags as soon as possible after purchase, using the fast freeze setting. It is a very good idea to freeze foods in small or individual portions or slices.

Fresh meats, dairy produce and all chilled food: These should be stored in the fridge. Store raw meat, ideally in a covered leak-proof container, in the bottom of the fridge, well away from cooked meats, to avoid cross-contamination and possible food poisoning.

Opened jars: These should be kept covered and stored in the fridge and once opened the use by dates no longer apply so eat up as quickly as you can for maximum safety.

Opened cans: As chemicals from the insides of cans may leach into food, leftover contents should be decanted into glass or china containers, or at least heavy-duty plastic ones, and the contents used within 24 hours. Once a bottle, can, jar, pack, etc., is opened, it will NOT keep indefinitely.

High-fat items, such as cheese, butter, pâté and fatty meats, shouldn't be wrapped in clingfilm, as this may contain chemicals which can migrate into these foods, and cling film makes cheese go off more quickly, research shows. Cheese should be stored in its own container, which should have airholes, or wrapped in waxed paper. Hard cheeses may even be stored in a cool larder.

Best before dates are a guide only. Using your eyes and nose to tell if a food or drink is still okay to eat is what people did for thousands of years. If something smells rancid, is covered in mould, dried out, discoloured or otherwise is something you do not wish to inflict on yourself or your family, throw it away. If you're unsure, throw it away. If it looks and smells normal, then have a tiny taste. If it tastes fine, it probably is fine. But if you are catering for children, elderly people, pregnant people or sick people it is better to err on the side of caution as these groups are more vulnerable to infection.

PREPARING FOOD

Careful food preparation can retain water-soluble vitamins B group and C and minimize risk of food poisoning.

Avoid chopping, peeling or tearing fresh fruits, vegetables and salads until the last possible minute before cooking or eating, as cut and exposed surfaces lose vitamin C and begin to oxidize.

Don't leave vegetables soaking in water (hot or cold) as this too leaches vitamin C. Cook vegetables for the minimum amount of time to retain nutrients – for more information on healthy cooking methods, see page xxx.

Defrost meats, fish and meat products thoroughly before cooking unless the label advises otherwise. Poultry MUST be thoroughly defrosted – feel the cavity to check before cooking and check portions with a sharp knife. Meat that comes out of the fridge very cold should also be brought to room temperature before cooking, (from half an hour to 2-3 hours depending on size and temperature of the room). Cook all meat thoroughly to prevent food poisoning. Minced meat, chicken, sausages and burgers should have no pink left in their centres at all. All microwaved food should be piping hot in the centre.

Food Waste

£17 billion of food is wasted every year according to WRAP (the Waste & Resources Action Programme), 70% of which comes from the home.

Don't stuff poultry as the stuffing may also prevent the inside of the bird from thoroughly cooking. Make stuffing and cook separately. Don't wash chicken (or other meats) before cooking it. This can easily spread food poisoning bacteria. You can buy whole chickens to roast ready prepared in foil tins and bags for almost total safety.

When handling raw meat in the kitchen, use a clean chopping board reserved just for raw meat. A marble board may harbour fewer bacteria than those made from wood or plastic. Wash hands, board and utensils in anti-bacterial cleanser after use. Steep utensils in boiling water if practical. Dry hands well before handling other foods, and clean tap handles which may have been touched with infected hands.

REHEATING AND LEFTOVERS

If food that you've just cooked is to be kept for later or another day after cooking, allow it to cool and transfer it to a fridge (or freezer) as quickly as possible in a suitable container. Vitamins B group and C will diminish in food kept warm for long periods. If hot food is to be kept for less than an hour, cover it and keep at room temperature then reheat to piping hot, or keep in a low oven just simmering. In general, it is better to allow a meal to cool and then reheat it than keep it hot for long periods. All reheated food should be heated until piping hot.

Leftover food, if still in good condition, should be wrapped or put in containers (preferably glass or china), covered and kept in a fridge. Use or throw away within 24–48 hours using the criteria explained above to tell whether the food is good or not.

FOOD POISONING AND HOW TO AVOID IT

Food poisoning is an illness caused by eating contaminated food. It usually causes sickness, diarrhoea and maybe other symptoms. Most people get better within a few days without treatment. However, it can cause serious illness and even death.

The UK Food Standards Agency (FSA) reported in 2014 that there are around half a million cases of food poisoning 'from known pathogens' a year, with campylobacter the most common, accounting for over half the cases. Most cases are caused by food 'eaten out'; the rise in restaurant, café and takeaway eating is an obvious cause. Food eaten in the home accounts for one in six cases. Poultry meat is the food linked to the most cases of food poisoning, with an estimated 244,000 cases every year, says the FSA. Produce including vegetables, fruit, nuts and seeds caused the second highest number of cases of illness (est. 48,000), while beef and lamb were third (est. 43,000).

Foods particularly susceptible to

Causes of food poisoning

The NHS says most cases are caused by:

* not cooking food thoroughly (particularly meat)
* not correctly storing food that needs to be chilled at below 5C
* leaving cooked food for too long at warm temperatures
* not sufficiently reheating previously cooked food
* someone who is ill or who has dirty hands touching the food
* eating food that has passed its 'use by' date
* the spread of bacteria between contaminated foods (cross-contamination)

contamination if not handled, stored or cooked properly include raw meat and poultry, raw eggs, raw shellfish, unpasteurised milk, and ready-to-eat foods such as cooked sliced meats, pâté, soft cheeses and pre-packed sandwiches.

Campylobacter can be found in chicken, meat and unpasteurized milk. Chicken and meat should be thoroughly cooked to kill it.

Salmonella: Salmonella is the food poisoning bug that causes the most hospital admissions – about 2,500 each year. It is found in eggs, meat and other sources, though a programme to eradicate it from our eggs has been very successful in recent years. Lion stamped eggs in the UK are all from hens which have been vaccinated against salmonella. Food should be as fresh as possible when eaten, as bacteria quickly multiply, and thoroughly cooked. Wash leafy salads thoroughly.

Clostridium perfringens comes mainly from undercooked meat or poultry and food that is kept warm but not hot enough for long periods.

Norovirus is becoming more common. Avoid eating raw, unwashed produce and only eat oysters from a reliable source, as they can carry the virus.

E. Coli has a very low infective dose and a common source of infection is meat, possibly contaminated during slaughter and processing. Undercooked meat may then cause poisoning. Minced meat and under-cooked burgers have been cited as particular risks because mincing may spread it through the meat. Dairy products can also be contaminated.

Listeria monocytogenes: bacteria found in soft cheeses, such as Brie and Camembert, in pâtés, and chilled ready-meals and deli foods, like pre-packed salads, pasta salads and hams. The bacteria can thrive at temperatures as low as 5°C (many domestic fridges function at around this temperature). It is dangerous for pregnant women, young children and people with weak immune systems.

FOOD POISONING PREVENTION TIPS

✳ Wash your hands after going to the toilet or changing a baby's nappy, before preparing food, after handling raw food and after touching bins or pets.

✳ Don't handle food if you are ill with stomach problems such as diarrhoea or vomiting, or you have any uncovered sores or cuts.

✳ Make sure the fridge is set to 0-5 degrees C. Many domestic fridges are too warm.

✳ Follow all the tips on these pages for food storage, preparation, cooking and leftovers.

✳ Make sure almost all meat, poultry and fish/shellfish is cooked thoroughly. The only exception is that large pieces of meat, such as steaks and joints of beef or lamb, can be served rare (pink in the middle), as long as the outside has been cooked properly, says the NHS. ◾

Food as Medicine

Twenty years ago, who would have believed that we would be being urged to eat dairy foods to help prevent diabetes, or would be told to eat up our tomato ketchup to help prevent cancer?

The last few years have seen a massive increase in interest in the idea of food as medicine – and yet it is nothing new. For thousands of years the medicinal value of plant foods has been appreciated throughout the world. Garlic was first used as a medicine at least four thousand years ago. Five hundred years ago it was known that fresh fruits and vegetables could cure scurvy. Two hundred years ago a powerful effect of the foxglove flower (Digitalis) in helping heart problems was discovered, and 150 years ago salicylic acid (the natural forerunner of today's aspirin) was first isolated from the bark of the willow.

Even as recently as the turn of the twentieth century, the largest proportion of medicines were herbal-based. It is only in relatively recent years that the Western world has become so sceptical of the power of plants – and so reliant upon man-made chemical drugs to effect cures.

Now people in their hundreds of thousands – including the medical profession and scientific world themselves – are realising the major drawbacks of a society dependent upon drugs for their health. Drug resistance, drug dependence and unwanted side effects are three main reasons why alternative, more natural methods of cure and prevention are regaining popularity. Diet is a first choice in this change. We all need to eat – so if what we eat can act like medicine, too, then isn't that a marvellous solution?

Now, with the advantage of modern scientific techniques, we know so much more about food, what is in it and how it works, that we can fine-tune our diets to suit almost any illness or condition. We are no longer reliant upon the local witch-doctor to provide cures without question. We have the greatest minds in the most well-funded laboratories in the world, seeking the answers to food as medicine.

Conditions and Solutions

A

ACNE AND SPOTS

Acne is caused by over-production of sebum – oil – which sits in the pores of the skin, particularly on the face and back. The pores become clogged and are then easily infected. This over-production of sebum often occurs in the teenage years, because of increased production of the sex hormones, and is more common in boys than girls. Acne can carry on into the 20s and can also occur in older people, in women before menstruation, and a mild version may also occur at menopause. Some experts believe that acne is exacerbated by stress, in which case see page 119 for tips.

Solutions

All teens should eat a basic healthy diet and follow the particular instructions for them given in Section Three, The Teenage Years.

Although the NHS says on its website that 'there is no evidence that diet plays a role in acne', many sufferers would disagree. For some people, dairy produce is known to aggravate acne, perhaps because dairy milk is a source of hormones and IGF-1 growth factor, so it could be worth trying a switch to non-dairy milk and milk product alternatives such as soya or almond milk and yogurt for several weeks to see if it makes a difference.

Many acne sufferers also find that if they avoid sugar and refined carbohydrates in the diet that their condition improves. It would also be worth trying to eat plenty of zinc-rich foods, such as shellfish and nuts (best sources list on page 41), as acne may be linked with a zinc deficiency. Vitamin E-rich foods, such as vegetable oils, avocados, nuts and seeds, can aid skin healing and most experts also agree that a diet high in vitamin C (fresh fruits and vegetables) to fight infection is also important.

It may also be useful to eat more foods rich in carotenes, such as carrots, apricots, sweet potatoes and broccoli (best sources list on page 30). In the body, these convert into vitamin A, which is known to be important in maintaining a healthy skin.

Doctors often prescribe antibiotics for acne, which can help the condition, but if antibiotics are taken for long periods they can upset the microbiome (gut microflora) which, ironically, may make acne worse! Regularly eating foods such as live yogurt, kimchi and sauerkraut, naturally rich in beneficial bacteria, is a very good idea, whether or not you are on antibiotics. For more on gut bacteria, see Gut Health.

ALCOHOL ABUSE

While there may be some health and wellbeing benefits for some from light alcohol intake (see pages 48–51 Section One), alcohol abuse remains one of the most important causes of ill health throughout the world. Alcohol is a drug and an intoxicant, and alcohol addiction and dependence is widespread. The safe drinking limits outlined on page 50 are exceeded by approximately 9 million people in England alone.

Experts believe that over 30,000 premature deaths a year in England and Wales are related to excessive alcohol consumption and it is one of the three biggest lifestyle risk factors for disease and death in the UK, after smoking and obesity. The higher above the safe limits your alcohol intake, the more likely it is that you will become dependent and incur a variety of side effects and illnesses. These can include abnormal heart rhythms, increased likelihood of some cancers, diabetes, obesity, brain damage, liver damage and early death.

Long-term drinking can impact on nutritional health. Alcohol affects the absorption and metabolism of many nutrients, including the vitamin B group and vitamins A and D, the minerals zinc, calcium and phosphorus, and the essential fatty acids, and may deplete the body of magnesium. It is therefore important to eat a very healthy diet rich in these nutrients (which means following a diet similar to that outlined in Section One) and avoid junk foods, particularly sugary low-nutrient foods like sweets, biscuits and fizzy drinks.

Including plenty of healthy fats such as from oily fish, olive oil, avocados, nuts and seeds may help the liver (which has the job of breaking down the alcohol and converting it into harmless components) to cope.

See also **Hangover**.

ALLERGIES AND FOOD INTOLERANCES

An allergy is an over-aggressive response by the body's immune system to a substance – for example, an airborne pollutant, a chemical, a plant, an animal's fur or feathers – or a food, and it is the latter we discuss here. A food allergy is caused by your immune system handling harmless proteins in certain foods as a threat. It releases chemicals then, such as histamine, that trigger an allergic reaction.

An allergic reaction can produce a wide variety of symptoms, the most common being skin reactions (eczema, urticaria, for example), digestive reactions (such as vomiting, stomach-ache, bloating or diarrhoea) or respiratory tract reactions (like wheezing, runny nose, rhinitis and other asthma-like symptoms). Other reactions can include headache, flatulence, fatigue, fluid retention and palpitations.

When an allergic reaction is so severe that it can be life-threatening, this is called anaphylactic shock. The immune system releases a 'hit' of histamine within seconds after the allergic individual has come into contact (even slightly) with the allergen; the throat may swell and make breathing difficult, so the sufferer will wheeze, the face may swell, rashes, stomach cramp and vomiting may occur, and unless adrenaline treatment is given quickly the sufferer may die.

Diagnosed anaphylactics – numbers of whom have doubled in the past few years – carry their own emergency kit for treatment. Anaphylaxis usually starts in childhood and is not outgrown. The most common foods to cause this type of reaction are peanuts, other nuts and seeds, fish and shellfish, and eggs. The tendency to be allergic (or 'atopic') may run in families.

Some experts say that up to one in six people in the UK suffer from allergic reaction to some degree; however, there is evidence that many more people think/say they are allergic to certain foods, etc., than actually are and other trials put the figure as low as less than 2% of the population. There is little doubt, though, that instances of food allergies and intolerances are on the increase and have been implicated in a number of other conditions such as arthritis, migraine, IBS, PMS, ME, Crohn's disease and hyperactivity in children.

Where there is an adverse reaction to a food but the traditional allergy tests are negative, the term 'food intolerance' may be used, although it is still possible that immune reactions may be involved in some way. The rise in the numbers of people in the UK feeling that they have a food intolerance is linked with the rapid rise in popularity and sales of 'free from' foods.

The term intolerance may also be used to describe a specific and medically recognised condition e.g. lactose intolerance. Normally the digestive enzyme lactase breaks down lactose, the sugar found in milk and dairy products. In lactose intolerance, this enzyme is deficient, so lactose passes into the intestines resulting in bloating and diarrhoea.

Diagnosing food allergy

There is now a scientific test for true allergic reaction, the RAST test, which measures the amount of immunoglobulin E antibodies (IgE) a person has to a specific substance. There are also 'skin prick' tests, in which a tiny amount of the suspected allergen is placed on the arm and a scratch made in the skin, then any reaction (swelling, redness) noted, but this method is more suitable for non-food allergens, such as dust mites, feathers pollen, etc., and is useless for most food intolerances.

Other tests, such as hair tests by post or unspecific blood tests

DEFINING COELIAC DISEASE, GLUTEN INTOLERANCE AND WHEAT INTOLERANCE

Coeliac Disease is a lifelong autoimmune condition caused by a reaction to gluten and is dealt with separately on page 136.

People who are coeliac have a reaction to gluten, but this is not the same as 'gluten intolerance' which, according to Allergy UK, is a comparatively newly recognised condition, although there is still a lot of controversy as to whether or not it exists and whether it is caused by gluten or another protein found in wheat. It is unclear if it is an intolerance or whether the immune system is involved, and it is also unclear if it is life-long or whether it is a temporary condition.

Currently there are no tests for gluten intolerance – diagnosis is made by excluding coeliac disease and wheat allergy and using the exclusion of wheat from the diet to see if symptoms resolve, followed by wheat reintroduction to determine if symptoms reappear. Patients should be referred to a specialist dietitian for help in following the diet.

offered by alternative practitioners, are probably of little real use in most cases. According to research, some private allergy clinics are notorious for giving out long lists of 'problem' foods to people with no known complaints while failing to spot true allergies.

The most reliable test for food sensitivity is the exclusion diet, which should be discussed with your doctor and supervised by a dietician. This involves a diet usually consisting of a few foods which almost never cause allergic reaction (lamb, bottled water and rice are prime examples), which is followed for a number of days and then, if symptoms have improved, one by one other foods are introduced, at intervals, starting with foods less likely to produce a reaction. If there is no reaction, that food can stay in the diet. Once any newly added food triggers a reaction, it should be removed from the diet (possibly for good, although see Living with a Food Allergy or Intolerance overleaf).

A simpler form of exclusion diet involves removing one or two suspect foods from the diet for about 2 weeks and if the condition clears the food is then reintroduced. If the symptoms return it is assumed that the reintroduced food is to blame. This type of exclusion diet is best attempted with professional advice.

Foods most likely to cause allergy

Almost any food, additive or drink can cause allergic reactions, though some, like rice and lamb, do so less often. Here are the most common food triggers:

Cows' milk and dairy produce: see lactose intolerance on page 158. Some people who can't tolerate cows' milk may be able to have goats' milk. Others find that they can drink skimmed milk

and low-fat milk products but not full-fat varieties. Common in babyhood and may be outgrown.

Eggs: often egg whites rather than the yolks are the problem. Eggs are an ingredient in many products, so label reading is crucial. This allergy is most common in toddlers and again may be outgrown.

Grains: wheat allergy is common; gluten is not always the 'culprit', though it may often be. Any grain can cause allergic reaction, but rice and corn are less likely to do so. Again, grains, particularly wheat and gluten, appear in many products and so vigilance is needed.

Fish and shellfish: allergic reaction to these is increasing, possibly because of increasingly polluted waters. Most common allergens seem to be prawns, oysters, crabs and white fish. Nuts and seeds: peanut allergy is the most common, and it is now thought that around one in 200 people are sensitive to peanuts, which actually aren't a true nut. Sufferers may be advised to avoid groundnut (peanut) oil, although a recent study showed that only 10% of peanut-sensitive adults tested were allergic to unrefined peanut oil and none to refined oil. Other common nut allergens are walnuts, brazils and cashews. There is a growing allergy to sesame seeds — found not only in hummus, tahini, sesame seed bread and sesame oil, but also often in vegetable burgers, Oriental meals and cakes. Mustard seeds are another common allergen. See also Box, Pollen Food Syndrome, below.

Fruit and vegetables: See Box, Pollen Food Syndrome, below.

Celery: Surprisingly, this vegetable figures in Allergy UK's top 14 most common allergens, see Pollen Food Syndrome box below.

Soya beans: soya beans and soya bean products, such as tofu and soya flour, can cause a reaction, particularly

POLLEN FOOD SYNDROME

One of the most common types of allergy in the UK, according to the Association of UK Dietitians, PFS is caused by the body reacting to proteins found in food from plants which are similar to pollen. It usually occurs in people who have hay fever in the spring. It may also be called Oral Allergy Syndrome (OAS) and it is the most common type of food allergy affecting adults, sometimes causing swelling of the lips, tongue, mouth and soft palate.

The foods most likely to cause this are raw apples, strawberries, kiwis, hazelnuts, Brazil nuts and almonds but others include celery, pears, peaches, carrots, oranges, nectarines and tomatoes for example. Cooked, these foods are much less likely to cause a problem. A skin prick test is available to see if you have PFS – see your GP.

digestive upsets. Soya is found in a multitude of commercial products and avid label reading is necessary for those with a soya intolerance.

Additives: artificial food additives, such as preservatives and colourings, may cause a flare-up of symptoms in people with pre-existing conditions. Likely 'culprits' are the azo dyes, such as tartrazine (E102), caramel (E150), benzoates (E210- 219), sulphates (E220-229) and sulphites, nitrates (E249-252), glutamates (621-623), and artificial sweeteners such as aspartame.

Living with a food allergy or intolerance

For most allergy sufferers, the most obvious course of action is for them to stick to a diet that excludes the food(s) to which they are allergic or intolerant. As self-diagnosis is often difficult, as has been proven by research, it is unwise to start any limited diet unless the allergy has been confirmed through your physician by using one of the techniques described above.

A suitable diet may then be a simple matter to follow (if, for instance, you are allergic to oysters only, it won't be too hard for you to follow a diet that doesn't include oysters). If a wider range of foods is involved, however, or if you have an allergy to one of our major foods or food groups, such as dairy produce or grains or even soya, the diet becomes much more restricted and advice from a dietician is needed so that you can safely avoid possible nutrient deficiencies.

The long-term outlook for an allergy sufferer isn't always bleak – sometimes your body will change and tolerate a food that you have had to avoid for a long time. In severe cases, however,

WHO GETS ALLERGIES?

People who produce too much of the IgE antibody (see page 116) are 'atopic' individuals, who are more likely to suffer allergic reactions, and the tendency to this is probably inherited. It may also be that babies are 'sensitized' to allergens even before birth by what the mother eats, but this is still the subject of much research. Food allergies do, however, seem more common in childhood. The simple truth is that the experts don't yet have any concrete answer to who will get what allergy, or even when, which means that as yet there is no means of prevention.

See also – **lactose intolerance**.

returning to a food, particularly for anaphylactics, is a risky business and needs professional supervision if undertaken at all.

ANGINA – see Cardiovascular Disease and Stroke

ANOREXIA – see Eating Disorders

ANXIETY AND STRESS

Anxiety states are often a response to an overload of stress in people's lives. When people are under stress, the body's 'fight or flight' system pumps adrenaline out in preparation for dealing with a crisis situation, but in modern life the crisis doesn't manifest itself physically – e.g. in a fight or a long run away from danger, and the adrenaline simply stays around, making the person tense, nervous or anxious.

This can be short-term or almost permanent state. Short-term anxiety can also be a perfectly natural response to worrying situations, such as a job interview or an exam. Anxiety and stress can trigger several other complaints, such as digestive problems, insomnia, muscular pain, skin complaints, palpitations and even heart disease.

Solutions

Long term, try to seek out causes of anxiety and think about what changes you can make to your lifestyle to minimize these. Tackle anxiety by taking more exercise – walking and yoga is an ideal combination.

Chronic stress depletes the body of B Vitamins, so eating plenty of B-rich foods (see best sources list on page 36) and perhaps taking a B-group supplement is a good idea. The same applies to vitamin C, which most experts believe a stressed person will need in much greater quantities than the DRV of 40mg a day — up to 200mg a day may be better.

Stressed people may turn to alcohol or smoking — but both further deplete the body of B and C vitamins and can hinder absorption of other nutrients. Alcohol can also disrupt sleep patterns (for example, middle of the night waking is typical) which may make anxiety worse.

Eat a good basic healthy diet including lettuce, which contains the calming chemical, lactucarium, and plenty of magnesium-rich foods. Magnesium has been called 'nature's tranquilliser' and is excreted in greater amounts when you are under stress. Eating plenty of complex carbohydrates, such as pasta and whole grains, will help the brain to calm down by releasing the chemical serotonin.

Over-consumption of caffeine can

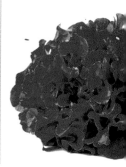

SYMPTOMS OF STRESS

Stress can produce many physical symptoms, such as fatigue, migraine, heartburn, impotence, insomnia, irritable bowel syndrome, memory problems and muscular pain – see individual entries for all of these. See also Depression.

heighten a state of anxiety so when you are stressed it may be wise to limit your consumption of caffeine-containing drinks and avoid caffeine in the hours before bedtime.

Herbal remedies for anxiety include valerian, camomile, passionflower and lemon balm, all of which are best taken as a tea infusion. Cloves, rosemary and lavender are all also said to be calming, can be used in cooking, and their essential oils are ideal in a bath.

ALZHEIMER'S DISEASE – see Dementia

APPETITE, POOR

Several conditions can bring about a loss of appetite – anxiety, stress, depression and shock are four typical situations. Illnesses of many kinds can cause loss of appetite, particularly digestive disorders such as irritable bowel syndrome or peptic ulcer, viral and bacterial illnesses and food intolerance. Colds, catarrh and allergic rhinitis can lessen appetite, partly by reducing the sense of smell on which our sense of taste largely depends, as can cigarette smoking. Drugs prescribed for various ailments can cause appetite loss.

Hormonal changes through the monthly menstrual cycle mean that women's appetite may vary, usually being greater in the week preceding a period and lower in the few days afterwards. Eating disorders such as anorexia nervosa may present themselves as poor appetite, though the sufferer may, in fact, have a normal appetite. Diminished appetite is fairly common in the elderly (see Section Three, Sixties Plus, page xxx).

Poor appetite can also be brought about by a deficiency in certain nutrients – zinc deficiency may contribute to loss of taste and smell and therefore appetite; potassium and magnesium deficiency may also be to blame – likely if the person with a poor appetite has been taking diuretic drugs for fluid retention, as some varieties cause these minerals to be excreted in the urine. Alcohol can reduce the appetite if taken in excess regularly – one drink can, however, be an appetite stimulant.

A short spell of poor appetite in an otherwise healthy person, when the reason is clear, is nothing serious to worry about and the appetite should return (often with a vengeance!) when the cause is gone. Any severe or long-term loss of appetite should be discussed with your physician.

To tempt a poor appetite, small amounts of tasty and attractive food should be offered frequently. If possible, low-nutrient 'junk' foods should be avoided, unless the main consideration is weight gain; meals and snacks should contain plenty of foods rich in vitamins B and C (which are water-soluble and the body can't store them for long), zinc, potassium and magnesium. High-protein drinks, smoothies and shakes are good ways to deliver plenty of calories and nutrients and are easy to swallow. For ideas see the recipe section on pages 214-257.

ARRHYTHMIA – see Cardiovascular disease and Stroke

ARTHRITIS

There are two main types of arthritis – osteoarthritis and rheumatoid arthritis. Osteoarthritis is a degenerative condition of the joints with a strong genetic component more common in older people. A normal healthy joint, such as the knee or hip (two very common sites of osteoarthritis), is covered by a smooth layer of shiny cartilage, which normally allows free gliding movement. In osteoarthritis, the cartilage becomes roughened, resulting in the underlying bone being worn. This is the commonest form of arthritis and is more common in women. Symptoms are pain, stiffness and loss of mobility in the affected joint(s).

Rheumatoid arthritis is determined by blood tests and history and is most common in adult women. It is a chronic inflammatory condition involving multiple joints and is thought of as having an auto-immune disease component. The immune system, which normally defends us against infection, appears instead to react against some part of the body. Rheumatoid arthritis often starts with pain and weakness in the hands and wrists. Joints may swell and may eventually become deformed. Inflammation may flare up and then disappear again, making it difficult to known exactly what 'works' to help. The causes of rheumatoid arthritis aren't fully understood, but there may be an environmental trigger such as a virus or bacterium. Even stress has been linked to rheumatoid arthritis.

Solutions

Diet doesn't really appear to play a big part in the prevention or management of osteoarthritis in most people, with the main exception that the symptoms of the condition – and the amount of trouble it causes – will be worse in someone who is very overweight or obese. The 'loadbearing' joints, such as the knees and hips, are put under much greater strain if the sufferer is too heavy. So, if you have osteoarthritis and are overweight, it is very important to lose the weight (see Section Four).

A variety of diets have been reported to be helpful for rheumatoid arthritis, but unfortunately, what works for one sufferer may well not work for another. Because symptoms often disappear for weeks or longer of their own accord, it is hard to know, when the sufferer suddenly feels better, whether it is diet or a period of remission.

That said, the essential omega-3 oils found in oily fish and fish oil supplements have been shown in several trials to help ease joint pain not only in osteoarthritis but also in rheumatoid arthritis. They seem to subdue the enzymes that cause inflammation. One trial found that patients given daily fish oil plus 10ml olive oil showed significant alleviation of joint pain, morning stiffness and fatigue over a six-month period. A diet low in saturated fat will help these fats do their work. Olive oil and pumpkin seed oil are two other oils that may help reduce inflammation while a high fibre diet, new research shows, can lessen pain.

Other work on individual nutrients is less clear-cut. One trial in the USA found that the progress of osteoarthritis can be minimized

with high intakes of vitamins C and E, and recently some studies have found that the condition is linked with low levels of vitamin D. There is also research showing that the spice turmeric can help relieve inflammation and evidence that a healthy vegetarian or vegan diet can help minimize symptoms in some people. Glucosamine sulphate supplements seem to work in offering pain relief for some. They are often made from shellfish, but vegetarian varieties are available.

Certain general guidelines seem to achieve the best results. Rheumatoid arthritis is linked with an increased risk of heart and circulatory problems, so the Healthy Heart Diet (page 134) may be a good idea, or follow a typical Mediterranean diet. A diet high in fruit and vegetables provides antioxidants, which may be important.

Many foods are reported by some sufferers as 'triggers' for attacks of rheumatoid arthritis. Dairy foods and grains, especially wheat and corn, are the most common triggers mentioned, along with members of the nightshade family such as tomatoes, potatoes, aubergines and peppers. Coffee, nuts and fruits with pips have also been cited, as well as red wine and citrus fruits. However, Arthritis UK says there is no proper evidence to support these foods causing or exacerbating arthritis and they don't recommend that they should be eliminated from the diet. If you want to try food elimination you need to read Allergies (page xxx) and get the advice and help of your GP as elimination shouldn't be attempted on your own.

Fasting has been shown to improve rheumatoid arthritis but Arthritis UK says they don't recommend fasting, as symptoms quickly return once the fast is finished.

People who are on anti-inflammatory drugs for their arthritis may well become anaemic and should therefore be sure to eat plenty of iron-rich foods regularly. People who are on steroids should be sure to take plenty of calcium-rich foods as steroids taken long term are a risk factor for osteoporosis.

See also **Gout.**

ASTHMA

The symptoms of asthma are wheezing, cough, tight chest and difficulty in breathing, due to air passages in the lungs narrowing. 5.4 million people in the UK are now diagnosed with asthma and it is the most common long-term disease in the West. This may be due to a number of factors, including air, chemical and food pollution, but asthma may be triggered by many things, including house mites, cigarette smoke, household sprays, cold air, exercise, pollen, animals, and less commonly by some foods.

Asthma UK says, 'A small number of people with asthma are also allergic to certain foods. Coming into contact with a food allergen can lead to an allergic reaction, which may include asthma symptoms such as wheezing, coughing and difficulty breathing. There's some evidence that if you have both asthma and a food allergy, you may be at greater risk of having an asthma attack that's life-threatening, so it's important to strictly avoid the food. You should also make sure your asthma is well managed, to lower your risk of having an asthma attack.'

For foods and ingredients that may cause allergies, see Allergies on pages 115–119. Check with your GP or asthma nurse if you think a food is affecting your asthma. A skin prick test should show whether you're allergic to the food you suspect. If you know you have a food allergy, you need to avoid the food completely, recognise the symptoms of a reaction and know what to do if it happens. Your GP should refer you to an allergy specialist to help you achieve this.

Research shows that people who eat a poor diet, low in fruits and veg, and therefore plant chemicals, are more likely to get asthma. Several recent studies have found that lung function and asthma symptoms improve in both adults and children who eat plenty of fruit and veg. Apples, tomatoes, carrots, leafy vegetables and citrus fruits appear to have the greatest effect. And regular oily fish intake by pregnant women is linked with an up to 30% lower risk of asthma in young children.

ATTENTION DEFICIT HYPERACTIVITY DISORDER

Symptoms of ADHD usually begin in early childhood, and it's thought that around 2% to 5% of school-aged children may have ADHD. There is some evidence that smoking, alcohol and drug abuse during pregnancy may be a potential cause.

Scientific research on whether or not diet can help prevent or improve ADHD is limited and results are mixed.

The UK National Institute for Health and Care Excellence (NICE) says healthcare professionals should stress the value of a balanced diet, good nutrition and regular exercise for the condition.

There may be a link between eating some types of food such as sugar, caffeine, wheat or dairy foods and ADHD symptoms becoming worse. It can help to keep a diary of symptoms and foods eaten at the time to see if there is a pattern, but the NHS cautions against changing the diet of a child with ADHD or cutting out foods without getting proper medical advice first.

Some food colourings or E numbers have been linked to hyperactivity and worsening of ADHD symptoms. These include sunset yellow (E110), quinoline yellow (E104), carmoisine (E122), allura red (E129), tartrazine (E102), ponceau 4R (E124). The Food Standards Agency is working with food and drink manufacturers to find alternatives. However, NICE says there is no evidence that cutting out foods containing artificial colouring and other additives helps people with ADHD.

NICE also says there is no evidence supplements such as essential fatty acids can help children with ADHD but a recent review of under 18s has found they do improve ADHD symptoms, helping with reading, behaviour and aggression.

See also – **Section Three.**

BAD BREATH – see Halitosis

BLOATING – see Digestive Health

BLOOD PRESSURE – see High Blood Pressure

B

BRAIN POWER

Our brains have a high water content and a high fat content of around 60%. The brain uses up a lot of energy compared with other parts of the body – it is approximately 2% of body weight but uses up to 20% of calories consumed. It benefits, just like the rest of the body, from good nutrition and a healthy lifestyle.

Research has found that what we eat – or don't eat - can affect learning ability, memory, concentration, problem-solving and thought processes as well as the preservation or otherwise of our 'grey matter' – the thinking part of the brain.

A quarter of brain fat is unsaturated essential fatty acids (see pages 20-22) and these have to be supplied through the diet, through foods such as plant oils, nuts and seeds for example. No wonder researchers have found that eating a diet rich in these fats increases brain power in almost every way. The special omega-3 fatty acids DHA and EPA, found in oily fish, seem to be particularly important, much research finds. A good balance of types of fat in the diet is also important – with a ratio of around 5:1 omega-6s to omega-3s being a good do-able amount.

Several researchers have found that blood flow and therefore oxygen can be increased to the brain with a diet rich in antioxidants such as those found in blueberries, broccoli, beetroot and cocoa, and this increase in oxygen boosts brain power while other research finds a lack of vitamin B12 is linked to memory and brainpower problems.

Protein is important for the brain, too because neurotransmitters – tiny chemicals that send signals within and from the brain – are made of proteins, and the brain itself needs protein to maintain its structure.

Eggs seem to be one particularly good brain food. They are not only high in protein, but also rich in the vitamin choline, a precursor to the neurotransmitters, and a nutrient linked to memory.

Eating less also boosts brain function – research shows that people on diets or who have lost weight have better organisational skills and memory, while overweight or obese people have more chance of having prematurely aged grey matter. High sugar intake has also recently been linked to negative changes in brain function.

Getting enough water is important for a healthy brain – it needs to be fully hydrated to work properly, and in fact it doesn't have to be plain water. But don't drink a lot of alcohol – moderate drinkers are likely to become forgetful over time.

However, slight loss of memory is quite common as we age. Many women report a deterioration in their memory at the time of menopause and others find their memory is worse

in the few days before a period, both of which are probably connected to changing hormone levels. The disorder hypothyroidism also produces loss of memory as one of its early symptoms. If you also have problems with tiredness, constipation and tend to feel cold all the time, it may be worth seeing your doctor to have them check out your thyroid function.

Supplements of ginkgo biloba are claimed to increase brain capacity and memory and Siberian ginseng is said to have a similar effect, but these supplements need to be taken with caution and are not suitable for all.

See also – **Dementia.**

BRONCHITIS AND COUGHS

Bronchitis is an acute or chronic inflammation of the bronchial tubes, the airways which lead to the lungs. There will often be an underlying infection. Bronchitis is accompanied by a mucus-producing cough and often a raised temperature.

The most common cause of bronchitis is smoking, but it can also be caused by infection or viruses, pollution or an allergic reaction to, say, dust or airborne fumes.

Avoidance of tobacco and known allergens is the obvious starting point in avoiding bronchitis. People who are prone to chest infections should also build up their immune system with a diet rich in antioxidants, zinc and other immune builders (see Immune-strengthening Diet, overleaf). Some nutritionists advocate avoidance of 'mucus-forming' foods, such as dairy products, saturated fats and white bread, although this has never been proved.

Once bronchitis has taken hold, it is important to take action quickly to minimize its duration and severity. Take plenty of fresh garlic; one of its active compounds, allicin, is a powerful antibiotic. To a lesser extent, onions and leeks are effective too. Increase your intake of vitamin C, with plenty of fresh fruits and salads. Manuka honey helps fight the streptococcus bacteria that cause sore throats – take twice daily with fresh lemon juice and a little warm water or use on bread.

The herbs hyssop and thyme are antiseptic and can be taken as an infusion daily. It is also useful to inhale their oils in recently boiled water. Bronchial and other coughs and sore throats can be soothed with liquorice and with the honey drink mentioned. A honey and cider vinegar gargle and zinc lozenges can also be effective in some cases.

BULIMIA – see Eating Disorders

CANCER

A quarter of all deaths in the industrialized world are due to cancers. One in three Britons is at risk of contracting cancer and about 160,000 a year die of the disease – but, according to Cancer Research UK, 42% of cases are preventable, and diet is an important factor, as is bodyweight.

In precis – a healthy balanced diet with plenty of fibre, wholegrains, fruit and vegetables, more healthy fats and fish and less red and processed meat can help cut cancer risk.

Increase intake of a wide variety of fruits and vegetables

Eating plenty of fruits and vegetables has been linked to a lower risk of mouth, throat and lung cancer. They

C

Immune-Strengthening Diet

Items in italics represent recipes in Section Four.

✐ DAY ONE ✐

Breakfast
½ pink grapefruit
75g muesli
3 Brazil nuts, chopped; 6 walnuts, chopped
½tbsp milled flaxseed
1tsp Manuka honey

Lunch
Chilli Lentils with Greens
2tbsp tzatziki
Wholemeal pitta bread

Evening
Scallops and Mussels in the Pan
Stir-fry of green beans, broccoli and
baby corn
Slice Cantaloupe melon

✐ DAY TWO ✐

Breakfast
1 boiled egg
1 slice seeded wholemeal bread
2tbsp mixed Brazil nuts, almonds and
sunflower seeds
1 orange

Lunch
Roast Tomato, Garlic and Pepper Soup
topped with 15g crumbled goat's cheese
1 small sourdough roll with a little butter

Evening
1 chicken breast fillet stuffed with thyme
leaves and crushed garlic and baked
Baked sweet potato drizzled with cold
pressed extra virgin rapeseed oil
1 large halved and baked tomato
Stir-fried shredded kale
25g dark 70% cocoa solids chocolate

✐ DAY THREE ✐

Breakfast
As Day 2, but with cantaloupe melon instead
of orange

Lunch
2 small slices dark rye bread topped with
sugar-free cashew nut butter
1 banana

Evening
Chilli Beef Fajitas
1 Apple Flapjack

DAY FOUR

Breakfast
As Day 1

Lunch
Spiced Lentil and Vegetable Soup
1 large slice dark rye bread
1 orange

Evening
150g cod fillet, baked and
topped with 30g peeled prawns
stir-fried in rapeseed oil with
crushed garlic, spring onions and
chopped mild chilli
Salad of cos lettuce, watercress
and rocket
Summer Berry Gratin

DAY FIVE

Breakfast
As Day 2

Lunch
*2 Mushroom, Spinach and
Chickpea Sliders*
Tomato and red onion salad
sprinkled with sliced black olives,
1 tbsp feta cheese and olive oil
French dressing

Evening
Miso-Marinated Salmon
New potatoes
Broccoli
Peas
100g natural yogurt with 2 tsp
Manuka honey

are an excellent source of fibre which has been linked to cancer prevention and can also help you keep a healthy weight – obesity is another risk factor for several cancers.

In one study, cancer deaths in vegetarians were found to be 39% lower than in meat-eaters, while another study found that eating just 10g extra of fibre a day can reduce the risk of bowel cancer by 10%.

They are also rich in vitamins and minerals needed for health as well as a very diverse wealth of plant compounds such as flavonoids, indoles, sterols and phenols, and within each group are yet more specific compounds, each with its own function(s). Many seem to help prevent, block, or suppress carcinogens or tumours. Here are some examples:

Tomatoes contain the carotenoid lycopene, one of the phenol group, which protects against cancer-causing pollutants. One trial found that men eating ten servings of tomato a week were 45% less likely to get prostate cancer though Cancer Research UK says more research is needed to be sure of a protective effect.

Broccoli and other members of the brassica family contain indoles, a group of cancer-fighting agents. Broccoli contains glucosinolates which convert to sulphorophanes and fight cancers of the lung and colon.

Brussels sprouts contain another glucosinolate, sinigrin, a compound which helps to suppress pre-cancerous activity.

Watercress is rich in phenethyl isothiocyanate, which is particularly good at helping to prevent lung cancer.

Beetroot is rich in anthocyanins which help to prevent tumours.

All dark green, red, orange and yellow vegetables contain carotenoids, which help to protect the immune system and may help fight lung cancer.

Yams are high in phytooestrogens, which may help to protect against breast cancer and other similar hormone-driven cancers.

Oriental mushrooms such as shiitake contain lentinan, which strengthens the immune system and helps the body fight cancer.

Red grape skins and many other fruit skins are rich in resveratrol, a compound which inhibits cancer development and is also found in red burgundy wines. Grapes also contain ellagic acid, also found in cherries and strawberries, another cancer blocker.

Citrus fruits such as oranges are high in special types of antioxidant flavonoids, such as hesperidin and naringin, which are highly anti-inflammatory and fight breast, colon and skin cancer for example.

And so on! For more information on phytochemicals, see pages 46–48. Many fruits and vegetables also contain rich levels of the vitamins C and E which also seem to offer protection against some cancers.

Aim for 5 a day minimum but try for eight or more a day!

Increase intake of starchy plant foods

Starchy, 'complex carbohydrate' foods, such as wholegrain cereals, rice, pasta, oats, pulses and potatoes, are high in fibre and high intakes have been linked to low levels of prostate, pancreas and breast cancer. Research also suggests that a substance called butyrate, produced by fermentation of complex carbohydrate in the bowel, and essential for colon mucosal health, helps prevent conditions which promote cancer and increases rate of death of cancer cells as well as helping the work of good gut bacteria.

Pulses have many benefits – isoflavones found in soya beans slow the growth of breast cancer cells so eating more tofu, edamame beans and so on has been shown to reduce the risk, for women who already have breast cancer, of dying by over 20%. All pulses are great sources of fibre (see above) and can boost the gut microbiome (see Gut Health).

Reduce intake of red meats and processed meats

Red meats (which are beef, lamb and pork) and processed meats, such as ham, bacon, salami and sausages, are linked with an increased risk of bowel cancer. There is also some evidence linking red meat to pancreatic cancer and prostate cancer, says the International Agency for Research on Cancer, (IARC) and processed meat to stomach cancer, however this is still uncertain.

In the case of processed meats, the IARC classifies them, without doubt, as 'a cause of cancer', while they say red meat is a 'probable cause of cancer'. Their estimate is that a quarter of bowel cancer cases in men and a sixth in women are linked to eating red or processed meat. And a recent UK study of half a million middle-aged people found an even stronger link – just four small (70g) portions of red meat a week make us 42% more likely to get the disease, they say, and other studies have found a similar link.

Nitrites and nitrates are used to preserve processed meat and may explain why studies find that processed meat increases the risk of cancer to a greater extent than red meat.

Overcooked meats, barbecued, burnt and chargrilled meats have also been linked with increased incidence of cancer, probably because the high cooking temperature creates carcinogenic compounds.

There is no strong evidence that eating fresh white meat, such as chicken, or fish increases the risk of cancer, nor that saturated fat in itself does so.

Increase intake of healthy fats

Many of us may need to increase the amount of the essential omega-3 fats and other healthy fats that we eat.

Adequate amounts of omega-3s appear to protect against cancer of the prostate, lung, breast and bowel, probably by having a 'calming' effect against the inflammatory prostaglandins in the system. Omega-3s are found in oily fish and linseed (flax) oil (and other foods such as those listed on page 22). It is therefore a good idea to replace some of the meat meals in the diet with oily fish meals as well as plant-based meals. Indeed, a 2012

CANCER AND ACRYLAMIDE

The chemical acrylamide is created when certain foods, particularly starchy foods, are cooked at high temperatures for long periods, so it is found in items such as crisps, chips, biscuits and even bread. Studies on animals indicate acrylamide has the potential to interact with the DNA in our cells, so could be linked to cancer, and in 2017, the UK Food Standards Agency launched a campaign to help people reduce the amount of acrylamide they may ingest at home (mainly by eating fewer of the culprit foods, and by making sure items such as chips, roast potatoes and toast are not overbrowned but cooked just to light golden). However, Cancer Research UK says that for most cancer types, there is no link between acrylamide and cancer risk.

study found that regularly eating all kinds of fish protects against bowel cancer.

According to latest research, there is also a link between high monounsaturated fat (found for example in olive oil and avocados) intake and lower risk of colon and breast cancers.

Increase intake of nuts/seeds

A handful – around 20g – of shelled nuts a day protects the body against cell damage and cuts the risk of cancer by about 15%. Walnuts may be particularly helpful, but all nuts and seeds are protective. Nuts and seeds also contain good levels of healthy fats (see above). The healthy chemicals in nuts and seeds include phytosterols, which help block colon, breast and prostate cancers, and gamma tocopherol, which may inhibit prostate and lung cancers.

Avoid obesity and overweight

Obesity is the second biggest preventable cause of cancer, according to Cancer Research UK, and is linked to 13 types of cancer. Abdominal fat appears to be a particular risk factor – adding 11cm to your waistline increases the risk by 13 per cent. By following a healthy diet and the guidelines above people who need to lose weight may do so naturally. For more advice, turn to Section Four, Food for Weight Control.

Limit consumption of alcohol

Excessive alcohol intake increases the risk of several cancers, including

TIPS

✳ The US National Cancer Institute says that population studies link garlic intake with reduced risk of various digestive system cancers, but there is little in the way of clinical trials to confirm these links.

✳ Adequate intake of vitamin D – found mainly in oily fish and egg yolks – is linked with cancer prevention. Nearly a third of the UK population is deficient in this vitamin and a daily supplement of 10mcg from October – April is advised by public health experts.

✳ Coffee – around 3 strong cups a day – may cut the risk of prostate and liver cancer because of the high levels of plant chemicals it contains.

✳ The mineral selenium is an antioxidant and is powerful in fighting the free radicals which are thought to increase risk of cancer. Brazil nuts and tuna fish are two good sources of the mineral. For best sources list, see page 41.

✳ Don't bother taking supplements of vitamins and so on to help prevent or cure cancers (apart from the vitamin D advice above). After a review of the results of 78 clinical trials on vitamin supplements, it's been found that these do not prolong life – they either have no effect or have a harmful effect.

✳ Polyunsaturated cooking oils can oxidize if heated too many times or kept too long and may be carcinogenic. Oils should be stored in a cool dark place and discarded after use. Use oils with a high smoke point for cooking at high temperatures (see page 217).

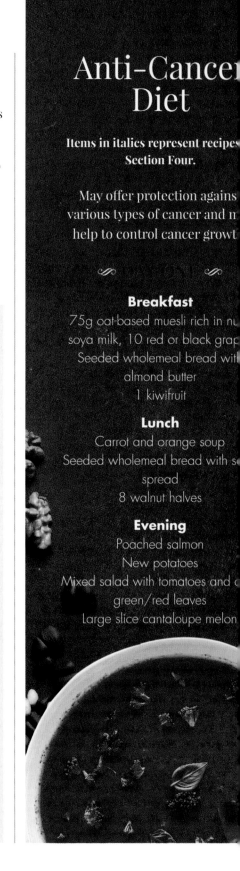

Anti-Cancer Diet

Items in italics represent recipes Section Four.

May offer protection agains various types of cancer and m help to control cancer growt

Breakfast
75g oat-based muesli rich in nu soya milk, 10 red or black grap Seeded wholemeal bread witl almond butter
1 kiwifruit

Lunch
Carrot and orange soup Seeded wholemeal bread with s spread
8 walnut halves

Evening
Poached salmon
New potatoes
Mixed salad with tomatoes and c green/red leaves
Large slice cantaloupe melon

Breakfast

Natural yogurt or soya yogurt topped with
sliced strawberries and raspberries
1tbsp almonds and pecan nuts
½tbsp milled flaxseed

Lunch

Salad of grated carrot, chopped hazelnuts,
chopped apple, 30g crumbled feta cheese and
2tsp dukkah on a bed of watercress and lamb's
lettuce with olive oil French dressing
1 slice seeded wholemeal bread with soya
spread

Evening

Winter Squash with Lentils and Ginger
Brussels sprouts
Mango Filo Tart

Breakfast

Pink grapefruit or orange
2 poached eggs on 1 slice seeded wholemeal
bread with soya spread

Lunch

Broccoli Soup
10 red or black grapes with 100g natural
fromage frais with 2 tsp honey

Evening

200g (cooked weight) wholewheat pasta with
Tomato Sauce, 80g cooked skinless chicken
breast and 2-3 pieces of red peppers from a
jar, chopped and stirred in
1 tbsp grated Parmesan
Salad of mixed lettuce leaves, watercress and
rocket with olive oil French dressing

Breakfast

125g natural yogurt topped with 30g oat-
based muesli, 4 chopped semi-dried apricots, 1
tbsp chopped walnuts, ½tbsp milled flaxseed,
25g blueberries

Lunch

Roast Beetroot, Feta and Pomegranate Salad
1 slice seeded wholemeal bread with soya spread

Evening

Roasted Turmeric Cauliflower
1 halved and roasted tomato
100g ready-cooked Puy lentils mixed with 50g
ready-cooked brown rice
Green salad with olive oil French dressing

Breakfast

100g natural fromage frais topped with 30g
oat-based muesli rich in nuts and 1 sliced peach
or nectarine
1 slice seeded wholemeal bread with almond
butter

Lunch

Salad of 90g fresh lightly pan-fried tuna, half an
avocado, sliced tomato, chopped crisp lettuce,
1 tbsp *Tofu Mayonnaise* stirred with 1 clove
garlic, well crushed
3tbsp ready cooked mixed whole grains

Evening

Artichoke, Aubergine and Spelt Warm Salad
Stir-Fried Fruit Salad

those of the mouth, pharynx, larynx, oesophagus, breast and liver. It may also increase risk of rectal cancers.

Beer can be a major source of nitrosamines, which are carcinogenic, and heavy beer drinkers appear to be more at risk from pancreatic cancer. Alcohol drinking should therefore be kept within safe guidelines (see page 50-51).

A protective effect for bowel cancer has been shown in red wine, which contains resveratrol, also found in grape skins, but safe limits should still be observed and red grape juice is probably just as good.

CANDIDA

Vaginal thrush is a yeast infection caused by Candida albicans or other types of fungus that occur naturally in the vagina, and thrush may also occur in the mouth.

Some people try a dietary approach in trying to prevent thrush, for example by eating more probiotic foods, or supplements. However, there is no firm evidence to support this and most experts do not believe adjusting what a woman eats is an effective approach to preventing Candida.

Also, various preventative diets have been promoted – such as a yeast-free, sugar-free diet – but most professionals agree that there is no evidence these diets are effective at preventing yeast growth or infection.

CARDIOVASCULAR DISEASE AND STROKE

Cardiovascular disease is an umbrella term for conditions affecting your heart and/or arteries and so this will include blood clots, heart disease, heart attacks, angina, heart failure, stroke, TIAs, arterial disease and aortic disease. Together these are the number one cause of death in the UK.

It develops when the arteries, which supply blood to the heart and brain, become narrowed by a build-up of plaque (cholesterol and other deposits). This is called atherosclerosis. Blood supply is reduced and in time the arteries may become completely blocked, either by more build-up of plaque and/or by a blood clot (thrombosis). In this case a heart attack or stroke may occur.

Men are more likely to get CVD than women, until after menopause when women appear to lose their hormonal protection. The exact cause of CVD isn't clear, says NHS UK, but there are lots of things that can increase your risk of getting it. The more risk factors you have, the greater your chances of developing CVD.

Some of the main risk factors are high blood pressure (see page 154), smoking, high blood cholesterol, diabetes (see page 142), lack of exercise, high alcohol consumption (see page 115), being obese or overweight, especially with excess abdominal fat (see Section 4), and an unhealthy diet.

CVD and Diet

While you will be protecting your cardiovascular system if you follow all the general healthy diet advice in Section One of this book, there are a few extra pointers it is worth reiterating here and this advice is incorporated in the Healthy Heart Diet that appears at the end of this information.

The balance of healthy fats versus other fats

The American Heart Association suggests that to lower the risk of CVD you should aim for no more than 7% of your total calories in the form of saturated fat. That is quite a low level compared with what we eat on average and can be achieved most easily by eating more plant-based protein foods such as pulses, nuts and seeds, by eating skinless chicken, turkey, fish and seafood rather than fatty cuts of red meat, and by limiting portion sizes.

A diet higher in the plant foods will also provide you with more of the various types of fibre that are good for lowering cholesterol, while a diet higher in fish, particularly oily fish, nuts and seeds, will increase your intake of the 'good' fats alpha-linolenic acid and the omega-3s, which are linked with protection from CVD. Also choose plant oils such as extra virgin olive oil or rapeseed oil for salad dressings.

However – research published in the *British Medical Journal* found that older people on low-cholesterol diets have a higher rate of stroke incidence, perhaps because cholesterol has a protective effect for more mature brains, while other research has linked eating probiotic yogurt with protection from stroke, high cholesterol and high blood pressure, and more research found that low-fat cheese doesn't lower cholesterol or heart disease risk.

Five or more a day

Getting plenty of different types of vegetable and salad items on your plate at each meal will help protect your cardiovascular system by providing fibre, vitamin C (one large trial of middle aged men found that those who had a vitamin C deficiency had a three

INFECTION LINK

There is now growing evidence that CVD may sometimes be linked with bacterial infections, particularly those that cause chest infections and gum disease, all of which may be controlled with antibiotics. To reduce risk of contracting infections, follow the Immune-strengthening Diet on page 126. See also Gum Disease and Tooth Decay, Colds and Flu, and Bronchitis and Coughs.

and a half times greater risk of heart attack), a variety of plant chemicals with anti-inflammatory and other protective benefits, and by helping you to control your weight. Whole fruits also provide vitamin C, fibre and various plant chemicals and are an ideal addition to your breakfast or as a quick dessert. Rutin, found in apples (and tea), may protect against blood clots.

Salt intake

Eating high levels of salt can increase blood pressure, one of the major risk factors for CVD, so use the tips earlier in the book to reduce your salt intake.

Sugar intake

While sugar isn't directly linked with heart disease and stroke, a diet high in sugar can lead to obesity and leaves less room for the healthy items that you need such as fresh fruit.

Weight control

It is important to maintain a healthy weight as obesity is linked with a much higher risk of cardiovascular problems. But equally important is the distribution of your weight – if you tend to be an apple shape, with a fat belly, you are at higher risk. While apple shape is partly hereditary, it can be minimised with a healthy diet, weight control and regular exercise.

Protect your healthy gut bacteria

Having a healthy colony of bacteria in your gut is linked with higher blood levels of HDL (good) cholesterol and triglycerides and with lower body weight, the American Heart Association reported in 2015, and may improve your blood pressure.

A diet rich in plant foods including fermented foods such as sauerkraut, tempeh and kimchi, pickled beetroot, olives, and in other foods containing healthy bacteria, such as yogurt, cheeses and kefir, is ideal for maintaining or improving your microbiome.

See Gut Health on page 151.

CATARRH – see Colds and Flu

CHRONIC FATIGUE SYNDROME – see ME

A NATURAL DIET

Sometimes it is hard and time-consuming to follow all the dietary advice for a healthy cardiovascular system but if you remember one thing, it should probably be this: try to follow a natural diet.

This means a diet low in processed foods and the items most likely to be high in saturates/calories/ sugar which may be takeaways, items from the local bakery and so on. Instead go for a diet high in unprocessed or minimally processed foods such as vegetables and salad, fish, chicken, eggs, nuts, seeds, pulses, olive and other virgin plant oils, natural yogurt, herbs and spices.

If you think this way at each meal, then you will naturally be getting a much healthier diet for your heart and arteries. The diet that follows is an example of the types and balance of foods that should help protect your cardiovascular system.

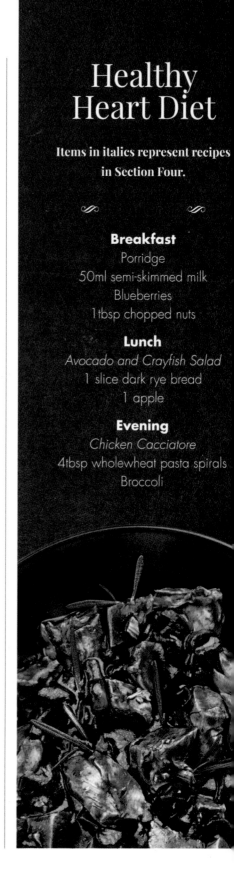

Healthy Heart Diet

Items in italics represent recipes in Section Four.

❧ ❧

Breakfast
Porridge
50ml semi-skimmed milk
Blueberries
1tbsp chopped nuts

Lunch
Avocado and Crayfish Salad
1 slice dark rye bread
1 apple

Evening
Chicken Cacciatore
4tbsp wholewheat pasta spirals
Broccoli

Breakfast
Home Baked Beans on
1 slice lightly toasted wholemeal bread with a
little butter or soya spread
1 orange

Lunch
35g Roquefort, Stilton or other mature
artisan cheese
2tbsp sauerkraut
2tbsp pickled beetroot
1 slice dark rye bread
Watercress and rocket salad

Evening
Potato and Mediterranean Vegetable Bake
1 apple

Breakfast
150g natural organic yogurt
50g oat-based muesli
2tbsp chopped walnuts and almonds
80g raspberries or blackberries

Lunch
Roast Tomato, Garlic and Pepper Soup
1 mixed grain roll

Evening
Baked Sardines with Pine Nuts and Raisins
New potatoes
Green beans, kale

Breakfast
Fresh fruit salad – chopped orange, grapes,
apple, pear
100g natural fromage frais

Lunch
4 *Lentil and Feta Koftes*
1½tbsp *Beetroot Hummus*
1 wholewheat pitta
Large green salad with olive oil and wine
vinegar dressing

Evening
Turkish Aubergines

Breakfast
75g oat-based muesli rich in nuts and seeds
125ml semi-skimmed or soya milk
1 apple

Lunch
Butterbean and Basil Spread
2 dark rye crispbreads
Tomato and red onion salad with olive oil
French dressing

Evening
Speedy Herbed Swordfish
Selection of summer vegetables steamed and
sprinkled with chopped fresh mint
Apple Flapjack

COELIAC DISEASE

Coeliac disease is not a food allergy or intolerance; it is an autoimmune disease, an inflammatory condition of the gastrointestinal tract, and is caused by the immune system reacting to the protein gluten in the diet. Coeliac UK says that one in every hundred people has the condition. But the average is higher in insulin-dependent diabetics and those who suffer from some other auto-immune conditions, and your chances of having the disease increase if other family members have it.

Once diagnosed, it is treated by following a gluten-free diet for life – currently there is no other cure, although Coeliac UK are hoping that one day a vaccine will be available.

Symptoms may include weight loss, diarrhoea or constipation, tiredness, lethargy, flatulence, mouth ulcers and sore tongue, painful joints, depression, hair loss. Once on a gluten-free diet, symptoms should improve but the time it takes for the gut to heal varies from person to person.

What causes coeliac disease?

Coeliac disease is caused by a reaction of the immune system to gluten – a protein found in wheat, barley and rye – which results in damage to the lining of the small intestine. This results in a reduction in the ability of the gut to absorb nutrients and can then result in malnutrition, anaemia, osteoporosis and other problems.

Solutions

If you suspect coeliac disease see your physician, who will make arrangements for diagnosis to be made. Specific dietary advice for coeliac sufferers should be obtained from a properly qualified dietitian (your GP should refer you).

Management involves avoiding all gluten-containing foods. These include ordinary breads, biscuits, pasta,

OATS

A small number of people are also sensitive to a similar protein, avenin, found in oats. If you are coeliac and have a reaction to oats you need to avoid them as well as wheat, rye and barley. Around a quarter of coeliacs don't eat oats.

Even if you are not sensitive to oats, sometimes oats are processed in factories where wheat, barley and/or rye are handled and so cross-contamination is a strong possibility. If you want to eat oats you need to find a source which is guaranteed suitable for coeliacs; i.e. they should be labelled gluten-free. Also, check with your dietitian before introducing oats into your gluten-free diet.

TIPS TO AVOID CROSS-CONTAMINATION

Minute amounts of gluten can be damaging to people with coeliac disease so it's important to be careful in the home that cross-contamination doesn't occur if you live with people who do eat gluten-containing foods.

Keep cooking utensils separate during food preparation and cooking.

* Use separate oil to fry foods.
* Thoroughly clean pans, grill, etc before use. If possible have your own toaster and breadboard.
* Have your own butter, spreads and so on – any items that people use to spread on bread/crackers, etc.

LIST OF GRAINS THAT ARE **NOT** GLUTEN-FREE*

Barley – including products that contain malted barley, such as malted drinks, beers, ales, lagers and stouts

Bulgar wheat – part cooked wheat

Couscous – granules made from semolina

Durum wheat – wheat used in making pasta and bread

Einkorn – an ancient form of wheat

Emmer – wheat, also known as faro or farro

Kamut ® – ancient wheat grain

Pearl barley – barley which has the hull and bran removed

Rye – closely related to barley and wheat

Semolina – coarse particles of wheat, used to make pasta and puddings

Spelt – an ancient form of wheat

Triticale – a cross between wheat and rye

Wheat – used to make bread, pasta, biscuits and cakes

* Coeliac UK

LIST OF GRAINS AND INGREDIENTS/ ALTERNATIVES THAT **ARE** GLUTEN-FREE*

Agar – from algae, can be used as an alternative to gelatine

Almonds – often ground and used as an alternative to flour in baking

Amaranth – a traditional plant used in Africa

Buckwheat – used to make flour and noodles

Carageenan – from red seaweed, used as a food additive

Cassava (manioc) – the white or yellow flesh can be boiled and used as an accompaniment for meat dishes

Chestnuts – ground and used for flour

Corn – also called maize, used for flour

Flax/linseeds – seeds can be added to muesli

Gram flour (besan) – from ground chickpeas

Hemp – flour and seeds used in bakery and cereal products

Hops – used in the brewing of beer

Maize – also called corn, used for flour

Millet/bajra – cereal used in porridge

Mustard seeds – used for flour and powder

Polenta – boiled cornmeal

Potato – used to thicken sauces and soups, flour/starch used in baking

Pulses (peas, beans, lentils) - can be ground into flour and used in a variety of dishes

Quinoa – closely related to beets and spinach, used in muesli, salads and baking

Rice – for example wild, arborio, basmati

Sago – starch extracted from sago palms, used as thickener

Sesame seeds – used in baking

Sorghum – sorghum malt is used in gluten-free brewing

Soya – beans are ground to make soya flour

Tapioca – starch from the root of the cassava, commonly used to make tapioca pudding

Teff – a grass with small seeds, used to make flour
Urd/urid/urad flour - ground lentils

* Coeliac UK

cakes, many breakfast cereals, pastry, puddings and pies. Because wheat, and to a lesser extent barley and rye, is present in so many manufactured foods, it is important to read labels of processed items. For example, soups, sauces, ready meals and sausages very often contain gluten.

The avoidance list may sound daunting at first, but in recent years there has been a huge increase in the number and range of gluten-free foods available and so following a gluten-free diet is very much easier. Sometimes, gluten-free foods are simply made from grains that don't contain gluten – such as corn and rice. Other times the gluten is removed from the grain.

Coeliac UK produces a list of manufactured foods that are guaranteed to be gluten-free and this list is regularly updated. Also, individual supermarkets will usually provide lists of gluten-free products in store and/or on their websites.

See also – **Gluten Sensitivity**

COLDS AND FLU

A recent Canadian overview of all the major studies done across the world on cold prevention and cures found that only zinc supplements may be beneficial (in helping to prevent them) – but long term supplements may be toxic so zinc is best obtained through diet (see page 40), though zinc lozenges sucked every four hours or so when you have a cold starting are unlikely to have any adverse side effects – experts say up to five days is safe.

Another recent review found that regular large doses of vitamin C supplements had no effect on cold incidence although they may shorten the time the illness lasts by a day or so.

Other work has found that they may reduce the severity of the cold as well. However, large doses of Vitamin C (more than 200mg a day) are also likely to cause nausea, diarrhoea and stomach cramps, the researchers advise. Getting more vitamin C via your diet – mainly by increasing your intake of fruits and vegetables rich in the vitamin (see page 34) could be a good idea.

The Canadian overview also found that the evidence for the usefulness of garlic was 'unclear' while both vitamin D and the popular cold cure, echinacea, appeared to have no benefit. As garlic has several health benefits in other areas, increasing your intake of real garlic is worth trying. The beneficial compounds in garlic are more potent if you crush the cloves and then leave them for ten minutes before using in your recipe.

There is encouraging research showing that getting plenty of probiotics into your diet can reduce the severity and length of colds and flu. For further information see Gut Health page 151.

The long-standing theory that eating dairy produce is mucus-forming has been knocked on the head by the few scientific studies done on the subject – it seems that they have no impact.

See also - immune-strengthening diet on page 126.

COLD SORES

Cold sores appear on the lips and mouth and are caused by the Herpes Simplex 1 virus – some people seem more prone than others. By keeping the immune system as strong as possible, the likelihood of frequent recurrence of cold sores is reduced, and if they do appear, they will be milder and of shorter duration.

Diet can help achieve this – such as foods rich in immune-boosting nutrients zinc, vitamins C, A and E, and the essential fatty acids found in oily fish and plant oils. Best sources of vitamin C are those that are also rich in flavonoids, such as citrus fruit and blackcurrants.

Use plenty of garlic, onions, ginger and thyme. Black and green tea are useful for the anti-viral quercetin and catechins they contain. Iron deficiency may be linked to cold sores as well.

There is evidence that the amino acid lysine helps block the herpes virus. Lysine-rich foods are lamb, fish, chicken, milk, eggs and potatoes. Similarly, the amino acid arginine helps the herpes virus to grow, so cut out arginine-rich foods, including chocolate, nuts, seeds, cereals and raisins, if a cold sore seems imminent.

See also - The Immune-strengthening Diet on page 126.

COLITIS – see Inflammatory Bowel Disease

CONJUNCTIVITIS – see Eye Problems

CONSTIPATION

Constipation – the infrequent passing of stools – is one of the most common physical complaints in the Western world. More than just an uncomfortable problem, if left untreated it can cause or contribute towards diverticular disease and haemorrhoids. Largely, it is our modern Western diet that is to blame, although lack of physical activity undoubtedly makes the problem much worse, and sometimes other factors can cause sudden constipation, especially stress or a change in daily routine.

To function correctly and regularly our bowels need adequate high-fibre foods as well as plenty of fluids to help bulk up the stools and make them easy to pass — about 3-4 pints of water a day is ideal.

Solutions

You need to increase the fibre-rich foods in your diet. In brief, these are pulses, vegetables, fruits (including dried fruits), wholegrains, nuts and seeds – all plant foods contain fibre, but if you choose highly-refined versions, such as white rice or refined breakfast cereals, you will be getting much less. Prunes and rhubarb are also known to contain further special compounds which produce a laxative effect, but they should not be relied on to the exclusion of a varied high-fibre diet. The addition of a little oat bran to meals may also help.

The food charts on pages 262–331 list the fibre content of over 300 foods and the best sources of fibre are listed on page 16. Olive and other plant oils and spices may have a laxative effect.

Millions of people currently rely on daily doses of branded laxative pills to try to help cure their constipation. However, these are best avoided except for really very occasional use as long-term they can make the problem much worse because your colon comes to rely on them instead of trying to work for itself. So when you stop taking them your constipation is likely to be worse.

CORONARY HEART DISEASE

– see Cardiovascular Disease and Stroke.

CROHN'S DISEASE

– see Inflammatory Bowel Disease.

CYSTITIS

Cystitis is a bladder infection, the main symptoms of which are a need to urinate very frequently, but then finding that you can only pass a few drops, a burning sensation when you do pass urine, and, if the attack is left untreated, pain in the kidneys (felt in the centre of the back). Urine may be cloudy, or even red, through traces of blood, and you may feel generally unwell.

Some anecdotal evidence shows that drinking cranberry juice reduces the risk of getting cystitis, and may lessen the severity of an attack, but NHS UK says large studies have shown it doesn't make a great deal of difference. At the onset of an attack it is essential to drink plenty of water, which helps to dilute the urine and so makes it less painful to pass as well as reducing infecting bacteria.

Some people try over-the-counter products such as potassium citrate to reduce urine acidity but again NHS says there's a lack of evidence to suggest they're effective. A basic healthy diet (see page 74), low in refined sugar and low-nutrient foods, may help to prevent infection.

DEMENTIA

Dementia is caused when the brain is damaged by diseases, such as Alzheimer's or stroke.

Alzheimer's disease is the most common type of dementia, but not the only one. In those with Alzheimer's, abnormal proteins damage the structure of our brain cells and in time this causes the cells to die. Often thought of as a disease of the elderly, it can begin at 50 or even earlier, often with barely noticeable small problems, such as poorer short-term memory, progressing at an unpredictable rate into severe memory loss and confusion.

Vascular dementia (VD) is when the oxygen supply to the brain is reduced because of narrowing or blockage of blood vessels, and then some brain cells become damaged or die. The symptoms can occur suddenly after a stroke or develop over time. because of a series of small strokes. The symptoms of VD vary and may overlap with those of Alzheimer's. Many people have difficulties with problem-solving and concentration and may get easily confused.

There are various other less common types of dementia, most of which have similar symptoms and outcomes to the above.

Minimising risk

Tobacco smoking is now known to increase the risk of dementia. High blood pressure, diabetes, stroke, obesity, high cholesterol and having a fat stomach are all also known risk factors for the disease. There is also a genetic link.

The starting point for everyone should be a basic healthy diet which can help to prevent or minimize all the conditions above. A traditional Mediterranean diet high in vegetables, leafy greens, fruit, fish, nuts, plant oils and fibre and low in red meat and saturates has been shown in many trials to help prevent brain disorders as we age. For example, a large 4-year US study found that people who ate a Mediterranean-style diet were up to 40% less likely to develop Alzheimer's.

A recent observational study has found a link between diet drinks and

D

dementia – just one fizzy diet drink a day produces almost three times the risk of someone suffering a stroke or dementia. In the wake of the research the American Heart Association recommends swopping diet drinks for plain water while more studies are conducted.

Meanwhile, a link between dementia and aluminium is still being studied and recently it has been suggested that drinking silicon-enriched water could reduce the amount of aluminium in the body/brain and in one trial at Keele University in the UK found 'drinking silicon-rich water over 12 weeks

NUTRIENTS AND SPECIFIC FOODS THAT MAY LOWER THE RISK OF DEMENTIA INCLUDE:

❋ **Folate** – found in pulses, wholegrains, green vegetables.

❋ **DHA** – the omega-3 fatty acid, found in oily fish. Fish oil supplements may not be so effective as eating actual fish.

❋ **Flavonoids** – tea, coffee, green tea and cocoa are rich in flavonoids which have been shown to help reduce the risk of Alzheimer's.

❋ **Vitamin E** – some evidence that the vitamin is linked with reduced risk of Alzheimer's but should not be taken as a supplement. E rich foods include nuts, seeds and their oils.

❋ **Vitamin A** – a deficiency of this vitamin, found in bright and dark-coloured vegetables and fruits, is linked with an increased risk of dementia. Supplements should not be taken.

❋ **Extra virgin olive oil** – reduces the formation of the plaques in the brain linked with Alzheimer's.

produced significant improvements in cognitive function without any known or observed side effects'.

DEPRESSION

Depression is usually treated medically with a variety of drugs that enhance mood but, unfortunately, few are free from side effects. However, with dietary alterations and other natural methods, many cases of depression can be helped or even cured.

Depressives sometimes lose their appetite, possibly because of a knock-on effect from the 'slowing down' syndrome that is so symptomatic of depression, and possibly because the will to 'look after yourself' goes. Poor or meagre eating habits will result in nutrient deficiencies, which can also contribute to depression. Other depressed people frequently turn to junk food for comfort, and an overview of studies in 2018 found that saturates, sugar and processed foods which boost body inflammation are associated with the risk of depression. This is a downward spiral, because comfort eating inevitably results in weight gain and even lower self-esteem.

Solutions

There are many ways that foods can affect how we feel, just as how we feel has a large influence on what foods we choose. Some of the mood/food effects are due to nutrient content, but a lot of effects are due to existing associations of foods with pleasure and reward (chocolate) or diet and deprivation (plain foods). Very many people experience a reduction in anxiety, stress or poor mood when they eat, for example, a high-carb meal or a bar of chocolate – the so-called 'comfort foods'.

However, it is not just high-carb foods that can change mood. There has been much interest in recent years on the link between mood and the amino acid tryptophan. Research in the UK showed that women deprived of tryptophan showed symptoms of depression within hours. Tryptophan is found in bananas, walnuts, turkey, sunflower seeds, milk, eggs, cheese, brown rice, chicken and fish.

Several studies have found a link between a low intake of omega-3 fatty acids, such as those found in oily fish, and high levels of depression and mental illness. As omega-3s are healthy anyway, it is worth including plenty of oily fish in the diet.

The basic healthy diet should also include plenty of foods rich in the vitamin B group including folate. This group keeps the nervous system healthy and research has shown that people who follow a diet low in B vitamins suffer from more mood swings and are less happy.

Vitamin C is depleted more easily in the body when it is under stress (which happens when we are depressed), so plenty of C-rich foods should be included. Vitamin C can also help in the production of serotonin. The herb hypericum (St John's Wort) works for many people to alleviate mild depression (see page 173).

Alcohol should be avoided – in small doses it has a stimulant effect but after the first drink or so it is a depressant and likely to have an adverse effect on those prone to depression. Alcohol also robs the body of the B group vitamins and C and can lead to insomnia.

DIABETES (TYPE 2)

Over 3.4 million people in England alone have diabetes mellitus (Type 2), the latest figures from Public Health England reveal – a 65% increase in the last decade. The likelihood of developing Type 2 diabetes is increased by being overweight – family history, ethnicity and age can also increase risk.

Type 2 diabetes used to be called 'adult-onset diabetes', but with the epidemic of obese and overweight children, more teenagers are now developing it. There's been a 40% increase in under 25s in just 3 years.

People with the condition either produce too little insulin (via the pancreas), or there is a defect in its use, e.g. the body cells are resistant to it. Insulin is responsible for regulating levels of sugar in the blood and its utilisation, so people with diabetes have levels of sugar in the blood that will easily rise too high. The first signs of diabetes are increased thirst, frequent urination, weight loss, excessive tiredness, and perhaps skin and fungal infections, wounds that won't heal and blurred vision. If diabetes is not treated it can damage the heart, kidneys, eyes and other organs, and having diabetes is associated with increased risk of cardiovascular disease and stroke.

DEPRESSION AND FOOD – NEW IDEAS

* The main component of turmeric, curcumin, reduces depressive feelings, a new US review finds.
* Women who have a low intake of zinc are more likely to be depressed.
* Probiotics found in dairy products may alter brain chemistry and help treat depression.
* Coffee seems to improve mood because caffeine helps the brain release dopamine into the prefrontal cortex, a brain area important for mood regulation. Dopamine is also vital to help you feel motivated.

Happily, recent studies show that diet, exercise and weight loss as necessary can actually be better at controlling, and even reversing, diabetes type 2 than is medication, though of course medication is sometimes necessary. It is vital if you have any of the signs of diabetes that you visit your practitioner to get tested – many people live with diabetes not realising they have it until one or more of the serious complications begins.

Diet, weight and diabetes

Most people with diabetes Type 2 are overweight or obese, and of the small percentage who are not clinically overweight, most have an 'apple shape' and intra-abdominal fat. Research finds that too much fat within the liver and pancreas prevents normal insulin action and secretion and that both are reversible with weight loss, which is why we are finding that substantial weight loss can reverse diabetes type 2 which was once thought to be a condition for life.

The type of diet that is best to follow to lose weight if you have diabetes type 2 is a healthy diet of the type outlined in Section One, but bearing in mind your own preferences. There has been much discussion in recent years about the benefits of a low-carbohydrate diet for diabetics, with some experts and studies showing that low-carb achieves the best results.

In the midst of controversy, in 2017 Diabetes UK released a statement on the low-carb diet which concluded that, 'Low-carbohydrate diets can be safe and effective in the short term in managing weight, and improving glycaemic control and cardiovascular risk in people with Type 2 diabetes'.

While there is no clear indication that low-carb diets are superior to other weight control approaches for preventing diabetes, they may help to better manage blood sugars once the condition is present. This reinforces Diabetes UK's call for an individualised approach to diet, taking into consideration peoples' personal preferences. Consistent evidence shows that total energy intake is the main predictor for weight loss.

'Whether people chose to follow a low-carb diet or not, they should be encouraged to include foods with good evidence to support health. This includes fruit and vegetables, wholegrains, dairy, seafood, pulses, and nuts. People should be encouraged to reduce their intake of red meat and processed meat, sugar-sweetened foods, particularly sugar-sweetened

DIABETES TIPS

✳ The antioxidants and anti-inflammatories in coffee can help protect against diabetes.

✳ A diet that promotes a healthy microbiome (friendly gut bacteria) seems to help prevent and control diabetes too. Such a diet, rich in nuts, fruit and other plant foods, is discussed under 'Gut Health' on page 151.

✳ Eating fish regularly reduces the risk of diabetic women getting heart disease by around 64%.

✳ Milk may help to protect against diabetes. A large 15-year study found that people with highest dairy intake had a 50% lower risk of developing diabetes than those with low levels. Full fat dairy also offers protection against weight gain in women, finds a very large study from the American Society for Nutrition.

✳ Moderate coffee consumption – 2-3 cups a day - is associated with a lower risk of getting diabetes type 2, according to a recent *British Medical Journal* study.

✳ Special foods manufactured for diabetics are not worth buying, says Diabetes UK. There is no role or benefit from the use of diabetic foods.

drinks, and refined white bread.'

So – go low-carb if you want – you will almost certainly see better weight-loss results in the short term. But if you don't want to do low-carb, you can still lose weight.

Weight loss results in being completely free of diabetes type 2 for many people – or at least, the condition is manageable without having to take medications.

For more information on weight loss and low-carb diets, see Section Four. For more information on a general healthy diet, see Section One.

DIGESTIVE PROBLEMS

Eating is rarely a pleasure if you have regular bouts of indigestion (heartburn), or perhaps bloating, stomach ache or nausea.

Heartburn can cause sharp and even severe chest pains and is the result of too much acid in the stomach when a meal is being digested. The excess acid spurts back up into the oesophagus, which connects the stomach and mouth, and the acid causes pain and discomfort, often known simply as indigestion. Heartburn is also a symptom of hiatus hernia, which is more common in people who are very overweight and may also be a common problem in late pregnancy, when the expanding uterus can literally 'squash' parts of the digestive system.

Certain foods such as acidic foods (pickles, sauces and vinegars) and fatty foods, such as fry-ups and pastries, are the most common culprits. Raw vegetables such as onions, chillies, radishes, and under ripe fruits are also best avoided, as are alcohol and fizzy drinks, all of which may promote irritation.

How you eat is also important. Have several small meals rather than one or two large ones; the digestive system will find this easier to handle. Chew food thoroughly, eat slowly and try to relax while eating. After you have eaten, an infusion of fennel or dill or apple mint leaves will help to prevent heartburn.

Lose weight, if necessary, and have a check-up, as there may be another underlying problem that needs attention.

Nausea, a feeling of queasiness or sickness which may or may not result in vomiting, can have various causes. A food allergy or intolerance could be the cause (see Allergies and Lactose Intolerance).

In women, nausea is a fairly common side-effect of PMS and can often be relieved by a small low-fat, high-protein snack such as a small piece of cooked chicken breast. It is also common in pregnancy (see the Pregnancy feature in Section Three pages 187–190).

If the problem is food poisoning, nausea will soon be followed by vomiting and diarrhoea (see advice on avoiding food poisoning on pages 110–111).

Another likely cause of nausea is the onset of an infection. Stress and worry can cause feelings of nausea, often associated with appetite loss. Eat small meals or take nutritious drinks until appetite returns and see entries on Anxiety and Stress and Appetite.

Travel sickness is a type of nausea that happens because of the motion of travelling. One of the best cures for this is fresh ginger — some tests have shown it to be more effective than travel sickness pills from the chemists.

Try an infusion of grated ginger root half an hour before travelling and eat a little crystallized ginger as you travel. Peppermint alleviates nausea – a few peppermint sweets will help, or peppermint tea. Any unexplained nausea lasting more than a day should be checked out by a doctor.

Stomach ache is a symptom of many different conditions and illnesses. Upper abdominal pain may be caused by indigestion, hiatus hernia, peptic ulcer, gallstones or infection. Central abdominal pain (around the front and sides of the waistline) may be caused by food poisoning, constipation (page 139), irritable bowel syndrome (page 157), diverticulitis (below), appendicitis (see your doctor immediately), or ulcerative colitis or Crohn's disease (see Inflammatory Bowel Disease page 156).

Lower abdominal pain may be caused by wind, constipation, cystitis or menstrual problems. General stomach aches may also be a symptom of allergies, anxiety, coeliac disease and stress, or, rarely, cancer of the stomach, colon or bowel, or elsewhere within the body. Stomach-ache which cannot be explained, and which persists longer than a few days or so, should be investigated by your doctor.

Mild bouts of stomach-ache caused by everyday problems such as indigestion, flatulence or over-indulgence can usually be eased somewhat by taking herbal infusions of basil, dill, fennel or peppermint. Also see the Fodmap diet page 158.

Bloating of the abdomen/lower belly is often caused either by wind in the digestive system or by fluid retention.

Flatulence (wind) is a fairly common side-effect of a diet high in fibre, particularly the insoluble types such as those found in high amounts in pulses, wholegrains and bread. Other foods to commonly cause flatulence are dried fruits and the cabbage family. Reducing the amount you eat and gradually re-introducing small amounts is a good idea, or in the case of pulses, eat them pureed or as soups. Or the cause could be eating too quickly and swallowing air with your food, or fizzy drinks. Irritable bowel syndrome (page 157), Crohn's disease (page 156) or coeliac disease (page 136) can also cause wind.

Wind in the stomach is usually expelled by burping, while wind in the small intestines and colon is expelled by the anus.

Fluid retention may be a side effect of PMS or of eating a large meal high in carbohydrates, which tend to 'mop up' fluids in the body. Another common cause is a high salt diet, as salt also retains fluid. Heart disease and kidney disease also predispose towards fluid retention.

See also – **Gut health, Peptic Ulcer, Inflammatory Bowel Disease, Irritable Bowel Syndrome.**

DIVERTICULAR DISEASE

Diverticular disease is a common problem in older people, when small pockets or sacs form in weakened areas of the wall of the colon. Half or more of the population over 60 may have diverticular disease, but only 25% or less will have the symptoms — abdominal pain, particularly in the lower left hand side above the groin, bloating, and a change in bowel habits, e.g. alternating diarrhoea and constipation. Symptoms may include fever and bleeding.

Research at Harvard has found a strong link between eating a lot of red meat and diverticulitis in a very large, long-term study over 26 years. Every portion of red meat that research participants swapped for white meat or fish resulted in an 18% reduced risk of developing the disease. It's thought that the balance of the gut microbiome may be altered unfavourably by a high red meat diet, and research continues.

Another cause of diverticular disease, some experts believe, is a highly refined Western diet, with inadequate amounts of fibre, particularly soluble fibre. This can easily lead to constipation and the diverticuli may form when straining to pass hard stools. In this case, follow all the tips in the separate entry for Constipation.

See also – **Gut Health**

DUODENAL ULCER – see Peptic Ulcer

EATING DISORDERS

It is estimated that around one and a half million people have an eating disorder in the UK and that they are more common than ever before. Many people with eating disorders go undiagnosed and untreated.

Anorexia Nervosa, Bulimia Nervosa and Binge Eating Disorder are the three categories of eating disorder which are most well-known, but others have been categorised in recent years, including SED (Selective Eating Disorder) also sometimes called ARFID (Avoidant/Restrictive Food Intake Disorder).

Most experts agree these disorders are often an outward expression of psychological conflict rather than simply a problem with food and body image. The earlier treatment is sought the greater the chances of recovery.

Anorexia Nervosa

The term means 'loss of appetite due to nervous reasons' but, in fact, at least in the early stages of the disease, most anorexics do feel hungry and do want to eat, but they don't allow themselves to do so. Later, appetite may indeed disappear and, even though the anorexic may want to be cured, they may find that that decision is no longer within their grasp (ironically, because anorexics frequently fear being out of control).

Neither is anorexia simply an obsession with becoming slim (although thinness is outwardly one of the anorexic's main goals), or a disease brought about by modern society's accent on good looks – anorexia was recognized as long ago as the Middle Ages and given its name nearly 130 years ago. Some cases, certainly, may be triggered by a need to have a particular body image (which is why the incidence of anorexia, and bulimia, is high amongst people such as dancers, models and actors).

The disease is ten times more prevalent in females than males. Fourteen to twenty-five year olds are most often affected, although it can affect people of all ages and quite often starts during the menopause.

Experts say that the two most common traits in the anorexic personality are perfectionism and obsessionality. The symptoms of anorexia are a preoccupation with weight and weight loss, and perhaps with eating only foods perceived to be low in calories, such as lettuce or celery. Weight loss may be disguised by wearing baggy clothes or thick layers. Anorexics may go to great lengths to avoid eating food and become adept at making excuses for missing meals. Often, though, they will enjoy preparing and serving delicious meals for the rest of the family. Weight loss is the obvious first symptom though may often be disguised e.g. with baggy clothes or thick layers.

Anorexics are often restless and hyperactive and may be obsessional about exercise and orderliness. In women, periods will eventually cease. If anorexia starts before puberty, development may be slowed. As anorexia progresses, the sufferer will face severe constipation, malnutrition, will feel very cold all the time and may grow hair on the body while hair on the head may be thin. As time goes on, anorexics will tend to eat less and less, until eventually their diet may consist of a lettuce leaf and some water every day. Unless the anorexic is treated, death through starvation or related causes, such as heart failure, will occur.

Help and recovery
It is very hard for an anorexic to make a recovery without the support and help of other people, as many refuse to admit that they have a problem. Various private clinics and residential homes now exist where the anorexic can be helped to work through problems and be taught to eat again. The National Eating Disorders Association in the UK has a database of treatment centres. BEAT, the UK eating disorders charity, has a network of support and self-help groups, phone helplines, message boards and so on.

Recovery often takes several years. About half of diagnosed and treated anorexics recover completely, others remain ill long-term, and about 5% die.

Bulimia Nervosa

This is the eating disorder with the largest number of sufferers – the Priory Group estimates 40% of people with an eating disorder are bulimic. It is a mental illness when people are caught in a cycle of eating large amounts of food quickly ('bingeing'), and then vomiting, taking laxatives or diuretics (purging), in order to prevent weight gain. Usually people hide this behaviour pattern and their weight is often in the healthy range.

Symptoms may be tiredness, feeling bloated, constipation, abdominal pain and irregular periods, while long-term frequent vomiting can cause tooth decay and gum disease. Laxative misuse can cause heart problems. Bulimia usually develops at a slightly older age than anorexia. In some instances, bulimia develops from anorexia.

The guidelines for getting help and making a recovery are similar to those of anorexia, above.

Binge Eating Disorder

People who binge eat consume very large quantities of food quickly and often eat even when they are not hungry. Unlike bulimics, they don't purge afterwards and thus may be overweight or obese.

Binges often involve the buying of 'special' binge foods and usually happen in private. After binges, people often feel guilty and angry with themselves for their lack of control. Binge eating affects both men and women and the condition tends to be more common in adults than in young people.

Self-help with support from appropriate groups, courses or books may often help with BED. If these don't help professional treatment may be recommended and this may include the use of anti-depressants.

Selective Eating Disorder

There are many types of eating problems that may come under the umbrella of SED/ARFID diagnosis – difficulty digesting certain foods, avoiding certain colours or textures of food, eating only very small portions, eating a very small range of foods or eating only certain types of food. Variations of this condition are fairly common in small children, but adults can also be affected. Eating may fill the sufferer with anxiety and some people with SED/ARFID may go on to develop another eating disorder such as anorexia. SED/ARFID does not tend to be connected to body image issues.

Orthorexia – an 'unofficial' (i.e. non-clinical) term invented by a US doctor back in the 1990s – is used to describe a person who is overly concerned or obsessional about eating only pure, natural, healthy foods, and this could also be within the SED umbrella. The motivation to follow such a diet may be similar to the motivations (maybe unconscious) of anorexia sufferers. Orthorexics may be socially isolated, and deficient in nutrients depending on the amount and types of food they will eat.

The recent 'clean eating' movement has some traits in common with orthorexia, differentiating as it does between 'clean' foods (usually fresh vegetables/fruits/nuts and some other items which are deemed natural) and those that are perceived to be 'dirty' or that must be avoided, and if taken to extremes may indeed be categorised as a SED. Indeed, mental health experts warn about the risks of the trend, with numbers of 'clean eating' proponents attending eating disorders clinics having doubled in the past two years.

Sufferers of SED and related disorders may benefit from all the options described in this article, including self-help, books, courses, or clinical treatment.

ECZEMA

Eczema is an inflammation of the skin, with a red itchy rash which may form small bubbles. If scratched, these may burst and infection may occur. There may be dry and flaky skin otherwise. Though there are several causes other than diet, several studies have shown that foods can provoke symptoms and up to 40% of sufferers could benefit from exclusion diets as explained in the Allergy entry.

Though it may start at any time, eczema is a common disease in childhood, with 50% of cases starting before six months of age. Recent research has found that if oily fish and fish oils are eaten regularly during pregnancy, the incidence reduces by over 30%. And indeed, sufferers of any age often find that inflammation is reduced if they follow a diet low in saturates and high in essential fatty acids and omega-3s.

Some anecdotal evidence exists that zinc supplements and evening primrose oils may also help.

See also – **Allergies**, **Skin problems**.

EYE PROBLEMS

Your grandma was right – good eye health really is a lot to do with eating up your carrots. She didn't know why, but we do now – the extremely high beta-carotene content of carrots, which is an antioxidant and converts to vitamin A in the body is essential for good eyesight, night eyesight and healthy eye tissue. For general eye health, it is essential that you get enough of all the main antioxidants in your diet – the carotenoids, vitamin C and vitamin E. Lists of good sources of all these appear in Section One.

The risk of **macular degeneration** can be minimised with a Mediteranean-type diet, rich in oily fish, vegetables, fruit – particularly orange – and nuts. It can also be helped with a diet high in the carotenoids lutein and zeaxanthin. Leafy greens such as spinach, kale and broccoli and egg yolks are good sources.

Blepharitis/bloodshot eyes/sties are often a sign of vitamin B2 deficiency. A daily B group supplement should be taken – and foods high in B2 include yeast extract, offal, nuts, seeds and pulses.

The risk of **conjunctivitis** may be minimised with the Immune Strengthening Diet (see pages 126–127) as it can be caused by an infection. Allergies may also be involved (see page 115).

Dry eyes may be helped with a diet rich in plant and fish oils and in vitamin E.

Puffy eyelids are often caused by fluid retention but you should see your doctor to eliminate other causes.

Cataracts are very common as people age, but their development can be slowed by a diet that is rich in the antioxidants explained left, in quercetin-containing foods, such as tea, onions and red wine, as well as in vitamin B2.

FATIGUE

There are many lifestyle and medical reasons why people feel fatigued or tired long-term and if you do, get checked out by your doctor for underlying reasons. Temporary fatigue can be natural in some circumstances – lack of sleep, overwork, stress, pregnancy and more.

A healthy diet containing plenty of vegetables and fruit, healthy fats, all the range of vitamins you need plus iron may help minimise fatigue symptoms. A frequent cause of feeling tired when you can count out all the causes listed above is that you have been eating too much refined carbohydrate/sugar. These can give you spikes in blood sugar levels – at first boosting energy and then bringing you down low. A big high carb meal can also divert blood and oxygen from the brain to the digestive system to handle it and this can result in feeling sleepy. The solution is to eat high-protein, moderate carb meals, especially during the day, and make any carb that you do eat 'complex' or minimally refined, as this has less impact on fluctuating blood sugar levels.

Being low on iron can make you feel tired so make sure you are getting plenty of the iron-rich foods in your diet (page 40) and see your doctor for an anaemia check.

F

Dehydration can make you feel tired, so get regular drinks throughout the day – but avoid alcohol as that can make you feel tired too.

Eat regularly and, if you are very physically active, consider that you may need to increase your calories.

If you are getting older and feel tired all the time, you may benefit from taking supplements of Co-Enzyme Q10, a compound that has an important role in the production of energy, and production of which can decline as we age.

Chronic tiredness may also be linked to gut bacteria – see ME and the entry on Gut Health.

See also – **Insomnia, ME.**

FOOD INTOLERANCE – see

Allergies, Lactose Intolerance.

GALLSTONES

Up to one in three of all women (men are much less likely than women to suffer) have gallstones, but only a minority of those will ever experience problems because of them. Pain in the upper right-hand side of the abdomen, which comes on several hours after eating, may be due to stones, which are generally caused by an excess of bile (which helps in the digestion of fats) and cholesterol in the gall bladder that can build up, particularly when the sufferer eats a high-fat diet. Inflammation or pain can occur if the stone tries to leave the gall bladder and becomes lodged in the bile duct. Pain can spread to the back and right shoulder and flatulence is another common symptom.

Gallstones are less common in vegetarians and in people who eat a basic healthy diet of small regular meals, low in saturated fats and sugars and high in fibre, fruit, vegetables, oily fish, folate, magnesium, and vitamin C. Some research shows foods that most often trigger symptoms are eggs, pork and onions.

GLUTEN SENSITIVITY

Some people who aren't diagnosed with coeliac disease (see page 136) still have symptoms such as abdominal pain, bloating, diarrhoea, constipation, headaches and chronic fatigue when they have gluten in their diet. This is sometimes called non-coeliac gluten sensitivity, and there doesn't appear to be damage to the gut lining.

Non-coeliac gluten sensitivity is something that is becoming more recognised, but research is in its early stages and the role of the immune system in it is unclear. Sometimes non-coeliac gluten sensitivity is defined as an improvement in symptoms when following a gluten-free diet, but Coeliac UK says it is difficult to rule out a placebo effect.

There is also some feeling that other component/s in gluten-containing foods may actually be the cause, such as types of fibre, a group of chemicals called fodmaps (found in a wide variety of foods including grains) or other types of protein. If you are experiencing symptoms when eating foods that contain wheat, barley, rye or oats and think you have a sensitivity to gluten, it's important to first rule out coeliac disease.

GOUT

A form of arthritis affecting around half a million UK people, gout is caused by the build-up of uric acid, a metabolic waste product, in the blood. Gout affects single joints, usually the big toe, and happens when not enough uric acid is passed in the urine, or too much is produced so crystals are formed, causing inflammation and pain.

Treatment is usually by drugs and diet. A generally healthy diet rich in vegetables, fruit, wholegrains, nuts and healthy fat, and low in rich foods has been shown to reduce incidence by a third, while a large Harvard University study has found that a diet high in red meats, soft drinks and fried and sugary foods increases the risk of getting gout. Overweight is another risk factor. Individual tolerance varies, but alcohol, particularly beer, often makes gout worse.

The UK Gout Society says it is advisable to reduce the amount of foods you eat that are high in purines, which may lead to increased uric acid in the body. These are:

* Offal, such as liver, kidneys and sweetbreads.
* Seafood, particularly shellfish such as mussels, crabs and prawns.
* Some oily fish, such as anchovies, herring, mackerel, sardines, sprats, whitebait, trout, as well as fish roes. Taking an omega-3 supplement might be advisable, to replace oily fish in the diet. This will not contain purines.
* Game such as pheasant, rabbit, venison.
* Meat and yeast extracts and gravy mixes.

Low purine foods include dairy produce, eggs, pasta, and most fruits and vegetables.

See also – **Arthritis**.

GUM DISEASE AND TOOTH DECAY

Gum disease, with symptoms such as sore, red, puffed, bleeding gums and perhaps bad breath, is most often caused by poor oral hygiene, such as not brushing regularly or properly, perhaps in combination with other factors such as long-term illness or being run-down. It is linked with an increased risk of heart disease, and if left, can cause teeth to fall out, so it's important to treat it via your dentist and/or doctor.

Diet can decrease the risk of gum disease – a diet that contains adequate vitamin C and zinc is important. Supplements of co-enzyme Q10 may help keep gums healthy, and tea is protective in both gum disease and tooth decay.

Tooth decay is also linked with poor oral hygiene and has a strong link with diet. Sugary food and drinks are one of the main causes. Bacteria breaks down the sugar, and then acid dissolves the tooth surface, which is the first stage of tooth decay. Sugars in many processed foods such as sweets, chocolate, biscuits and cakes are the main culprits. Other items to watch are sugary items that are kept in the mouth a long time, such as chewing sweets, fruit juices and sugared soft drinks that are sipped or sucked through a straw over long periods, and even some healthy items such as dried fruits.

GUT HEALTH

Way back in the 1980s, 'bio' yogurts were first manufactured by the French company Danone and were probably the first 'functional' foods we bought in the UK. These were promoted as containing probiotics – 'friendly' gut

bacteria said to improve digestion, and perhaps with other benefits.

We still buy them today – but thirty-plus years later the knowledge of gut bacteria – or the microbiome, as it is now called – and its importance to our health has increased tremendously, although research is still in its infancy.

It is estimated our bodies each contain – or should contain – between 1-2kg of bacteria – more than a trillion – living deep inside the gut. Our gut bacteria help to produce micronutrients (like vitamins and antioxidants) from the food we eat, as well as break down macronutrients (carbohydrates, proteins and fats) to ease digestion. They're also very important in helping our uptake of nutrients along the intestines.

But in addition, researchers now believe that the amount and strains of these bacteria not only affect gut health directly, but that they also have wide-ranging effects on almost every function and faculty of our bodies – they have been linked to pain and inflammation reduction, mood, brain power, the immune system, appetite,

weight, food cravings, protection from major illnesses, and more.

The survival of a healthy microbiome

In recent years our Western diet has meant that many people eat a lot of processed foods that are heat-treated, pasteurised or otherwise compromised, and often quite a small range of foods, particularly plant foods. This, coupled with the wide use of antibiotics and the obsession with cleanliness, reducing our exposure to bacteria, has lowered the amount and variety of bacteria in our guts and, experts now think, this is a main reason for many of the illnesses of our modern life.

Prebiotics and probiotics

We can encourage a thriving colony of gut bacteria by eating the right diet. The Basic Healthy Diet on page 74 is a good starting point. Probiotics are still being much researched and it seems that though they may not be of great use for everyone, they do help most people some of the time (more research needs to be done!). though it seems the good bacteria in natural foods work better than those in supplements). Good food sources are live yogurts and some cheeses, including most traditionally made hard and soft cheeses, blue cheeses, Gouda and feta. But perhaps the absolute best sources are highly-fermented foods such as traditional sauerkraut, kimchi, miso, tempeh, kefir and kombucha which are teeming with beneficial live bacteria (this doesn't include canned/pasteurized versions which have been heated to high temperatures and the bacteria will mostly have been killed, or pickles made with vinegar).

Much recent research shows that even better than probiotics are prebiotics - the foods containing types of fibre such as inulin and various oligosaccharides that gut bacteria love to eat. These include the onion family, Jerusalem artichokes, bananas, barley, oats, apples, beans, pulses, the cabbage family, root vegetables, asparagus, cocoa and flax seeds.

You should also consider cutting back on too many highly-processed foods, to make room for these microbiome friendly foods, and next time the kids come in the house covered in dirt from an outdoor game – don't be too worried. It could be just what they need for health.

See also – **Pre and probiotic supplements**, page 173.

HALITOSIS

Some foods can cause short-term bad breath – halitosis – and perhaps garlic is the most well-known of those, particularly if it is raw or present in the food in large amounts. Regular garlic-eaters find that over time the odour is very much diminished every time you eat it, as the body becomes used to digesting it. Some other foods such as curries can also cause odour. Often bad breath is little to do with food and more about poor mouth hygiene, sleeping with your mouth open, having an infection, taking medication, or constipation.

There is evidence that eating natural yogurt will lessen the odour as it neutralizes one of the causes – hydrogen sulphide. In one trial the yogurt helped beat odour in 80% of volunteers. It is also important to drink plenty of water, clean your teeth and floss regularly, and get a healthy diet.

HANGOVER

The after-effects of drinking too much alcohol can be debilitating, and prevention is better than cure. If you know you will be drinking, make sure to eat something beforehand as alcohol on an empty stomach is more quickly absorbed into your bloodstream.

Drink slowly, having a glass of water on the table, and sip from this every time you have a sip of alcohol. If you've been drinking in the evening before bed, have more to drink than usual at bedtime and during the night. Dehydration is a major cause of hangover.

Some research finds that paler drinks are less likely to cause a hangover than deeply coloured ones because they contain fewer congeners (impurities in alcohol that come about as a result of fermentation) so, for instance, white wine should be better than red and vodka better than Scotch. Researchers have found that on average, bourbon has 37 times more chemicals than vodka.

Also, it may pay to pay more – expensive spirits should contain fewer congeners.

HAY FEVER

A healthy diet rich in plant foods and anti-oxidants is the first protective measure you should take if you suffer from hay fever each year. This will boost the immune system (try the Immune Strengthening Diet on page 126–127). An overview of hay fever research in the USA has found that a probiotic-rich diet will also help by cutting the severity of the symptoms (see Gut Health).

Histamine-containing foods and drinks may exacerbate hay fever –

these are, for example, grapes, pickled foods, cured meats and cheeses. Beer and particularly red wine are high in histamine and studies have found that hay fever sufferers were more likely to have symptoms after they had consumed wine. Vitamin C may reduce histamine in the body as may the plant chemical quercetin, found in red onions, broccoli and red-skinned apples for example.

See also – **Allergies**.

HEART DISEASE – see
cardiovascular disease

HIGH BLOOD PRESSURE

An extremely common disorder, affecting approximately a third of adults in Western countries, if left untreated high blood pressure (hypertension) can cause strokes, heart attacks and kidney disease, and yet symptoms are not easy to spot. The middle-aged and elderly, people who smoke and those under stress are more prone to it.

Medication can help to reduce hypertension, but there are also various nutritional methods of helping to prevent or control it. One of the major factors is body weight – overweight and obese people are much more likely to have raised blood pressure. Alcohol is another factor so if you drink more than

the safe limits (see pages 50) you should cut down. Even 2 pints of beer or half a bottle of wine a day increases blood pressure.

Reducing salt in the diet does lower blood pressure – and combining a low-salt diet with increased fruit and vegetables has an additional beneficial effect as the potassium they contain balances out salt. A list of the major sources of salt in the diet appears on page45.

There are several salt substitutes available which you may find helpful, and nowadays there are many commercial foods which are 'reduced-salt'.

Two other minerals, calcium and magnesium, have also been shown to lower blood pressure as have omega-3 essential fatty acids, garlic, dark chocolate, soluble fibre and vitamin C. Foods high in polyphenols also lower it – these include all purple and black vegetables and fruits – as does the anti-oxidant lutein, found for example in kiwi fruits, kale and tomatoes.

Data from the Vegetarian Society shows that vegetarians have less incidence of hypertension than meat eaters and this is probably because of their high plant diet (see above). There is also recent research from Harvard University, showing that well-done

meat cooked using a high temperature produces chemicals that raise blood pressure, while rare meat does not have the same effect.

See also – **Cardiovascular Disease and Stroke**.

INFECTIONS

As bacteria are becoming more and more resistant to antibiotic drugs, it is important to find natural ways to fight infection. We now know that several foods and herbs do have strong anti-bacterial (as well as anti-fungal/anti-viral) effects.

To ward off infections of the respiratory system, digestive and urinary system and the skin and eyes, and to help minimize the effects of bacterial problems such as food poisoning, a general healthy diet (Basic Healthy Diet, page 74) should be followed, or at times of particular stress or vulnerability, the Immune-strengthening Diet (page 176) can be followed.

If an infection has set in, try the following:

✳ **Garlic** and its less powerful but still effective relatives, onion and leek have been used as infection-fighters for thousands of years all over the world by alternative practitioners. Scientists are now beginning to discover raw garlic can not only kill bugs such as listeria and salmonella but will also kill the new 'superbugs' that antibiotics don't work on any more. Its main active ingredient is allicin.

✳ **Honey** is very useful for skin infections. Rubbed on wounds and burns, it has been shown to heal the skin, leaving minimal scarring, and can also be used to treat ulcers, the fungal infection athlete's foot and the eye infection conjunctivitis. The famous manuka honey from New Zealand and some other single-source honeys have been shown to have especially powerful anti-bacterial effects – and can be more effective than medication for wound healing.

✳ **Green tea** has been shown to help kill bacteria when taken as an infusion and can also be used as a bathing fluid for skin infections.

✳ **Ginger root** is thought to be a mild anti-bacterial food which will also help to clear up chesty coughs and colds. Use it grated in meals or infuse for a drink with honey and lemon.

✳ **Lemon** is rich in vitamin C and antioxidants. Taken as juice, with ginger and honey, it is an ideal drink for sufferers of coughs, colds, bronchial problems and flu.

✳ **Vitamin C** – long talked about as a 'cure' for colds, a daily supplement of up to 500mg with added bioflavonoids (phytochemicals which help the vitamin be effective) may shorten length and severity of an infection.

See also **Colds and Flu, Bronchitis** and **Coughs**.

INFERTILITY

The inability to conceive may be due to several different medical or physical problems, but diet does play an important role. Regular menstruation and a reasonable body weight are both linked to ease of conception. Women who over-exercise and/or who follow over-restricted diets, which contain neither enough calories nor enough nutrients, may cease menstruation and therefore, at least temporarily, fail to ovulate.

A certain amount of body fat, which helps regulate hormone levels, and a Body Mass Index (page 201) over 20 are important factors in conception. Anorexics and people who exercise a great deal professionally, such as sportswomen and dancers, are frequently unable to conceive; if a sensible diet is followed and less exercise taken, however, periods can usually be restored to normal.

On the other hand, obesity can also cause infertility, probably by hampering ovulation, so a BMI over 30 should indicate a weight-loss diet. A general basic healthy diet, containing all the nutrients for good health, will help to facilitate conception. New evidence shows that the polyphenols in tea may increase fertility. For more information see Section Three.

Male fertility can be boosted with an adequate intake of zinc-rich foods such as nuts (see best sources list on page 40) and with a diet naturally rich in vitamin C and essential fatty acids and with adequate selenium. All males intending to father a baby should eat a general basic healthy diet – preferably organic, as chemical residues may reduce fertility – cut down on alcohol, caffeine and smoking, and get plenty of exercise.

INFLAMMATORY BOWEL DISEASE

This is an umbrella term that covers both Crohn's Disease and Ulcerative colitis. It is thought that both may be caused by an abnormal reaction of the digestive system to bacteria in the intestine – along with an unknown 'trigger' that could include viruses, other bacteria, diet, stress, or something else in the environment. Genetic inheritance is also a large factor.

These conditions cause inflammation of the digestive system or gut, are a little more common in women, and can affect any part of the gut, though the area most commonly affected is the lower part of the small intestine, or colon. Crohn's and ulcerative colitis are long-term conditions often with periods of remission and then flare-ups.

Symptoms may include abdominal pain, diarrhoea, tiredness, mouth ulcers, loss of appetite and weight loss. Although there's no clear evidence that any food directly causes or improves Crohn's and UC, some people have found that certain foods seem to trigger symptoms or make them worse, says the UK's Crohn's and Colitis Organisation, and very new research from the US links healthy plant fats with a reduction in gut inflammation. Prebiotic supplements may be useful too.

Generally, for both conditions, the most important thing is to eat a nutritious and balanced diet to maintain your weight and strength, and to drink sufficient fluids to stop you getting dehydrated. And sufferers may find during flare-ups that bland, soft foods may cause less discomfort than raw vegetables, spicy and high-fibre foods.

INSOMNIA

Lack of sleep is linked to many health problems including heart disease, diabetes and weight gain. As prescription medication can be addictive with unwanted side-effects, natural sleep remedies are a more sensible idea.

While a large meal, particularly late in the evening, may keep you awake while it is being digested, there is a lot to be said for having a medium-sized supper fairly early, and then a small snack before you go to bed.

But it has to be the right kind of snack, containing a mixture of carbohydrates, which promote the production of serotonin, a calming chemical, in the brain, and certain high protein foods, such as dairy produce, poultry and almonds, walnuts and Brazils which contain tryptophan, that converts to serotonin as well. Prebiotic foods (see page 152–153) encourage production of serotonin in the gut. Lettuce contains lactulacin which is a natural calming chemical.

The minerals calcium and magnesium are important for good sleep. They have both been called 'nature's tranquillisers' and calcium helps the body to utilise tryptophan. Research has found a lack of both minerals is linked to disturbed sleep. For good sources, see pages 38 and 42.

Some herbal remedies can be useful – chamomile, passionflower, valerian and lemon balm all have reported success in helping people to sleep and can be taken as teas or as herbal supplements.

Other foods and drinks can be detrimental to good sleep. These include alcohol – while one small drink may be fine, any more can cause middle of the night waking and general

disturbed sleep. Caffeine can also keep you awake, so while tea, coffee and cocoa are good healthy drinks, they are best reserved for earlier in the day.

Some people find that certain cheeses give them bad dreams, while other people don't sleep well after a high-fat meal especially if it includes fatty cuts of meat and fried foods.

Regular exercise is an important factor in good sleep – according to research, a daily walk or other activity in fresh air effects a 50% improvement in sleep patterns.

IRRITABLE BOWEL SYNDROME

One in five people may suffer from IBS, and it affects twice as many women as men. Symptoms are abdominal pain related to bowel function, with either constipation or diarrhoea, and a range of other symptoms which may include nausea, wind, bloated stomach, sharp pains in the rectum, depression, fatigue, dry eyes and backache.

There are no specific tests for IBS, as it isn't classified as a disease. Sometimes the symptoms of IBS can be confused with those of other digestive disorders such as Coeliac disease or IBD, but your doctor can arrange blood tests to rule those out.

The exact cause of IBS is not certain, says NHS UK, but most experts think

BEDTIME SNACKS THAT MAY HELP YOU SLEEP WELL

* Smoothie of ground almonds, honey, banana and milk.
* Slice of cooked lean chicken on a small piece of calcium-rich white bread.
* Warm malted milk drink.
* Almond butter spread on an oatcake.

that it's related to increased sensitivity of the gut and problems digesting food, perhaps caused by 'bad' bacteria in the gut. A low-sugar and low-yeast diet may help, as may a diet containing prebiotic foods or drinks, particularly in IBS with constipation. Virtually any food or drink may provoke an individual response. But many sufferers improve on the Fodmap Diet – a diet that reduces intake of foods high in types of fibres, such as fructooligosaccharides, found in some fruits, vegetables, milk and wheat. Intolerances should be investigated with the help of a dietitian. See Allergies, page 115.

There is also an association between IBS and psychological factors. One study reported that two-thirds of IBS sufferers have experienced severe stress before onset of symptoms.

See also – **Digestive problems. Gut Health**.

KIDNEY STONES

These are formed of chemicals within the urinary tract and can be very painful but they can be prevented.

You should drink plenty of water every day so that urine is very pale – about 2 litres. Ensure you have enough calcium in your diet (see page 38) and not too much salt. Eat only moderate amounts of animal protein foods such as meat, which boost uric acid levels in the body and can lead to stones forming. Also, avoid foods rich in oxalates, substances that encourage stones to form. These are beetroot, rhubarb, spinach, tea and cocoa and some nuts.

LACTOSE INTOLERANCE

Lactose intolerance is when your body doesn't produce enough of the enzyme lactase to break down the lactose

sugar naturally found in milk. Because the sugar can't be broken down and digested, it causes problems such as bloating, cramps, wind, and even sickness and diarrhoea.

LI may be temporary or permanent – most cases that develop in adults are inherited and tend to be lifelong, but cases in children are often caused by an infection and may last just a few weeks.

The severity of symptoms often depends on the amount of lactose consumed, and it isn't the same as a milk or dairy allergy. Some people may still be able to drink a small glass of milk without triggering any symptoms, while others may not even be able to have milk in their tea or coffee. If you are mildly intolerant you may be able to handle aged cheese, bio yogurt, kefir, and some people can even take goat's milk. Some processed foods, such as creamy dressings, chocolate, biscuits, cakes and bread, can contain lactose so read the labels.

People who have LI need to replace the nutrients found in milk and dairy products in their diet in other ways. See section one for alternative sources of protein and calcium, vitamin A, D and B12.

ME

Myalgic encephalomyelitis, sometimes called chronic fatigue syndrome, is said to affect 150,000 people in the UK at any one time. It can last for months or even years, is highly disabling and sufferers frequently have to give up work or school.

As ME is not a medically recognised disease, it's diagnosed by ruling out other conditions that could be causing symptoms, and treatment simply aims to relieve those symptoms.

The NHS says that the cause of ME is not known, but it may result from an infection such as glandular fever, a hormone imbalance, immune system problems, mental health problems or a genetic predisposition. Recent research at the USA Columbia University has discovered that there are differences in the gut bacteria of those with chronic fatigue syndrome compared to their healthy counterparts. This may eventually lead to more positive and targeted help for sufferers, but more research needs to be done.

The Immune-strengthening Diet (pages 126–127) may be useful in helping to prevent ME, otherwise follow a basic healthy diet, including plenty of potassium-rich foods such as fresh fruits and vegetables, as well as oily fish and whole grains.

For some, various dietary supplements seem to help. One trial showed quite significant improvement in symptoms with a regular combination of evening primrose oil and fish oils. Another showed that a course of magnesium injections helped – oral magnesium may also be helpful, as may co-enzyme Q10. Regular moderate aerobic exercise has been shown to improve wellbeing in some sufferers.

See also - **Fatigue**.

MIGRAINE AND HEADACHE

Common migraine – a severe headache, which is often one-sided and may be associated with nausea, vomiting and aversion to bright lights or noise – affects one in ten of the population and is twice as frequent in women.

There are very many triggers for migraine. In general, skipping meals and any crash or severe diets are to be avoided as they can cause hypoglycaemia (low blood sugar), which may precipitate an attack. The Migraine Trust says that this is one of the most important dietary triggers. An analysis of many migraine studies has found that being obese raises the risk by nearly a third, while being underweight increases it by 13%.

Food related triggers occur in about 10% of people with migraine, says The Migraine Trust. Excessive caffeine may contribute to the onset of a migraine attack and 4–5 cups of tea or coffee a day is a sensible maximum. Even caffeine withdrawal may well set off a reaction. Red wine contains tyramine which can cause migraine, and tyramine is also found in some cheeses, smoked meats, some soya products, and other products.

Chocolate has often been cited as a major cause, but it now appears it doesn't play a significant role in triggering migraine, though it does contain caffeine so it's wise not to eat too much if you are prone.

Some food additives such as monosodium glutamate, nitrates and aspartame, may trigger an attack.

Regular meals, adequate fluid intake and plenty of foods rich in magnesium and oily fish are all thought to help prevent migraine. One US study found that fish oil supplements halved the number of attacks and reduced severity. Another study shows that feverfew helps 3 out of 5 people.

'Ordinary' headaches can be caused by many factors, including eye problems, hangover, allergy, catarrh, infection, high blood pressure, stress and hypoglycaemia. Check out the different entries for all these. Other causes can be poor posture, dehydration,

and a diet that is high in protein and low in carbohydrate. See the Basic Healthy Diet on pages 74–75 for information on improving the balance of your diet. Persistent headache or migraine should be checked by your physician.

MOUTH ULCERS

Certain food intolerances may cause mouth ulcers and can be a symptom of coeliac disease (see page 136). Dairy products, wheat, strawberries, Marmite, tomatoes, and even oranges may be a cause.

People who are run-down or recovering from illness, or are under great stress, may be more likely to get mouth ulcers. Try the Immune-strengthening Diet and see also Anxiety and Stress (page 119). A diet that is low in vitamins, minerals and other nutrients, and high in junk and processed foods, may also be a factor.

A few food ideas may help – a natural bio yogurt rich diet for instance; try to keep it in your mouth for as long as possible as the good bacteria may help clear up the ulcer. Put honey (set, not runny) on the ulcer – honey is antiseptic, soothing and healing, and will stay in place for longer than most of the gels that are sold for ulcers. Manuka honey is particularly effective.

Eat plenty of garlic, also an antiseptic. Try crushing a fresh garlic clove and dabbing the contents on the ulcer.

OSTEOPOROSIS

Osteoporosis, a common condition – when skeletal bone loses its substance and density, becoming thinner, more fragile, more porous, and therefore much more at risk of fracturing – affects one in three women aged 50

plus, and one in 12 men. It can affect all ages, but is most common in post-menopausal women, due to reduced levels of oestrogen in the body after the menopause, which causes acceleration of loss of calcium and other minerals from the bones.

The best method of dealing with osteoporosis is in prevention by building strong large bones in childhood and early adulthood. The human skeleton is a constantly changing structure. A child's skeleton is totally rebuilt every two years, and an adult's every 7–10 years. The bones increase in density until about 30–35, when 'peak bone mass' is reached. After this time, bone mass should be maintained by sensible precautions such as taking plenty of weight-bearing exercise throughout your life and eating an appropriate diet.

Diet factors that may have a positive effect on bone density.

Mineral intake – both calcium and magnesium are needed in large amounts to build and maintain bone. For adequate intakes, see pages 38 and 42. The mineral boron also plays a part, and it is found in, for example, green vegetables, avocados, potatoes, fruit, dried foods, nuts, eggs, milk and wine. Potassium has an alkaline influence on the diet and can reduce the loss of calcium in urine, and zinc is also involved in bone building.

Vitamin intake – vitamin D helps your body absorb calcium (for daily amounts and good sources see page 30). Often people struggle to get enough Vitamin D in their diets and so a 10mcg supplement may be a good idea. Vitamin K is necessary for bone building and healing, and is found in a wide variety of foods; few people are deficient – Crohn's and coeliac sufferers may be. Vitamins B group, C and E may also have their own roles to play in bone health – and so a general healthy diet, high in plant foods as described in Section One, will help ensure adequate intake of all these nutrients.

Protein intake – Protein is essential for bone health and collagen structure (the protein mesh in bone to which minerals are attached). Most of us in the Western world get more than enough protein for our needs, but the need for protein increases with age, and elderly and frail people are at risk of not having enough in their diets if, for example, appetite is poor. This can contribute to bone loss, an increased risk of falls and delayed healing of fractures.

Fatty acid intake – Omega-3 and Omega-6 essential fats appear to have a beneficial effect on bone health, says the UK's National Osteoporosis Society. Fats also help the body absorb the fat-soluble vitamins A, D, E and K, all of which have a role in bone strength.

Weight maintenance – Thin people are more prone to osteoporosis than people with a recommended body mass index of between 20 and 25. This is because thin people may have lower levels of the hormone oestrogen, which helps to prevent bone loss, and because they have less weight to carry around, thus minimizing the beneficial effects of weight-bearing exercise on the bones. Also, if diet is seriously inadequate, nutritional deficiencies will compound the problems, and menstruation may become infrequent and this will have a similar effect to early menopause, which is a risk factor for osteoporosis.

Dietary factors that may have a detrimental effect on bone density.

Alcohol intake – binge drinking and/or regular high intake can have a detrimental effect on bone mass though moderate drinking doesn't seem to increase the risks.

Fizzy drinks which contain phosphorus in the form of phosphoric acid, such as cola drinks, may be detrimental if taken in excess. Our body needs some phosphorus for proper bone formation, but it needs to be taken in balance with calcium. If phosphorus intake is high this has been found to contribute to bone loss over time, especially when calcium intake is low.

High caffeine intake has been found to increase the amount of calcium lost in urine and in theory this may lead to loss of bone strength if enough calcium is not taken to replace it.

High intake of salt may cause an increased loss of calcium in the urine.

High intake of pre-formed retinol. This is a type of vitamin A – we all need vitamin A in our diets (see page 29) but some studies show that if you eat too much of the 'pre-formed

PHYTOESTROGENS AND BONE HEALTH

Phytoestrogens, such as isoflavones, are plant substances that act like weak forms of oestrogen, the female hormone in the human body, and are sometimes taken to improve menopausal symptoms. They are found in, for example, soya beans and flaxseed. There has been much debate in recent decades about whether they may help bone density, but the National Osteoporosis Society now says that the evidence is that they have no effect, or at best a very weak effect.

types' there may be increased risk of lower bone density and fractures in later life. Pre-formed retinol comes from animal products - and liver (and fish liver oils e.g. cod liver oil) contain high amounts. It is also present in smaller amounts in oily fish, dairy foods and eggs, but as part of a healthy varied diet all these nutritious foods are considered valuable. However, it makes sense to get plenty of your vitamin A requirement from plant sources (see Carotenoids page 30).

PEPTIC ULCER

A peptic, gastric or duodenal ulcer is an open sore on the wall of the stomach or intestinal muscle, where the protective lining has worn away, made worse by the acid secretions in the stomach which aid breakdown of food.

Peptic ulcers occur in about 10% of the population, are more common in men and also have a hereditary factor. Ulcers may often be caused by the bacterium Helicobacter pylori which can be treated by antibiotics and can be caused by taking NSAIDs such as iboprofen long term or by Crohn's disease. Symptoms of a peptic ulcer are upper abdominal pain and for example nausea, bloating, wind, loss of appetite and weight loss.

Medicines that neutralize the stomach acids will take away the pain. Diet is not as important a factor in managing ulcers as previously thought, although small frequent meals and avoidance of late night eating, as well as eating foods that are easy to digest (such as soups, purees and mashes), chewing slowly and thoroughly, may be helpful in easing some of the symptoms. Smoking should be avoided, and it is best to avoid alcohol too.

There may be slight continual blood loss from an ulcer, which may result in anaemia, so a diet high in iron-rich foods may be important once an ulcer is formed.

See also – **Digestive problems.**

SKIN PROBLEMS

Dry or flaky skin with no other symptoms (such as rash, redness, swelling or itching) is a common complaint, and even people who have oily or normal skin in youth and young adulthood may suffer from dry skin as they get older, which may wrinkle more easily.

To help maintain the skin's natural moisture balance, eat the Basic Healthy Diet (pages 74–75) with adequate essential fatty acids from plant and fish oils. The fatty acids EPA and DHA found in oily fish may be especially

useful. Don't try to follow a diet too low in fat, and don't try to maintain too low a body weight, either.

Get adequate vitamin E in your diet (for best sources list, see page 31) and drink plenty of fluids (about 2 litres a day).

Avoid getting sunburnt by limiting your exposure to sun in the summer months and especially in the hours from 11 a.m. to 3 p.m. Wear a high sun protection factor cream suitable for sensitive/dry skin. A diet high in carotene-rich foods, such as many orange, red and dark green vegetables and some fruits (see page 30) can protect the skin against sunburn. Zinc-rich foods may also help the healing process.

See also - **Eczema; Acne and Spots**.

TIREDNESS – see Fatigue

TONGUE, SORE

A sore tongue which is smooth and bright or fiery red may be caused by a type of anaemia due to deficiency of vitamin B12 and sometimes iron and folate, or a vitamin B2 or B6 deficiency. Other symptoms such as tiredness may also be present, and your physician should make a diagnosis and then supplement your diet as necessary.

A well-balanced nutrient-rich diet, such as the Basic Healthy Diet (pages 74–75), should help with prevention. High alcohol intake can deplete the body of B vitamins and should be avoided.

A sore tongue accompanied by furring and, possibly, bad breath is probably caused by oral thrush, which may be linked with vaginal thrush (see Candida) and may also be present after being treated with antibiotics. Regular spoonsful of live bio yoghurt containing the bacteria *acidophilus* may help, and see also Gut Health.

Ulcers on the tongue may be a symptom of coeliac disease, but can also be due to allergies or food intolerances, or possibly sensitization to substances used in dental treatment. See also Mouth Ulcers. Occasionally, a sore tongue may be caused by a severe protein malnutrition, but this should be diagnosed professionally.

THRUSH – see Candida: Tongue, sore.
ULCERS – see Peptic Ulcers

Healing Herbs and Spices

IN THE PAST few years our use of herbs and spices in cooking has increased hugely as our taste in food has become more international and sophisticated, our choice in the supermarkets has become immense, and many people grow their own herbs and fresh spices such as chillies and coriander seed at home.

But herbs and spices are not just great culinary aids – they are also good, or very good, sources of a variety of nutrients, so that even when used in relatively small amounts, if you use them regularly they can help protect you from disease, boost your vitamin and mineral intake and help beat everyday ailments, aches and pains.

PICKING, BUYING AND STORING HERBS

❋ Herbs bought in growing pots are likely to last longer than those in cut packets. Put the pots in a tray, water regularly, cut as needed and many types will regrow too.

❋ Pick your own herbs in the morning when the weather is dry and use as soon as possible for maximum nutrition.

❋ Cut back after flowers, or cut off budding flower stalks before they come into bloom, as it is the leaves that contain most goodness and once flowered the plants will be less keen to produce more leaves.

❋ Store cut herbs in a plastic bag in the fridge; they should remain usable for up to 2 days (soft herbs like basil and coriander) and up to a week for hard herbs such as rosemary and thyme.

❋ Think about drying fresh herbs for winter use – hang bunches of hard herbs in a warm dry place; dry soft herbs on a tray in the oven on its lowest setting.

❋ Even better for soft herbs – freeze them in water to make herb ice cubes, ideal for many cooked dishes. And you can freeze chopped parsley as it is, in sealed bags.

＊ Use herbs to make flavoured oils or herbal teas – steep the leaves in near boiling water for 5 minutes, strain and drink.

THE TOP HEALTHY HERBS

Use the herbs listed below – and other healthy herbs such as tarragon, chervil and fennel – as often as you can.

BASIL

Health benefits: Anti-bacterial, anti-inflammatory, Excellent source of vitamin K, good source of pro-vitamin A and C, calcium and iron, with some omega-3 fats too.

Uses: Highly fragrant, a glut is ideal for making your own pesto or sprinkle the leaves on pizza, toss them with sliced mozzarella and tomato for salad, or use in pasta sauce. Best added at the end of cooking.

CHIVES

Health benefits: Chives contain allicin, the compound also found in garlic and onions, which may improve heart health and reduce blood cholesterol. Good source of vitamin C and iron.

Uses: Chop into salads, dips, over soups and sauces, use in omelettes with other soft herbs.

CORIANDER LEAF

Health benefits: Contains several beneficial plant chemicals including limonene and quercetin, which can help protect against heart disease, as well as having anti-bacterial properties. Said to be soothing for the digestive system and to stimulate insulin secretion and lower blood sugar levels.

Uses: Sprinkle liberally on curries before serving; make coriander pesto, stir into carrot soup, chop into guacamole and salsas.

DANDELION

Health benefits: Strong diuretic, potassium-rich, blood detoxifier, root is aid to liver action and has also been used to treat arthritis, eczema and constipation.

Uses: Pick fresh young leaves and use in green salads or add to stir-fry. Make dandelion wine with the flowers and dandelion tea with ground root.

DILL

Health benefits: Both the leaves ('dill weed') and seeds are rich in plant chemicals, particularly monoterpenes which can prevent cancers, including those of the liver and lung. Dill is also anti-bacterial, a traditional digestive aid, and a good source of iron and calcium.

Uses: The leaf fronds are ideal sprinkled over fish such as salmon; added to fish sauces, and in any egg recipe, or try sprinkling seeds and/or leaves into yogurt dips.

LEMON BALM

Health benefits: Calming; anti-viral (infusion good for treating cold sores);

may also help over-active thyroid.

Uses: Makes a delicious tea and the young leaves can be used in a mixed, leaf or herb salad or in summer soft drinks and cocktails.

MINT

Health benefits: Most studies have been carried out on the variety called peppermint, which is anti-viral, anti-bacterial, anti-cancer. It can also relieve various digestive disorders such as indigestion, as it relaxes the gut muscles, and may help breathing problems such as rhinitis and even asthma.

Uses: In the classic UK mint sauce or in tzatziki; in omelettes with other soft herbs, as a tea, chopped into cooked peas and broad beans, with melon dishes and in soups.

OREGANO

Health benefits: A good source of vitamin K, fibre, iron and calcium, oregano is also a powerful anti-oxidant, four times stronger in action than blueberries, and is strongly anti-bacterial, anti-fungal, anti-viral and anti-inflammatory and may help prevent development of colon cancer.

Uses: Chop and use in a fresh herb mix for omelettes and casseroles; sprinkle on pizza before cooking, use in stuffing for poultry and meats; add to marinades; make infused oil.

PARSLEY

Health benefits: Excellent source of vitamin C and carotenes and a good source of folate, iron and a range of other vitamins and minerals. Contains myristicin which may help prevent lung cancer. Said to help freshen the breath and act as a diuretic.

Uses: Traditional ingredient in many dishes including tabbouleh (see page 248), gremolata (Italian garlic, parsley and lemon zest rub or topping), in savoury white sauces for fish, ham and pies. Add chopped parsley to pan-fried prawns and garlic, make parsley pesto, use flat-leaf parsley in tomato salads.

ROSEMARY

Health benefits: Helps boost the immune system, increases circulation, and improves digestion. It is also anti-inflammatory, has been shown to improve concentration and may also be helpful in minimising the severity of asthma attacks.

Uses: Strong flavour marries well with many chicken and lamb dishes; good finely chopped in stuffings and marinades or make a dip with pureed rosemary and extra virgin olive oil. Classic component of mixed herbs and herbes de Provence.

SAGE

Health benefits: Has many similar benefits to rosemary (both from same mint family) and may help to minimise severity of inflammatory conditions such as rheumatoid arthritis and asthma, and of arterial disease.

Uses: Goes very well with most pulses, duck and pork. ideal sprinkled on pizza and mixed into stuffings, good with onions and in mixed vegetable dishes.

THYME

Health benefits: Good source of vitamin C and iron; contains the oil thymol which seems to protect the quality of 'good' fats, particularly DHA, in the body and is

also strongly anti-bacterial and anti-fungal.

Uses: Ideal in meat stuffings and rubs, with egg dishes and pulses, in casseroles and soups.

THE TOP HEALTHY SPICES

ALLSPICE

Health benefits: Also called Jamaican pepper, the spice is anti-inflammatory, helps relieve wind and indigestion, boosting the immune system, may reduce blood pressure, and has a mildly analgesic effect.

Uses: Use to pep up sweet dishes such as apple crumble or dark chocolate mousse; add to stews, curries and soups to add subtle peppery flavour; essential in Jamaican Jerk recipes.

BLACK PEPPER

Health benefits: A digestive aid particularly useful when eating protein foods, also helps reduce discomfort in the gut and stomach and helps prevent wind. Diuretic, anti-oxidant and anti-bacterial, some research seems to show that pepper can help breakdown bodyfat.

Uses: Widely as a condiment in and on savoury foods, can also be used on sweet foods, such as strawberries and melon.

CARDAMOM

Health benefits: Very useful fibre content, as well as iron and manganese, and some studies have shown it can reduce the risk of cancer.

Uses: Can be ground and added to casseroles, curries and rice dishes. Try sprinkling it on cauliflower slices before roasting or add to lentil or chick pea soup.

CINNAMON

Health benefits: Anti-bacterial; anti-clotting effect on the blood; may relieve pain of arthritis, boosts the immune system; digestive aid. Some evidence it can lower blood sugar in people with type 2 diabetes and may be anti-fungal, offering help in yeast infections including candida.

Uses: Ground cinnamon can be sprinkled on sweet and savoury dishes and stirred into milk. A tasty addition to Mediterranean casseroles and tagines; goes well with aubergine.

CLOVES

Health benefits: contains eugenol, a plant chemical with analgesic and anti-inflammatory properties. Rich in anti-oxidant flavonoids and with a good content of fibre, iron, calcium and iron.

Uses: Add to fruit compotes, curries, vegetable stews and stuffings.

CUMIN

Health benefits: Good source of iron and several other minerals and vitamin B1. A digestive aid and may also help protect from stomach and liver cancers as well as regulating blood sugars.

Uses: Staple ingredient of curries; goes well with Mediterranean vegetables, e.g in a ratatouille. Add to rice in pilafs.

CHILLIES

Health benefits: Fresh chillies are a good source of vitamin C, carotenes, fibre and vitamin E, as well as capsaicin, the plant chemical which gives the hot hit and is linked with several health benefits

including pain relief from arthritis and psoriasis and the prevention of prostate cancer. It may also help prevent inflammatory diseases, reduce blood cholesterol, is anti-bacterial and can help clear lung and nose congestion. Chillies also boost the metabolic rate so may be useful for weight control, and may even help reverse diabetes and colitis.

Dried chillies have similar effects but have lost most of their vitamin C.

Uses: Slice into all kinds of savoury dishes and even salads. Add to dips, make chilli oil, use dried chilli as a condiment, sprinkle over chicken before cooking, make your own chilli paste.

CORIANDER SEED

Health benefits: As coriander leaf.

Uses: Roughly grind using pestle and mortar and stir into vegetable dishes – goes particularly well with peppers, aubergines and butternut squash. Stir into steamed spinach and home-made hummus. Mix with lemon juice and olive oil to dress winter salads.

GARLIC

Health benefits: Sometimes classed as a vegetable rather than a spice, but as it is usually served as a flavouring I have included it here. A member of the onion family, its main active ingredient is allicin which can help to lower blood LDL cholesterol and reduce the 'stickiness' of the blood, protects against stomach and bowel cancers, and may regulate blood pressure. Also a good source of vitamin C and B vitamins.

Uses: In very many savoury dishes, either chopped, crushed, minced or left whole. Also in rubs, seasonings, sauces. Crushing garlic and letting it stand for ten minutes before cooking helps protect the allicin, as does adding the garlic to your dish towards the end of cooking time. Note – (dried) garlic salt contains around $^7/_8$ salt and $^1/_8$ garlic and thus will not offer the same health effects.

GINGER

Health benefits: Long used as a natural remedy for digestive problems including indigestion, wind and bloating. Helps prevent motion sickness and general nausea. Contains plant chemicals called gingerols which are strongly anti-inflammatory. Shown to help improve movement and pain in people with osteoarthritis, and may also help prevent some cancers.

Uses: In stir fries and many other Chinese inspired dishes; mince and add to sweet potato purees. Good in sweet dishes and with fruits, and makes a refreshing drink.

TURMERIC

Health benefits: A good source of iron and vitamin B6, turmeric's main active chemical is curcumin, and there is some evidence this reduces the levels of inflammation-causing cytokines in the body. The chemical may also help in preventing insulin resistance, in promoting heart health and in cancer treatment, but the evidence for these latter benefits is mostly via research on animals. More research needs to be done on humans before we can be sure of turmeric's true benefits.

Uses: Classic ingredient of spice mixes and pastes and goes very well with cauliflower and eggs. Can also be stirred into mash and salad dressings, used as a drink.

Vitamin, Herbal and Food supplements

WHATEVER HEALTH CONDITION you are looking to cure or prevent, there will be probably dozens of different supplements promising to help you. We spend over £414 million a year on over-the-counter herbal and vitamin pills in the UK – and yet there is little clear evidence that they are worth the expense.

The most popular supplements are fish oils, multivitamins, and single vitamins, but literally hundreds of different products exist in varying combinations, and new products are appearing all the time.

VITAMINS AND MINERALS

Most research on their efficacy has come to the conclusion that taking vitamins and minerals in pill form is nowhere near as good for your health as having the same vitamins and minerals as a natural part of your food. Just because a particular food nutrient might be protective, it does not mean that taking it in tablet form will have the same effect.

It seems that vitamins and minerals work closely with other nutrients in what we eat – and isolating them in a pill may mean that they don't have the same effect. They may also be made from synthetic, rather than natural ingredients. No wonder that several minerals in pill form are not easily absorbed in the body so you may be paying for a 'nutrient' that goes straight through your digestive system and out the other end.

And in some cases, supplement pills can actually do you harm. For example, beta-carotene supplements can increase the risk of lung cancer in those who already smoke by around 28%. Large doses of vitamin E can increase the risk of heart failure and higher death rates.

Some supplements are toxic in excess, unsuitable for certain groups of people (e.g. in pregnancy or for many people taking prescription medicines) and can create nutritional imbalances, meaning that for most people, supplements, with few exceptions, are probably best avoided.

The exceptions may be supplements recommended by your doctor – for example, vitamin D pills to help prevent osteoporosis during winter months or for the elderly, an iron supplement for anaemia, and vitamin B12 is often recommended for vegans as it is naturally present in very few vegan foods.

Tablets may contain binders, fillers and other ingredients, including sugar, artificial sweeteners, yeast, colourings and/or fat, and they may contain non-vegetarian or vegan ingredients.

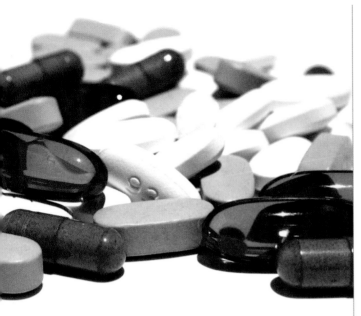

VITAMIN AND MINERAL SUPPLEMENTS ABSORPTION

＊ The UK independent watchdog, The Food Commission, has found that many supplements are hardly absorbed at all. Fat-soluble vitamins (A, D, E) are less well absorbed when taken without food; iron tablets are notorious for being badly absorbed – help absorption by taking with vitamin-C-rich food or drink.

＊ Don't take mineral supplements with tea or coffee as these hinder absorption.

＊ 'Time release' capsules may help vitamin absorption.

＊ Mineral supplements are sold with the mineral bound (or 'chelated') to other compounds.

Minerals which are chelated to organic compounds, such as amino acid chelates, gluconates, picolinates or citrates, may be more easily absorbed than those bound to inorganic compounds such as sulphates or phosphates (check label).

HERBAL AND FOOD SUPPLEMENTS

This category includes manufactured items that aren't foods as such – i.e. you would not use them in the kitchen for meal preparation – and are taken as a supplement often under the umbrella term of complementary, herbal or alternative medicine. However, if they don't make actual medical claims, a lot of the products sold in the UK come under food regulations.

A herbal/botanical product will be considered a medicinal product if claims are made that it can prevent, treat or cure disease. Such products for sale in the UK must display the Traditional Herbal Registration (THR) logo if they have been approved for sale. For further info see the Appendix.

Tests carried out by the BBC for a health programme found that products that come simply under food regulations in the UK may not contain what is on the label. For example, 27% of food supplement products labelled as Ginkgo and 36% of milk thistle products contained little or none of the advertised ingredient.

And the actual herbal ingredient may not be harmless. The NHS says, 'Many people have a false sense of security about herbal products because they are seen as natural. But natural does not always mean safe. Anybody considering taking complementary or alternative medicine alongside their own prescribed medication are advised to discuss this with a doctor, nurse or pharmacist first.'

Here we look at the most popular herbal and food supplements used to promote wellbeing or health.

AGNUS CASTUS

Several studies support the use of this herb for helping PMS, but a review of all these in 2017 found that 'most of the trials are associated with a high risk of bias. There is a clear need for high-quality trials'.

ALOE VERA

The gel or oral juice/capsules are a traditional remedy for treating wounds, burns, various skin conditions as well as complaints from IBS to constipation. Scientific reviews have concluded the evidence is mixed and the US National Center for Complementary and Integrative Health concludes that, 'There's not enough evidence to show whether aloe vera is helpful for most of the purposes for which people use it'.

BEE PROPOLIS

A hive sealant made by bees, this is often taken as an immune booster and hay fever remedy, but proper evidence for its efficacy is very limited. People with pollen allergies may have allergic reactions to bee products, such as bee pollen, honey, royal jelly, and propolis, so care needs to be taken.

BETA-GLUCAN

Beta glucans are soluble fibres found in the cell walls of bacteria, fungi, yeasts, algae, and lichens (and some cereals and other plant foods) which have been shown to improve blood glucose levels in diabetics and improve blood cholesterol levels, reducing LDL cholesterol by around 7% if taken regularly, but supplements may not be necessary if you eat good sources including oats, barley, legumes, and your minimum five a day veg/fruit.

BLUE-GREEN ALGAE

Freshwater algae supplements (including spirulina and chorella) have for decades been popular for the range of vitamins, minerals, protein and other nutrients they contain, but the algae can be contaminated with microcystin which could cause liver, kidney and nervous system poisoning. One US study found that 72% of blue-green algae supplements tested contained microcystin levels higher than the regulatory limit. Not to be taken during pregnancy.

CO-ENZYME Q10 (UBIQUINOL)

Often taken to help heart function and help prevent gum disease. The US NCCIH says supplements may benefit some patients with cardiovascular disorders, but research on other conditions is not conclusive. It has mild side effects and is generally well tolerated. However, it may make warfarin, an anticoagulant (blood thinner), less effective.

ECHINACEA

Said to help prevent or shorten the duration of colds, and a 2014 overview of the research found that some products may reduce the risk by 10–20% but that in general the evidence for their efficacy was weak, especially in reducing the length of colds.

EVENING PRIMROSE OIL

Rich in omega-6 fatty acid GLA and often taken to treat menstrual problems, but NCCIH says, 'There's not enough evidence to support the use of evening primrose oil for any health condition. A comprehensive 2013 evaluation found evening primrose oil, taken orally, is not helpful for relieving symptoms of eczema. Most studies of evening primrose oil for PMS have not found it to be helpful.'

FISH OILS

The fish oils EPA and DHA have been widely studied and found to be helpful for health in many ways (see pages 20–22), but it is generally accepted by experts that these omega-3 oils are better eaten in oily fish such as salmon and mackerel, rather than taken as supplements. In 2018 the Cochrane Library conducted a huge review of 79 trials and concluded that there is no evidence they reduce the risk of heart disease, stroke or early death but can improve brain health and ADHD in some.

GARLIC

There is very little evidence that taking garlic supplements can help prevent colds, according to a review of the trials in 2014, and other analysis of trials has found similar results for cardiovascular disease and high blood pressure but there is some evidence that supplements may reduce the risk of some cancers including prostate, ovarian and colon. While safe in the amounts found in food, supplements may increase the risk of bleeding if you are on anticoagulants such as warfarin and may interfere with the action of some other drugs.

Real garlic is discussed on page 168.

GLUCOSAMINE

A component of body cartilage, several trials have shown supplements may help ease symptoms and pain of osteoarthritis, especially in combination with chondroitin. One large recent trial published in the *Annals of the Rheumatic Diseases* found similar pain relief to prescription drugs in those with knee arthritis. However, several other trials found a very weak link and some patients continued to find pain relief when the glucosamine was replaced with a placebo.

KELP

Kelp – a brown seaweed – is a concentrated source of iodine, but can provide excessive amounts which may be unsafe, especially during pregnancy or if you have thyroid disease, or are taking other medication. Therefore, the British Dietetic Association advises against using kelp as an iodine source.

MILK THISTLE

Used in Europe for hundreds of years to help treat liver disorders including cirrhosis, the herb's extract, silymarin, may also help blood sugar control and kidney disease in people with diabetes, according to various trials, but more research needs to be carried out before its effectiveness can be graded.

PASSIFLORA

Passionflower supplements have long been used to treat anxiety and insomnia and there is plenty of anecdotal evidence for their worth. But there is only a small amount of scientific evidence that they may be effective. There is also some evidence that passiflora may help children with ADHD but again, more research needs to be done.

PREBIOTICS AND PROBIOTICS

It is now known that maintaining a thriving level of gut bacteria is vital for good health.

Probiotic supplements usually in capsule form have been popular for several years – these contain live 'good' bacteria such as Lactobacillus and Bifidobaterium. Most research shows that a high percentage of these bacteria don't survive the journey from mouth to gut, and several studies show that even if they do, they fail to colonise. Of eight popular brands tested only one contained bacteria that flourished in the intestines.

Prebiotic supplements consist of particles of the foods that gut bacteria thrive on – and these seem to be much more effective. While many foods (see page 152) are prebiotic, it is not that easy to get enought of them in the diet so supplements can be useful. See Gut Health, pages 151–152.

ST JOHN'S WORT

Several reviews have found that the leaves of this plant can be an effective anti-depressant when taken as a supplement, but it should be avoided if pregnant or breastfeeding, and not taken with prescription anti-depressants or by people with bipolar disorder. It also may have interactions with several drugs including hormonal contraceptives, warfarin and other blood thinners, calcium channel blockers, statins, anti-convulsants and anti-cancer drugs, for example. Check with your doctor before taking St John's Wort (Latin name *hypericum perforatum*).

VALERIAN

While valerian is a long-used remedy for insomnia, anxiety, depression and menopausal symptoms, the NCCIH finds that the evidence on whether valerian is helpful for sleep problems is inconsistent, and that there's not enough evidence to conclude that valerian can relieve anxiety, depression, or menopausal symptoms.

WHEAT GRASS

Wheat grass (young wheat shoots) is said to protect us from inflammation, improve circulation and even build red blood cells – but there is no scientific evidence to prove this. Tests show that weight for weight there is little difference in the nutrient value of wheat grass compared with other greens such as broccoli and spinach. ∎

Food for the Time of Your Life

Everyone knows that a baby needs different food from an adult—and that there are special dietary requirements for pregnant women. However, eating right for the time of your life is important at ANY age.

So here, for instance, we look at the many problems that parents face in getting their young children to eat well, and their teenagers safely through the 'food fad' years. Then in pregnancy, we need to consider how best to fuel our bodies for the needs of this busy and often challenging time.

We move on to the middle years and, for women, the menopause. Many of the less wanted symptoms of these years can be reduced or prevented with a suitable diet. For men, middle age can be a tricky time healthwise, too, and diet is equally as important not least to help protect us against the diseases of older age.

Today, old age doesn't officially begin until you are 75 – and there is plenty to be done in the later years food-wise to keep your body and mind fit and healthy. So whatever the time of your life – start here for the advice you need.

Childhood and Teenage Years

THE IMPORTANCE OF a suitable diet in childhood is recognized by every health professional, and yet a recent Government report says only two out of five children eat properly. Find out how much your child's diet affects their health, growth and wellbeing – and what a healthy diet for most children really is.

BIRTH TO SIX MONTHS

Up to six months, most babies need nothing other than breast milk, apart from vitamin K, which is routinely given at birth by injection. Few will need vitamin supplements or any other food (there are always exceptions, particularly if nutrition during pregnancy was inadequate).

BREAST FEEDING

Breast feeding is beneficial to the baby's health in many ways:

✳ Breast milk contains antibacterial compounds which reduce risk of vomiting, diarrhoea and infections.

✳ It is rich in pre- and probiotics (see page 172).

✳ Breast feeding can offer protection against sudden infant death syndrome, leukaemia, diabetes, coeliac disease, asthma, eczema, jaundice and food allergies.

✳ Breastfeeding helps reduce the risk of obesity in childhood, as well as of strokes, CHD and high blood pressure later in life.

✳ Breast milk is high in the long-chain omega-3 polyunsaturated acids e.g. DHA (contained in fish oils) and also high in oligosaccharides, both of which may have an effect on cognitive development.

✳ Breast milk is natural, free, convenient and easily digested, with a perfect balance of nutrients in a highly available form.

In the UK, approximately 73% of mothers begin breastfeeding when their baby is born, 43% breast-feed until 8 weeks old, and around 34% until six months of age.

✳ The World Health Organisation recommends that all babies are breastfed for up to two years or longer.

BOTTLE FEEDING

Bottle feeding is necessary for some and provides adequate nutrition until the baby is around 6 months old. An approved infant formula should be used, not ordinary cows'-, sheeps' - or goats'- milk. It could be beneficial to choose a brand that contains probiotics (check the information and ingredients list) and brands which are organic, free from pesticide residues and so on are now widely available.

About 2% of babies develop an allergy to the protein in cows' milk, which can cause vomiting, diarrhoea, skin and respiratory problems. Some babies are intolerant of the lactose in cows' milk, which will also result in intestinal upsets (see Allergies, page 115).

Alternatives in these cases are infant formulas based on goats' milk (to which some are also intolerant or allergic) or soya milk, to which up to 10% of cows'- milk-intolerant infants are also intolerant. Soya milk is also high in natural oestrogens which may affect sex hormones and should only be given to babies on medical advice. Cows' milk intolerance may be only temporary in infants, and medical advice should be taken.

SIX TO TWELVE MONTHS

The DoH says weaning can be started at six months. Earlier weaning has been linked with the development of coeliac disease, food sensitivity, infection and possibly with obesity in infants, and there is no advantage for most babies in introducing solids at an earlier age.

However, by this time a baby has often doubled his or her birth-weight, and breast milk supplies of iron, zinc, copper and vitamin D and A, protein and energy may not be adequate. Research indicates a link between poor growth rate in infancy and disease in adult life. Low-weight infants at one year old have an increased risk of CHD in later life, for example.

Breast feeding may continue to advantage as long as possible, but if breast feeding is discontinued at weaning, your infant should have a 'follow on' milk formula until age one. Cows' milk can be introduced too, as part of the baby's food (see box on page 179 re allergies).

Foods traditionally offered in the first few weeks of weaning from 6 months are bland, puréed gluten-free cereals, such as rice, potatoes and some vegetables. These can be home-cooked or commercial, and a wider variety of items can be introduced from day to day – yoghurt, fruit, pulses and other vegetables, cereals and meat can be offered.

As the weeks progress, finger foods and foods with more texture, to encourage chewing, and wheat-

containing foods and bread can also be introduced. Baby-led weaning, when your baby feeds himself finger foods rather than being spoon-fed by an adult, has seen a huge increase in popularity and often seems to result in infants enjoying a wider range of foods and textures and with fewer feeding problems as they progress, and may help to prevent obesity.

From 9 to 12 months plus, infants can begin to eat a diet similar to that of the rest of the family, with three meals a day plus snacks if required, and infants should be encouraged to feed themselves as much as possible.

An infant diet shouldn't mimic the diet of a healthy adult exactly – a high-fibre diet should be postponed and salt should not be added to weaning foods at all. And it is important to avoid offering infants choke-hazard foods such as whole nuts and other hard small items.

Water or milk should be the main drink; fruit juices (although most contain good amounts of vitamin C) also contain free sugars and should be limited, diluted and offered only with a meal (when the vitamin C will help iron absorption in the food), unless no fresh fruit is eaten. Fruit squashes, cordials and fizzy drinks, tea or coffee should not be offered, and neither should 'diet' drinks containing artificial sweeteners. Sweet drinks should not be given in a bottle – infants can drink out of a cup after 6 months to avoid tooth decay. Bottles containing sweet drinks should never be given at bed- or nap-time.

COMMERCIAL BABY FOODS

It is possible for a weaned infant to get all his basic nutritional requirements from a diet based on commercial, ready-made (or dried) baby foods and formula milk. Artificial flavourings and other additives are normally not allowed, and sugar content should be stated on the label. Organic baby foods are available. However, the EC recognizes the importance of home-prepared food for the infant and suggests that it is ideal if home cooking is introduced to the diet early. There is evidence that infants fed only, or mostly, on commercial baby foods may be reluctant to change to home cooking as they grow older. It is also likely that the range of phytochemicals present in fresh foods, which we now know are so important to health, are just as important whatever one's age.

AGES 1-4

Young children need to enjoy their food and be encouraged to eat as wide a variety of new foods as possible. Research has confirmed that a love of healthy foods – such as vegetables, fruit, wholegrains and fish – can be instilled in children by parental example. If you enjoy healthy food, they will too.

And the old adage – 'start as you

Daily maximum salt intake for children by age

❋ 6m or less: less than 1g.

❋ 6–12m: 1g.

❋ 1–3 years: 2g.

❋ 4–6 years: 3g.

❋ 7–10 years: 5g.

❋ 11 years and above: 6g

mean to go on' – is a sensible idea. Before children begin socialising much, going to pre-school/school and eating out/in other kid's homes, virtually all of their food will be provided by you. It's also been found that pre-schoolers are sometimes more willing to experiment with new foods than are school-age children. So this is your window in which to instil in them a love of good, healthy food. Don't be put off by a first or second refusal – research shows young children may take up to ten 'tries' before deciding they like a new food!

It is important not to make an issue of food refused or the odd meal where a child doesn't seem hungry. Negative associations with food can begin through a child being made to feel 'naughty' or guilty through refusal.

How do you tell if a young child is getting all the nutrients he or she needs? If the child is growing well, has a good appetite, seems strong and active, and is neither fat nor thin, then all is well. A child who doesn't appear to be thriving, eats only a few foods, has an under- or overweight problem, is ill a lot, or suffers problems which may be linked to food intolerance, should see a physician and perhaps be referred to a dietician. Poor growth-rate in young children has been linked with heart disease, stroke and diabetes in later life.

From weaning to the age of five, children need more of some nutrients than adults and less of others. They need:

✳ More fat. Breast milk is over 50% fat; follow-on milks about 42% fat. Children should only gradually reduce the amount of fat in their diets, down to the recommended adult level of 30-35%. Under 2 years old, whole milk should be given, and from 2 to 5, semi-skimmed can be given, but skimmed milk not used until after 5. Whole-milk yogurts and cheeses are also preferable. The higher fat levels are important because of the high energy needs of young children and fats provide the fat-soluble vitamins A, D, E and K.

✳ Less fibre. Young digestive systems are not equipped to deal with large amounts of high-fibre foods. High-fibre diets may hinder absorption of vital minerals, such as iron and calcium, and because high fibre foods tend to need more chewing and appear to satisfy appetite more quickly than low-fibre foods, may also mean that a small active child may have trouble consuming enough food at each meal to take in adequate calories.

NEW THINKING ON INFANTS AND FOOD ALLERGIES

Don't avoid giving your infant peanuts, eggs and milk – allergies are less likely if they try these foods at the start of weaning. Infants not fed milk in their first year had quadruple risk of adverse reaction and the chances of sensitivity were double for egg or peanuts when introduced later, according to the US National Institutes of Health and recent Canadian research. Avoiding these foods increases risk of asthma, eczema and allergic rhinitis. A 2018 report from the UK's Scientific Advisory Committee on Nutrition broadly agrees with these findings.

✳ By the age of 4, no more than 40% of children eat any green vegetables except peas, and only a quarter eat any salad.

✳ Biscuits, fizzy drinks, crisps and confectionery are eaten by more than 70% of pre-school children.

AGES 5 TO 11

Did you know that:

❋ UK schoolchildren eat more sugar than any other age group; approx 25% more than the recommended limit.

❋ Our children are still on average eating too much salt and too much saturated fat.

❋ Few children of all ages get the recommended one portion of oily fish a week with the average being just one tenth of a portion.

❋ Nearly a quarter of children are deficient in vitamin D and nearly half of girls are not getting the recommended amounts of iron.

❋ Only half of children aged up to 10 get their five a day.

But good groundwork in previous years pays off so that by the age of five, he or she should be enjoying a wide variety of healthy foods. Children of this age usually have good appetites and, if plenty of activity is undertaken, may eat as much as an adult in order to gain enough weight and growth but inactive kids will need many fewer calories to prevent obesity. The chart, right, lists nutrient requirements of children aged 1 to 11.

SCHOOL MEALS OR PACKED LUNCHES?

As I write, currently most kids in their first 3 years at a local authority school are entitled to free hot lunches and these are obliged by the government to meet a set of nutritional standards set in 2015 so are a good option.

A packed lunch can also be good – it should contain at least one high carbohydrate item (e.g. bread, pasta), some protein (e.g. cheese, egg, tuna), some fruit, something sweet but nutritious (e.g. malt loaf, a slice of fruit cake), and a drink of milk or water. To that you can add what your child will need to satisfy his or her appetite. In winter, a small flask of soup is good. Try to vary content as much as possible from day to day to prevent boredom. Check with the school on what foods are allowed to be taken in as various rules will be in place.

EATING AT HOME

In a recent survey by The Children's Food Trust in the UK, parents of all ages, regions and social backgrounds identified cooking as an important element in helping their children to eat more healthily. Cooking meals for the family and letting children help in the kitchen can make a big difference to a child's food tastes and their future wellbeing. The Trust identified pasta, pizza and roast meals as three of the most popular dishes nominated by children.

CHILDHOOD DIET, WEIGHT AND HEALTH

Obesity levels in schoolchildren are rising. Recent statistics from Public Health England have found that by the time children finish primary school over a third are overweight with over 20% obese or severely obese. Mainly

Selected Daily Nutritional Needs of Children aged 1 - 11

Age	Calories (boy/girl)	Protein	Vitamin C	Calcium (boy/girl)	Iron (boy/girl)
1	765/717	14.5g	30mg	350mg	6.9mg
3	1171/1076	14.5g	30mg	350mg	6.9mg
5	1482/1362	19.7g	30mg	450mg	6.1mg
7	1649/1530	28.3g	30mg	550mg	8.7mg
9	1840/1721	28.3g	30mg	550mg	8.7mg
11	2127/2032	42g	35mg	1000/800mg	11.3mg/14.8mg

because of this, illnesses such as type-2 diabetes and heart disease are increasing in the young, year on year.

If your child looks fat or has a high BMI (see link in the Appendix) or school has sent a letter saying they are overweight, the best course of action is first to reduce portion sizes, cutting back on the very high-fat, high-sugar and/or highly-refined items, like puddings, cakes, biscuits, chocolate and sweets, and offer more items like yogurts, fresh fruit, veg, wholegrains, lean proteins and so on. Much of the advice in Section One applies to children as well as adults. Don't mention the word 'diet' to your child; if they ask why there are changes, say you want all the family to be as healthy as possible, and explain why.

Over the months, most children will grow taller, while staying the same weight or maybe losing a little. Without appearing over-anxious about childhood overweight, it is more sensible to do something about it early on, in as relaxed a way as possible, rather than leaving it and hoping the child will 'grow out of it'. It will, of course, help, if your child is active every day.

Around 5% of children are underweight and if your doctor advises they should gain weight, and their appetite appears normal, simply try increasing portion sizes, offer between-meal snacks such as a banana or oatcakes with nut butter, and offer higher-nutrient/calorie drinks such as milk and fruit smoothies.

FUSSY EATING DILEMMAS AND SOLUTIONS

How will you persuade your child to eat what you want him or her to eat, rather than the 'junk' so many kids seem to want? And what can you do with a child who will eat only one or two types of food for weeks at a time?

If you followed the 'start as you mean to go on' advice (see 'ages 1-4') you stand a much better chance of not facing these problems. But if you do have a reluctant or fussy eater there is still plenty you can do.

Here are some general ideas for helping your child develop a good relationship with food, from the NHS:

✳ Eat your meals together if possible.
✳ Give small portions and praise your child for eating, even if they only manage a little.

* If your child rejects the food, don't force them to eat it. Just take the food away without comment. Try to stay calm even if it's very frustrating.

* Don't leave meals until your child is too hungry or tired to eat.

* Your child may be a slow eater so be patient.

* Don't give too many snacks between meals. Limit them to a milk drink and some fruit slices or a small cracker with a slice of cheese, for example.

* It's best not to use food as a reward. Your child may start to think of sweets as nice and vegetables as nasty.

* Make mealtimes enjoyable and not just about eating. Sit down and chat about other things.

* If you know any other children of the same age who are good eaters, ask them round for tea.

* Children's tastes change. One day they'll hate something, but a month later they may love it.

Some practical tips:

* Fruit can be converted into smoothies and fruit ice creams (try ripe banana frozen and then pureed into instant banana ice cream, it is really good and needs no added sugars).

* Don't add salt to children's food; they don't need it. Look for reduced-salt products such as baked beans when at the supermarket.

* For kids going through a 'hate vegetables' phase, puree them for soups, very finely chop and add to pasta sauces, meat sauces, and so on. Kids who hate boiled and steamed veg will often enjoy roast ones (try butternut squash, sweet potato, red peppers and sweetcorn roast in

delicious extra virgin rapeseed oil). Greens can be stir-fried.

* Often children prefer raw vegetables to cooked ones. So try carrots cut into batons to nibble on, or grated into salads or cherry tomatoes with a nut butter dip.

JUNK FOOD — THE TRUTH

The fact is that a lot of the foods that you may consider to be complete junk actually contain a lot of valuable nutrients. The truth is that there are few completely 'junk' foods (see panel below).

The exceptions are the sweet and sugary products that offer little if any nutritional benefit, but too many E numbers and too much added sugar or artificial sweeteners for comfort – the coloured fizzy drinks and squashes, bags of brightly coloured sweets, commercial ice-lollies and packet dessert mixes that line our

supermarket shelves. Don't buy them, and don't give your child the impression that these are 'treats' for special occasions – explain in the simplest terms that they are poor food, lacking in real substance.

It's also wise to limit the amount of commercial pies, pastries, biscuits, cakes and bakery items that you let your child eat, especially the cheaper ones. They are often extremely high in saturated fat and some may still contain hardened margarines (trans fats) and (in the case of sweet items) sugar, but little else in the way of good nutrients, and are also often high in salt.

Active children may be able to eat these foods and stay slim and apparently healthy, but a diet high in saturated fat is linked with heart disease and obesity in adult years. Tests have also shown that children as young as 10 who eat such a diet already show signs of atherosclerosis.

'JUNK' FOOD THAT ISN'T SO BAD …

Chips: can be a good source of vitamin C, calories and some fibre and, if brushed in a healthy oil such as olive or rapeseed, and oven-baked, have no negatives unless smothered in more than a little salt.

Burgers: made with lean meat and grilled or dry-fried are an excellent source of iron, B vitamins and protein for children. Vegeburgers are a great choice which most children love – choose those containing some pulses such as lentils/chickpeas as well as vegetables.

Baked Beans: high in protein and fibre and low in fat – choose lower-salt and sugar versions.

White Bread: good source of calcium and ideal for children who generally don't need as much dietary fibre as adults. Try to buy good-quality bread made from hard wheats, and sourdough is a great option.

Chocolate: contains iron, calcium and healthy plant chemicals and, if a child isn't overweight, is a better occasional snack than sweets.

Pizza: good food for children, containing calcium, vitamin C and fibre. Go for vegetable-topped pizza rather than the high-fat meat and salami versions.

White Pasta: fine for children, who don't necessarily need the extra fibre that wholewheat pasta provides and an ideal base for healthy sauces and additions.

Sweet tooth: children have a naturally sweet tooth, probably because breast milk and formula milk is sweet. Try to satisfy this throughout childhood with fruits first. Sweet drinks consumption in kids is linked to obesity, a US survey found, and tooth decay. An average child's palate can be re-educated to accept less sugar in a few weeks.

Dislike of vegetables: Children whose mothers ate a lot of green vegetables during pregnancy are more likely to enjoy vegetables themselves, 2017 research has found.

Asthma: childhood asthma, coughing and wheezing has been shown to be reduced in children who eat enough fresh fruits, vegetables and essential omega-3 acids. There is also evidence that a diet low in vitamins E and A may increase risk of asthma-type illnesses. For foods high in these vitamins, see the lists on pages 29 and 32.

Breakfast: is an important meal for children, tests show. Energy, concentration and brain power are all better in children who get a good breakfast. They are also more creative and have more physical endurance. If a child is having a packed lunch, a hot breakfast such as beans on toast, porridge or a boiled egg and toast is a good idea. A small bowl of highly refined sugary cereal does not really provide enough calories.

Oily fish: trials have concluded that regular intake of omega-3s in oily fish can help improve children's brainpower, concentration, memory and performance, and improve anti-social behaviour, but few eat the necessary 1–2 portions of oily fish weekly (also see ADHD page 123).

THE TEENAGE YEARS

Teenagers (especially those aged between 14 and 18) have greater nutritional needs than any other age-group in terms of calorie, protein, vitamin and mineral requirements. This is the crucial time for making height and muscle, for building bone-mass and for sexual development. Health problems later in life, including osteoporosis and heart disease, may be influenced by what people eat in their teens. Yet many teenagers get a poorer diet than most other social groups.

VITAMIN AND MINERAL DEFICIENCIES

Iron: The iron RNI for female teenagers is higher than that for boys of the same age (see chart) because iron is lost each month in the blood during menstruation, and teenage girls tend to have heavier periods than older women. However, research suggests that optimum iron intake is actually being met by few girls. Iron deficiency can, research shows, affect academic performance and physical ability.

There seem to be four reasons why teen girls don't get enough iron in their diets:

✳ Many follow faddy and/or low-calorie diets, so they don't eat enough food to provide the iron.

✳ Many avoid red meat which is our main source of easily-absorbed iron, and don't replace this by increasing their intake of other iron-rich foods.

✳ Many others eat a 'junk' diet low on variety and particularly low on iron-rich dark green vegetables.

✳ Many drink fairly high levels of coffee and caffeine drinks and/or don't get enough vitamin C from fresh fruit and vegetables, both of which can affect iron absorption.

Parents can help by providing foods in the home rich in iron (see list page 40) and in vitamin C for absorption. For an anaemic teen, iron tablets can be prescribed.

Two other potential deficiencies to be aware of in all teens are calcium and vitamin D, both of which are vital to build bone mass at this time.

WEIGHT ISSUES AND EATING DISORDERS

Only about half of UK teens fall within the recommended bodyweight with a body mass index between 20 and 25. Half of the remainder are clinically overweight or obese, and the information in Section Four offers solutions.

The other half are clinically underweight. For underweight teens, practical ideas on increasing calorie intake are in Section Four on pages 212–13.

However, a surprisingly large proportion of teens may suffer from one of a variety of eating disorders and may need medical attention or referral to a clinic for treatment. The Walden Center in the USA says that up to 40% of teenage females may have an eating disorder and that they are increasing in male teens too.

Many teens with eating disorders are adept at keeping them from the rest of the family. For example, anorexics often wear bulky loose clothes and/or find plausible reasons why they don't eat.

The recent trend (amongst all ages but particularly older teens and young women) of adopting restrictive 'fad' diets is a form of eating disorder, many experts believe, and often results in severe underweight and malnutrition.

If you believe a teenager is suffering from an eating disorder you should take them to see your physician. See also Eating Disorders on page 146-8, Appetite on page 120 and Anxiety and Stress on page 119.

VEGETARIAN AND VEGAN TEENS

Teenagers make up the highest percentage of non-meat eaters in the

✳ Teens drink an average of 200g sweetened soft drinks a day.

✳ Under 10% of 11 to 18 year olds get their 'five a day', with average consumption of fruit and veg only half that amount.

UK, according to the NHS. As we've seen, both vegetarian and vegan eating can be a very healthy choice, but teens need to be especially careful to get their complete range of essential nutrients, and by limiting their food choices (avoiding meat and fish and dairy products for example) increase the chance of deficiencies.

Special points to watch out for if you are a teen, or you have a vegetarian/vegan teen:

* Make sure to replace meat in meals by dairy produce (if not vegan) and plenty of high protein plant foods such as pulses, nuts and seeds.

* Ensure plenty of iron-rich plant foods in the diet.

* For vegans, ensure plenty of calcium-rich plant foods in the diet. Suggest a daily vitamin B12 vegan supplement.

For more on vegetarianism see pages 82–88 and for lists of foods rich in vitamins and minerals see Section One.

TEENS AND JUNK FOOD

A high percentage of teenagers seem to have a particularly strong liking for fast/junk type foods during these years and because these are the years they may spend more time outside the home environment and may be choosing more of their own food, it can be a worry for parents/carers trying to ensure they get a healthy diet.

As we saw in the 5–11 section, many foods that are often perceived as junk actually have health benefits but, equally, a diet very high in burgers, chocolate bars and pizza and low in fresh vegetables and whole foods is to be avoided.

Teens who have been brought up in a home where the meals provided were usually health-promoting and nutritious, and especially if they had a real part to play in preparing meals, are often more likely to eat well as they grow and into adulthood.

While parents cannot keep an eye on everything their teenagers may eat, it is still important to keep good food values so that when they do eat at home, they get the opportunity to catch up on all the nutrients they may have missed while out for the day or in friends' homes. So try to keep sugary and high saturated fat items out of the home if possible and instead make sure you have a full fruit bowl and a fridge containing healthy snacks such as yogurt, cheese, and so on.

Lastly, if possible let them take packed lunch to school and make it a healthy one (but containing enough calories for an active teen of course) – or if that's not possible, at least check out that the meals offered at their school are well balanced and with plenty of tempting vegetables, salads and fruits on offer.

Selected Daily Nutritional Needs of Teens

Age	Calories	Vitamin C	Calcium	Iron	Fibre
Boys					
12	2247	35mg	1000mg	11.3mg	25g
14	2629	35mg	1000mg	11.3mg	25g
16	2964	40mg	1000mg	11.3mg	25g
18	3155	40mg	1000mg	11.3mg	30g
Girls					
12	2103	35mg	800mg	14.8mg	25g
14	2342	35mg	800mg	14.8mg	25g
16	2414	40mg	800mg	14.8mg	25g
18	2462	40mg	800mg	14.8mg	30g

Note: For protein and salt needs, see adult values, Section One.

Pregnancy

YOUR HEALTH BOTH before and during pregnancy may have a bearing not only on your baby's health in infancy but on their health right through to adulthood, and even on their lifespan, and good nutrition is an important factor.

PRE-PLANNING

If you are planning to have a family, for women, this means following a healthy diet and maintaining a reasonable body weight, as a low BMI may increase the risk of periods ceasing and therefore will reduce fertility. Good pre-conceptual care will also reduce the risk of birth defects or a low birth weight in the infant.

For men, a healthy diet high in zinc, selenium, and vitamins E and C has been shown to help fertility. There have been studies linking high coffee intake to lowered fertility levels and the Royal College of Obstetricians and Gynaecologists reports that alcohol intake affects female fertility too.

EARLY PREGNANCY AND FOETAL HEALTH

The mother's diet both before conception and during the first few weeks after conception is important for the growth and proper development of the embryo, as from conception for the first few weeks it grows more rapidly than at any other time. Any abnormal cell development also seems to happen at this early stage.

To help prevent neural tube defects, such as spina bifida, adequate amounts of the B vitamin folate should be taken. The normal RNI for non-pregnant adult women is 200μg a day, but preconception and for the first three months of pregnancy it is recommended that a supplement of 400μg is taken and that an extra 100μg is taken in the diet. (More than this will be prescribed for women who have already given birth to a baby with a neural tube defect.) This means eating a basic healthy diet containing plenty of

naturally folate-rich foods (for list see page 37). Even with a healthy diet the supplement is important, though.

Low-birthweight babies are more at risk of CHD, high blood pressure, stroke and diabetes in later life. They also appear to suffer poorer cognitive (brain) function in childhood. Low birth-weight is 2.5kg (5½ lb) or less. Nutritional factors that may produce a low-birth-weight baby include:

Inadequate calorie intake: Most researchers agree that those who don't put on adequate weight and/or don't eat adequate calories during the pregnancy may run a greater risk of having a low-birth-weight baby. See the section below for more information.

Poor diet: Shortages of B vitamins, magnesium, iron, phosphorous, potassium and zinc in the first three months of pregnancy have been associated with low birth-weight.

Inadequate essential fats intake: the essential fatty acids and their derivatives such as GLA, EPA and DHA (see page oo) may be very important to a healthy pregnancy and baby.

Research has linked a diet rich in EFAs with longer pregnancies and therefore higher birth-weight.

Alcohol intake: See box.

DIET, MATERNAL HEALTH AND PREGNANCY

As the pregnancy continues, it is important to continue to live healthily, eating a balanced and adequate diet. This is not only for the sake of the growing foetus (research even shows that what you eat also affects the baby's taste buds and food preferences after birth and henceforth!), but for your health and wellbeing too.

Surprisingly, the need for most nutrients, including calcium and iron (because absorption of both increases during pregnancy, less iron is lost without menstruation and less calcium is excreted in the urine), doesn't increase by much, if at all. The chart here lists the recommended nutrient intake for all major nutrients.

However, it IS vital to get enough of them all – a child's potential adult bone density (and risk of osteoporosis) is linked to vitamin D, magnesium, phosphorus and potassium levels in the mother's diet during pregnancy (but there is evidence that the foetus will deplete maternal bone if calcium runs short during the pregnancy).

Extra vitamin C is needed, especially in the last trimester. Regular intake of essential fats is linked to a reduced risk of high blood pressure in the mother, and optimum brain and eye development in the baby. Adequate fibre intake is important as constipation can be a problem for many women during the later stages of pregnancy. Drinking more fluids such as water will help as well. Adequate protein, carbohydrate

ALCOHOL AND PREGNANCY

Experts are still unsure exactly how much alcohol is completely safe for you to have while you're pregnant, so the safest approach is not to drink at all while you're expecting, says the NHS, especially in the first three months of pregnancy, when it may increase the risk of premature birth (or miscarriage) and your baby having a low birth weight (see below). The risks are greater the more you drink. Drinking heavily throughout pregnancy can cause your baby to develop a serious condition called foetal alcohol syndrome (FAS). However, the occasional drink is unlikely to cause harm and if you have had some alcohol in early pregnancy (for example if you didn't realise you were pregnant) do bear that in mind.

Additional Daily Nutrient Requirements for Pregnancy

(for nutrients not listed here the requirement is the same as for non-pregnant adult females)

Calories +200*
Protein +6g
Vitamin A +100mcg
Vitamin B1 +0.1mg*
Vitamin B2 +0.3mg
Folate +400mcg**
Vitamin +10mg
Vitamin D +10mcg

* For last 3 months only
** Preconception and until 12th week of pregnancy.

and fat is important.

For the basics of a healthy diet, see Section One.

CALORIE INTAKE AND WEIGHT GAIN

While it's vital to eat enough nutritious food throughout your pregnancy, 'eating for two' during most of the course of pregnancy is not necessary, i.e. you do not need to double your food intake! A mere 200 calories extra a day for the last three months will be enough for most women's needs – representing a small baked potato or 300 ml (½ pint) of skimmed milk and a small piece of cheese.

It is thought that part of the reason why pregnant women don't need to eat a lot extra is that the metabolic rate slows down during pregnancy, and also that they naturally become less active. However, women who are significantly underweight at the start of their pregnancy may need to consider eating more than this.

The optimal amount of weight to gain during pregnancy will depend on your initial weight. For women who

FOODS TO AVOID

✻ Excess vitamin A (in the form of retinol, not beta-carotene) is toxic in pregnancy and can cause birth defects. For this reason, pregnant women are warned not to eat liver or liver products, as liver contains potentially toxic amounts of vitamin A. They should also not take supplements containing retinol (e.g. cod liver oil) unless prescribed by their physician.

✻ Soft mould-ripened cheeses, like Brie and Camembert, and unpasteurized cheeses, such as most Parmesan, and blue-veined cheeses like Stilton and Danish Blue, which may harbour listeria. Cheddar and cottage cheese are fine.

✻ Pre-packed salads and beansprouts, deli salads in dressings, and other items sold loose from chill cabinets in shops and restaurants.

✻ Raw or lightly-cooked eggs and anything containing them, e.g. real mayonnaise, and tiramisu, in case of salmonella.

✻ Pâté, unless pasteurized, in case of listeria, and raw or partly cooked meat, unpasteurized milk, soil-dirty fruits and vegetables, to avoid toxoplasmosis.

✻ Shark, swordfish and mackerel which may contain harmful levels of mercury.

✻ Herbal supplements and Chinese herbs and medicines which may contain toxins.

✻ More than 5 cups of coffee a day – higher levels may increase risk of miscarriage.

are underweight with a BMI less than 20 the official UK recommendation is a gain of 12.5-18kg (27-38lb). If you are of average weight (BMI 20-26) the recommended gain is 11.5-16kg (25-34 lb), and for a BMI of 27 – 30 it is 7-11.5kg (15-25lb). For obese people with a BMI over 30, the recommended gain is from 6 kg (13 lb), with the maximum to be decided in individual consultation.

Gaining too much weight is not a good idea – gains over those listed are associated with several complications in pregnancy, such as high blood pressure and prolonged labour, as well as overweight after the pregnancy.

TIPS FOR A TROUBLE-FREE PREGNANCY

The three most common complaints mentioned by pregnant women and how to deal with them:

Morning sickness: this can occur at any time of day but *is* usually worse in the morning. Probably caused by low blood sugar levels and so eating several small high-carbohydrate snacks throughout the day will probably effect a cure, or at least minimize the nausea. Sickness on waking may be helped by eating a snack such as a banana or oatcake as soon as you wake. While ginger is a recognised help for nausea.

Tiredness: especially common in the first three months of pregnancy and is often the first sign that a woman is pregnant. Good pre-conception care will help, including a healthy energy-giving diet and an exercise programme to increase heart/lung capacity. Follow this on with a healthy diet for pregnancy (The Basic Healthy Diet, pages 74 and 75, plus supplementary nutrition as described on these pages) and make sure to get enough calories. Dieting is out. Check with a doctor that you aren't iron-deficient. For more information see Fatigue, page 149.

Food cravings: many women do find themselves craving foods that they possibly wouldn't even usually consider. There is little scientific basis for the idea that the cause is the need for a food high in a particular nutrient that the mother is lacking; e.g. if she craves oranges she must be lacking vitamin C. If cravings are for reasonably nutritious food then there is no great problem, unless the craved food is eaten regularly and to such an extent other types of foods are avoided, which will create nutritional shortages, or to such an extent that too much weight is gained, in the case of the higher-calorie foods. Your pre-natal dietitian should be able to help with your own cravings strategy.

AFTER THE BIRTH

After the birth, you'll want an easy and nutritious diet – and if you're breastfeeding, you'll need a range of nutrients in increased amounts from a normal diet, as well as additional calories. The chart here shows what is needed.

If you aren't breastfeeding you can return to a normal Basic Health Diet (see Section One and the diet on pages 74–75), and if you need to lose some weight, see Section Four but don't try to lose baby weight too quickly – you need plenty of energy at this time so be kind to yourself.

Additional Daily Nutrient Requirements for Lactation

(for nutrients not listed here, requirement is the same as for adult females as described in Section One)

Calories:

up to 1 month +450	Folate +60µg
1-2 months + 530	Vitamin C +30mg
2 to 3 months + 570	Vitamin A +350µg
4-6 months +570*	Vitamin D +10µg
over 6 months + 240**	Calcium +550mg
Protein +11g***	Phosphorus +440mg
Vitamin B1 +0.2mg	Magnesium +50mg
Vitamin B2 +0.5mg	Zinc +6mg****
Vitamin B3 +2mg	Selenium +15µg
Vitamin B12 +0.5µg	

* Assumes baby is not starting on weaning foods until 6 months.

** Assumes non-breast milk foods form majority of baby's diet.

*** 6 months plus, reduces to +8g (due to weaning).

**** 6 months plus, reduces to +2.5mg.

The Middle Years and Menopause

ONE OF THE main dietary mantras when you get into your middle years is perhaps not only to enjoy your food but also to ensure that what you eat helps to provide you and your body with immunity against the ill health and also the aches, pains and disabilities that for many people are still part of old age. Indeed, because we're living longer than ever before, old age doesn't now officially begin until we are 75, so the middle years are a vital time to look after yourself and pay even more attention to a healthy diet.

Some changes – such as the menopause in women – are natural and inevitable, while others which many people regard as natural may, in fact, be undesirable and possibly preventable.

One large study published in the *British Medical Journal*, which examined the link between the diet of men aged 50 to 70 and their death rates, found that a healthy diet is associated with a reduction of 13% in all causes of death in men of those ages. And we now know that all kinds of health problems and signs of 'getting older' — from Alzheimer's and osteoporosis to hair-loss and lack of libido – can be minimized, or even prevented, by particular diets or foods. Middle-age really is the time to pay attention to your diet.

The best place to begin is the Basic Healthy Diet on pages 74–75, and if you have particular health problems or perhaps your family history may put you more at risk of getting particular health problems as you age – then diet tips for these appear in the Food as Medicine section A–Z.

CALORIE RESTRICTION AND ANTI-AGEING

Over the past two decades, several studies have found that life-span can be increased by up to 50% on a calorie restricted but highly nutritious diet and that such a diet also reduces the risk of CHD, cancer, stroke and diabetes, and increases the functioning of the immune system.

Two studies published in 2017 confirmed these findings. One, from the University of Wisconsin, found that restricting food intake by around 20% in middle age appears to make people more able to fight off the illnesses of old age.

Meanwhile another study at Duke University, North Carolina, found that a 25% calorie restriction observed for at least a year reduced participants' biological age considerably compared with people not following the restriction. It appears that reducing food intake reduces inflammation in the body, a major cause of disease and cell damage and loss.

THE MENOPAUSE

For many, the menopause brings a variety of symptoms, ranging from the mildly upsetting to those severe enough to disrupt their lives. The majority of these symptoms – such as hot flushes, tiredness, mood swings and depression, libido problems and insomnia – can be alleviated by correct diet or, on the other hand, made worse by a poor diet.

Bone density: During and after the menopause the female hormone oestrogen is greatly diminished in the body and this is what causes loss of bone density and possibly osteoporosis in susceptible women. There are, however, various dietary means by which bone-loss can be slowed. A diet high in soya and soya products has been shown in studies to mimic the effects of oestrogen. Other foods which may have an oestrogen-like effect include nuts, yams, linseeds, pulses and grains, and most fresh fruits and vegetables.

Adequate calcium intake during menopause and beyond is also essential – 1,500mg per day is ideal. Vitamin D supplements are important for calcium absorption. Zinc and magnesium are also important for bone health. For more on the minerals, see page 37 and on osteoporosis see page 160.

Hot flushes: In the West, approximately half of menopausal women suffer from severe or prolonged 'hot flushes', with flushing of the face and neck, a feeling of suffocating heat and sweating, often followed by chilling. There is some evidence that these can be alleviated by soya based foods as outlined above. But more research needs to be done and meanwhile it seems that phyto-oestrogens don't work for all women to reduce these symptoms. Other foods that may help include yams, which contain a natural type of progeterone, and foods rich in the amino acid tryptophan, which is known to help the brain produce serotonin, the 'mood-calming' chemical. Cutting down on alcohol and caffeine have been shown to have some benefit. Various herbal supplements are said to help menopausal symptoms – see pages 170-3 – but proper evidence is lacking for most of them.

Mood swings, depression and insomnia can be helped by adequate intake of B vitamins, zinc, magnesium and tryptophan (see pages 141–142 and 157). A calcium-rich snack before bed can induce sleep.

Headaches can be minimized by regular meals and snacks, complex carbohydrates and foods rich in vitamin B group.

Fluid retention can be largely avoided by a diet low in sodium, junk foods and highly refined foods, and high in natural diuretics like parsley and asparagus, and potassium-rich vegetables such as celery and tomatoes.

Dry skin and poor hair condition is improved by eating plenty of the antioxidants selenium and vitamin E, and omega-3 oils as well as other plant foods rich in healthy oils, such as avocados, nuts and seeds.

Weight gain: It's been estimated that most women put on about half a stone during the menopause – much of it around and inside the abdomen. The British Dietetic Association says that diminishing oestrogen levels cause diminished muscle mass, which then causes the metabolic rate to slow by up to 10%. There are various other reasons why some women tend to eat more during the menopause, thus compounding the problem – both insomnia and depression can increase calorie intake, for example. If you are overweight in your middle years, whether or not this is due to gain during your menopause, Section Four offers a variety of tools to help you lose weight without risking your health.

Herbal remedies for the menopause, such as Black Cohosh, St John's Wort and sage, are often taken to help alleviate symptoms such as hot flushes, sweats and insomnia. Scientific research on these shows very mixed results. There is some evidence for soya products as relief for hot flushes. Herbal supplements are discussed in more detail on pages 170–173.

THE MALE MENOPAUSE – DOES IT EXIST?

The 'male menopause' (or 'andropause') is much discussed and many males in their midlife do feel as if they are going through their own set of menopausal symptoms. These can include loss of sex drive, irritability, depression, poor memory or concentration, loss of muscle, weight gain (like menopausal women, often around the middle), and other negative symptoms.

The menopause label in men infers the symptoms are the result of a sudden drop in testosterone, similar to what occurs in the female menopause with diminishing oestrogen and progesterone. But while testosterone levels do fall as men age, the decline is steady – less than 2% a year from around the age of 30–40 – and this is unlikely to cause any problems in itself.

Many experts believe that in most cases the 'male menopause' symptoms are nothing to do with hormones and that perhaps the term 'midlife crisis' would be more appropriate as midlife is a time when many people (of all sexes) do worry e.g. about lack of achievement in work and/or personal life. Problems may be compounded by increased alcohol intake and reduction in regular exercise (which has huge physical and mental benefits at this age).

The advice given in previous sections about healthy diet is especially important, and see also Anxiety and Stress, Insomnia and Depression, all in Section Two.

The Later Years

AS POPULATIONS ARE living longer and longer, so the age at which 'old age' begins is being pushed back – measured by how long people have, on average, left to live. One recent study concludes, by that measure, that old age now doesn't begin until our mid-seventies. But whether you are 75 or 95, your diet is still important for your health and your prospects of getting that big 100 under your belt.

'EARLY' OLD AGE

The average requirements for nutrients in 'young' older people (mid-seventies to mid-eighties) in reasonable health are similar to those in younger adulthood. The main differences are that older people often require fewer calories (2,342 for males and 1,912 for females aged 65-74, and 2,294 for males and 1,840 for females aged 75+) because their metabolic rate decreases as lifestyle becomes more sedentary and muscle mass decreases too. However, this isn't always the case, as the modern 75-plus 'baby boomers' tend to stay more active, fit and healthy for longer than their grandparents and even their own parents did at the same age.

Older women also need less iron (at 8.7mg/day compared with 14.8mg in younger women) due to cessation of periods. But in general, the requirements for vitamins and minerals (micronutrients) stay the same, although more vitamin D may be needed if an elderly person gets little sunshine exposure (the RNI is set at 10mcg a day for people over 65).

Absorption of some micronutrients seems to decrease as we age, added to which many seniors are on prescription drugs, which can also hinder absorption. This means that, if deficiencies aren't to occur, food needs to be selected carefully especially if fewer calories are being eaten.

This means choosing foods with a high ratio of nutrients to calories (which translates to the Basic Healthy Diet on pages 74–75 and to the many tips on healthy diet in Section One) and having only small, occasional portions of foods with a low ratio of nutrients to calories (for example foods such as highly refined carbohydrates and soft drinks).

NUTRITIONAL GUIDELINES FOR THE ELDERLY

A balanced diet, rich in plant foods and healthy fats as well as some protein and 'good' carbs, is still important – perhaps even more important – as the years progress, as this type of diet helps keep the diseases of age at bay. Over 60% of new cancers occur in people aged 65 plus, and a similar proportion of new cases of CHD and stroke, for example. And daily leafy greens help prevent mental decline.

And yet many people in the UK in the older-old age bracket (85-plus) suffer nutritional deficiencies, partly because, UK Government research shows, they eat considerably less fish, fruit, vegetables, meat and cheese than younger affluent adults, but considerably more bakery goods, including cakes and biscuits, many more beverages and twice the amount of sugar. In other words, they are

OLD AGE AND YOUR WEIGHT

Simply – whatever your age, if you are neither too fat nor too thin you are probably eating the right amount of calories. But what is 'neither too fat nor too thin'? In the last few years there have been several large studies which have found that the BMI (body mass index) charts which can help all adults decide whether they are a healthy weight (see more on page 201 in Section Four) may not apply to older adults. Each one of these major studies found that people with a BMI of around 27 lived longer than those with the 'recommended' BMI of between 20 and 25. Indeed, having a BMI in the low 20s was associated with an increased risk of earlier death (as was having a BMI over 30, which is clinically obese).

These studies are fascinating, especially when viewed alongside the apparent benefits of 'calorie restriction' (see above) in middle and later middle age. It seems that while we may be healthier if we eat less in our middle years, we will live longer if we eat a little more in our later years!

eating almost the opposite of the high-ratio nutrient to calorie diet described above.

In addition, as we get into 'old' old age (over the mid-eighties) the body systems that ensure we get the most out of food may begin to be less efficient – the digestive system of a 90-year-old is unlikely to be as efficient as that of a 30-year-old, for example.

Also, appetite can diminish, and taste buds change so that we begin to prefer sweeter tastes, some studies show. Mouth, teeth and gum problems can mean we may have trouble chewing or swallowing items such as some vegetables, meats, pulses and so on.

Most of these practical problems in eating well can be overcome with a bit of commonsense and/or ingenuity.

✳ Make food softer – the goodness in your fruits and vegetables is still there even if you puree them into a soup, sauce or dip, or make them into mash. Pureed peas, spinach, butternut squash, even broccoli, are all delicious, nutrient rich and easy to eat.

✳ Many naturally soft and easy to digest foods are nutritious – think of milk, yogurt, softer cheeses, poached or scrambled eggs, fish, wholemeal pasta.

✳ Iron can be found in cocoa, lentil soup, lentil dahl, liver pate, dried soaked apricots and fortified breakfast cereals even if you no longer fancy eating much meat or too many leafy greens.

✳ Your sweet tooth can be satisfied by having fruit and yogurt smoothies, banana ice cream (just freeze very ripe bananas then puree them in a blender and eat!), fresh fruit.

✳ Make sure you get enough fibre to avoid constipation by having cooked pulses (e.g. baked beans, hummus, lentil soup) dried fruit, wholegrains (e.g. porridge, wholemeal bread) and drink plenty of fluids.

There is evidence that the immune system becomes weaker in old age, which may also lessen immunity

against cancer – a diet high in zinc (see page 40 for rich sources list) will help to boost the immune system. Adequate calcium (perhaps with supplements, especially for women, who are four times more prone to osteoporosis than men) and vitamin D intake will help to prevent or minimize osteoporosis, which can result in hip and other fractures in the elderly, who are also more prone to falls. Body weight is also a factor – thin people are at greater risk of bone fractures (another reason to maintain a BMI a little higher than for young adults).

Alzheimer's disease is discussed on page 140, but, briefly, research indicates that a Mediterranean-type diet high in antioxidants and essential fats, fruit and veg, and low in saturates (similar to the Healthy Heart Diet on pages 134–135) may help stall the progress of the disease.

As with younger adults, there is no harm in older people having an occasional alcohol drink, although alcohol tolerance often decreases with age, so it makes sense, if necessary, to drink alcohol in later years at the minimum end of the safety guidelines rather than the maximum.

Lastly, older people may have financial worries and feel that healthy food is too expensive. Items that are fairly or very low-cost and also provide a good nutrient/calorie ratio include: Dried or canned pulses, milk, eggs, fruit in season, vegetables in season, wholemeal bread, root vegetables such as carrot, swede, sweet potato, wholemeal pasta. Potatoes, too, contain good amounts of vitamin C, protein and fibre. ■

Food for Weight Control

Average bodyweight in the Western world is on the increase and has been since the 1950s. Globally, a recent report published in *The Lancet* showed that deaths from excess weight (calculated to be 4.5 million) increased by 29% in 2016 compared with levels ten years earlier.

In the UK since 1980, the proportion of those clinically overweight has risen from about a third to around two-thirds – and one in five of us are clinically obese (severely overweight). Eight out of ten adults become overweight by their fifties and the average middle-aged man is almost two stones overweight. £40 billion a year of the UK NHS budget is spent on treating obesity and its consequences.

Overweight and obesity are linked with many health problems and increased mortality. In fact, obesity has now been declared an endemic disease by the WHO and is recognized as one of the most common avoidable causes of death.

So, with all the health advice on offer, just why are so many of us overweight? Our global propensity for sugar, for eating out, for snacking in between meals and taking large portions is partly the reason. And the Obesity Health Alliance has found that 'junk' food manufacturers spend 27 times more on advertising than the UK Government does on it's health campaigns! Although some research shows we in the UK don't eat any more calories than we did fifty years ago, this is a debatable figure as it is nearly impossible to track food and calorie intake outside the home.

A big factor is that we are much less active than we used to be, taking a third less exercise than we did in the 1950s, largely because of a sharp decline in the amount of everyday physical chores we do and the huge increase in powered tools, cars, and even online shopping.

Our hobbies, too, have become more sedentary – it's estimated that we spend between six and nine hours a day watching TV or the internet, time that, a few decades ago, would have been spent being active and outdoors. So our vastly decreased activity levels means that we don't need as many calories – and yet we haven't reduced the amount we eat to compensate. So surplus food is stored as body fat.

The cure, therefore, is not only to eat fewer calories but also to take more exercise, which will redress the balance. It only takes relatively minor regular adjustment to the energy out/energy in balance to achieve steady and healthy weight-loss. Or even better, to avoid putting weight on in the first place. In the following pages we will look at how best to achieve this; and will discuss the questions most often asked about diet and weight control. We will also look at the opposite dilemma – how to put ON weight.

Your Top Ten Questions Answered

1. HOW DO I KNOW WHETHER I REALLY AM OVERWEIGHT OR NOT?

There is a fairly broad band of 'acceptable weight' for your height, within which you're not, clinically, over or underweight. The scale used by most professionals to determine acceptable weight is the Body Mass Index (BMI), which some believe has its faults, but it is still the most used measure.

Your BMI (for adults) is easy to work out with the formula: BMI=Weight (kg) ÷ height (metres) squared. The easiest way to do this is to get your height in metres and then square it (multiply it by itself). Then get your weight in kg and divide this figure by your squared weight. That is your BMI.

The result is then interpreted as follows:

Below 20 = underweight
20-25 = acceptable weight range
25-30 = clinically overweight
30-40 = clinically obese
Over 40 = morbidly obese.

The acceptable range of 20-25 allows, for example, a woman of 1.65 metres (5ft 6in) to weigh anything between 54.5kg (8st 8lb) and 68kg (10st 10lb). And if you are over 65 several studies appear to show that a BMI of up to 27 seems to improve your chances of living longer!

Another good indication of genuine overweight is the 'waist circumference' test, because surplus weight around the waist ('central fat distribution') is more likely to be linked with health problems (particularly heart disease and diabetes type 2) than surplus weight around the hips, bottom and thighs.

A waist measurement of less than 94cm (37½ in) for men and 80cm (32in) for women is all right; between 94cm-101cm (37½-40½ in) and 80-87cm (32-34¾in) respectively indicates further weight gain should be avoided and perhaps weight should be lost; and over 101cm (40½ in) and 87cm (34¾ in) indicates weight should be lost.

If you are 'borderline' on the BMI system (say, just on or over 25), then the waist circumference theory may help you decide, or vice versa.

2. COULD BEING OVERWEIGHT BE SOMETHING TO DO WITH FACTORS OTHER THAN OVEREATING?

Well, it is absolutely true that many people who are overweight don't eat all that much compared with their slimmer friends. But they are probably eating more than they need to maintain a reasonable weight. The answer in this case is most likely a very sedentary lifestyle, which burns up a lot fewer calories than an active one. The main reason that obesity is such a major issue in our world today is – we eat and drink more calories than our bodies burn up for energy and so the surplus is stored as fat.

Some genetic and medical factors can cause obesity or at least leave you more at risk of becoming overweight. These include genetic syndromes such as Prader-Willi syndrome; endocrine disorders such as hypothyroidism or Cushing's syndrome; and certain medications, such as antidepressants, and others, can affect weight too.

There is also some evidence that various other factors can influence your weight. For example, many studies have found a high BMI in people who don't get enough sleep. Lack of sleep may affect how our bodies use nutrients for energy, and/ or our hormones that control hunger urges. It may increase levels of an appetite-stimulating hormone called ghrelin and decrease levels of the hormone leptin, which makes you feel full. Stress may have similar effects.

There is even research that finds obesity may be caused by chemicals dubbed 'obesogens', a growing problem in the modern world, and which may also affect our hormones. These pollutants include such things as cigarette smoke, phthalates, Bisphenol A and some pesticides. Your family genes and even your ethnicity may affect your weight, too.

Factors like those above that may make the right 'energy equation' harder to maintain.

Many people believe that the type of food that you eat, rather than the amount of calories you take in, is the most important factor in weight control. While some types of food can help to control hunger/blood sugars and can help you that way (see page 210), and some can maybe help you in other ways (see page 205), the calorie equation still can't be denied.

A simple way of looking at it is, a plate full of salad and low-fat, protein-packed grilled white fish, you've found, helps you lose weight. The same plate, full, instead, of battered fish and chips, does not help you lose weight, so you believe in the high protein diet as the best way to lose weight.

The fish and salad plate, applied in principle regularly to what you eat, will certainly make your slimming/weight control life easier. But that outcome isn't just because it is high in protein and low in carbs and unhealthy fat – no, it is because it is much lower in calories (at about 300) than the second plateful, which is at least 800 calories. This higher calorie content is because the foods on it are dense with less water content, the food on the plate weighs much more than your salad plate, and it contains more fat, which is a very calorie-dense food. In other words, the average high-protein diet works because, fundamentally, it provides a simple way to reduce your calorie intake. For more on the calorie discussion see page 206.

3. MY BMI IS OVER THE RECOMMENDED LEVEL BUT I AM HAPPY WITH MY SIZE. WHY SHOULD I DIET?

As we've seen on page 201, a slightly higher BMI may well be perfectly healthy for older adults. It may also be that you have a high proportion of lean tissue (muscle) to fat. Muscle weighs more than fat and in some people can lead to a high BMI even when their body fat level is perfectly fine. But in this case, you probably know whether muscle is the cause. It often applies to certain sportspeople and some people with very physically active jobs, but for most of us, it doesn't apply.

Lastly, you may have a slightly high BMI but as we saw in Q1, your waist measure may be fine, in which case you needn't worry. If your BMI is high and your waist also large, then you do run the risk of suffering from various health problems, if not now, then later in life – particularly if your BMI is over 30.

4. WHAT REALLY IS THE BEST SLIMMING DIET TO FOLLOW?

It needs to offer a good level of nutrition – a balance of the nutrients you need for health. It needs to be easy to follow (helping you reduce your food intake without endless calculations, and fitting in well with your daily life). And it needs to give you food that you will eat and enjoy. If you don't enjoy it, you're unlikely to stick to it. Lastly, some diets are more prone to have you put all the weight back on quickly – you want a diet that helps you avoid that.

All that said, the best diet is the one that works best for you and keeps you healthy. There are plenty of variations to suit everyone. One well-known diet plan will not work for all.

We look at the question of popular diets and what is the best method of slimming for you to choose in the pages ahead.

5. IS IT HONESTLY A BAD IDEA TO LOSE WEIGHT RAPIDLY?

According to the vast majority of research done in the last 20 years, rapid weight loss can lead to problems ranging from short-term dehydration to malnutrition, excess muscle (lean tissue) loss and additional weight gain in the long term. This is because very low-calorie diets can slow your metabolic rate, meaning you burn fewer calories.

Rapid-loss meal replacement diets can work well for some and produce good results initially. But many people find them hard to stick to – although ensuring they contain adequate protein can help reduce hunger. Recent research projects that find people have great success in losing weight – and keeping it off for up to 3 years on very low calorie diets and meal replacements- have all offered support and/or supervision, and it is widely acknowledged that this is a great contributory factor to success.

Perhaps the most sensible rapid loss diet for most people is one that forms the start of a longer-term diet – a week of, say, 800 nutrient-packed calories a day, producing encouraging results to motivate you to continue on a normal reduced-calorie plan until you are down to a suitable goal. But that said, even on a normal calorie-reduced diet, you will see good results in the first week as you are losing a lot of body fluid as well as fat (and some lean tissue). I'd say the best plan for almost all of us having to 'go it alone' is to take things more steadily.

6. CAN YOU LOSE WEIGHT WITHOUT DIETING?

It depends what you mean by 'dieting'. If you mean creating a negative calorie balance, so that you eat fewer calories than your own body needs to maintain its current weight, and thus you begin to lose weight, then it is hard to do that without reducing the calorie content of your total food and drink intake.

You can go a long way to creating the negative calorie balance by increasing your exercise/activity levels each day, but research shows that most people find it hard to lose weight by activity increase alone, and that a combination of fewer calories in, and more calories burnt through exercise, works best of all. It will also make you fitter and help protect your long-term health!

But you don't need to go on a particular diet – a named regime, a popular book, or so on. And you really don't even need to count calories or worry about weighing/measuring foods all the time. You just need to use the commonsense strategies and tips that appear on the following pages and you should reach a healthy weight naturally.

Alternatives to this are quite drastic and not things I'd like to recommend – over-the-counter or prescription diet pills, liposuction, a gastric band and so on – although some can be useful under medical supervision for clinically obese people.

7. WHY DOES WEIGHT LOSS SLOW DOWN AS YOU LOSE WEIGHT?

In the short term, this is because when you begin a slimming diet, in the first week or two you will lose several pounds of weight which are fluid, not fat. After this, weight loss will be mostly fat.

For long-term slimmers, the main reason is that when you lose weight, your metabolic rate gradually slows down simply because you are getting smaller. The heavier a body, the more energy (calories) it uses up. This can be exacerbated by lean tissue (muscle) loss. Muscle is very metabolically active and therefore uses up a useful amount of calories – if you lose a lot on a diet, it

will further slow your metabolic rate. This is one good reason not to try a very low-calorie diet as these have often been shown to increase lean tissue loss.

The best solution to weight loss slowing down is to accept it as a natural progress on the way to your eventual goal – long-term weight maintenance. However, if you reach a plateau (where you are losing nothing at all) first double check that your target weight is suitable and not too low. If it is suitable, then try a combination of a further slight decrease in your food/drink intake daily coupled with increased activity, particularly weight bearing exercise such as lifting weights, which helps to build/maintain lean tissue.

8. I LOVE EATING OUT AND ENTERTAINING – HOW CAN I LOSE WEIGHT?

Much of what you eat when you lunch or dine out isn't really essential to the spirit of the occasion, and that is the best attitude to take if work or a busy social life means that you have to eat out a great deal.

If you only eat out/entertain only occasionally, plan for it! Simply cut back a little for the rest of the day and enjoy yourself, while attempting to eat sensibly. That tends to work better than trying to cut back the day after you've eaten out/entertained!

Lastly, it does pay to eat out at places where the menu is more suited to healthy eating – the best idea is to check menus online beforehand and decide what you will eat that fits in with your slimming plans. And many restaurants will be happy slightly to alter dishes to help – e.g. not serving the French fries.

And skip the things you won't miss – e.g. the bread and butter or oil; no-one will mind and it will help you enjoy your meal more. Decide on starter or dessert, no-one needs both! Or choose one of each and share both with your partner or friend.

9. ARE THERE SPECIAL FOODS THAT CAN STOP ME FEELING HUNGRY/BURN UP MORE FAT?

In general, foods high in protein, and foods high in fibre, are two of the best food types to help you beat hunger. Fat also takes longer to digest and will help, too. More information on this appears in the following pages.

Protein also helps burn more calories because it uses a lot more calories in the digestive process than do either fats or carbohydrates. A few other foods have the ability to increase your metabolic rate, which in effect is what fat-burning means. These include, for example, chillies and several other spices, green tea and coffee, while there is some evidence that almonds and coconut oil can help, too.

10. WHAT IS THE POINT OF SLIMMING WHEN THE WEIGHT ALWAYS COMES BACK AGAIN?

Research indicates that a high percentage of successful dieters – perhaps as many as 90% – do eventually put the weight back on again. However, this seems as much to do with social, lifestyle and psychological factors as it is a consequence of dieting having lowered their metabolic rate.

So the idea that 'diets don't work' perhaps should be replaced by 'diets can, and often do work to help people achieve a healthy weight, but it does take commitment and dedication to maintain that new weight for life'. What is needed are permanent changes in our behaviour around food and in lifestyle.

Some experts remind us that in years gone by, humans were programmed to find food to eat when they became hungry, in order to avoid starvation. It may be that the newly-slim modern person still has that programme within themselves, urging them to eat more to keep themselves alive. Well known obesity science researcher Dr Stephan J. Guyenet says, 'A key reason for this is that weight loss decreases the circulating concentration of the hormone leptin, activating a negative feedback process … the "starvation response".'

One way to help avoid the lost weight returning is to settle for a goal weight that is maintainable, rather than maybe a bit too low. Remember, a BMI up to 25 is healthy for most adults and yet many slimmers' goal weight represents a BMI of no more than 20.

Because of the many health problems associated with obesity, it seems to be well worthwhile to get that surplus weight off and do all we can to keep it off. The rest of this section will help you do just that, in the best way for you. ■

Retrain Yourself

THE SKINNY ON DIETS

There are hundreds of different named diets and dieting methods out there, if not thousands. Each year one becomes popular, another goes out of favour. One or two tend to be the big hits of the season.

Low-carb, low-fat, high protein? No sugar, no processed, no meat? And so on, and so on. There are so many conflicting methods, and foods that are 'in' or 'out' that most of us end up totally confused about the 'best' 'healthiest' way to lose weight.

'People have these unbelievably strong beliefs against fat or carbs,' says obesity researcher Tim Church, professor of preventative medicine at Louisiana State University. 'But despite the never-ending list of best-selling books that exist on weight loss, there is no macronutrient that wins the day.'

That I agree with. Having researched the subject for many years, and in the past few months alone, having read all the available new research on 'which diet is best for weight loss', I think I can safely say that the answer to which diet works best is this:

It is a way of eating that ensures you create a negative calorie balance – you take in fewer calories than you burn up in energy – and it is an eating plan that you like enough to be able to stick to it over time while you lose your weight, and then will also help you keep it off for good. There are many different ways to achieve this. Dozens of different perfect dieting methods. Yours is something that works well for you and continues to work.

Find a way of eating that becomes your new normal, your new lifestyle. That's the programme that will work. And for that to happen, you have to enjoy it, be in tune with it, be happy with it.

And the best for health? I will say that this will be an eating plan that takes note of everything in Section One and offers a good balance of nutrients such as is illustrated at the front on pages 10–11. To lose weight, you need simply eat smaller portions of this kind of balanced food. Which individual foods you choose to make up that balance is up to you. When you reach your suitable weight, you may be able to increase your portions slightly, but fundamentally you are not suddenly 'ending the diet' and beginning a new regime which, as we've seen, is how weight comes back on so readily.

To summarise – all the diets that have been around and popular for the past couple of decades or more – from Atkins to F Plan to Paleo to Low Fat to Intermittent Fasting – each has at least some benefits and each may have drawbacks (for example, a very high protein, low carb diet can be dangerous for people with kidney disease).

THE QUESTIONS TO ASK YOURSELF BEFORE YOU CHOOSE YOUR WAY TO LOSE WEIGHT

If you do want to try a named or well-known diet, ask yourself – and it – some pertinent questions before you begin:

✳ Will I enjoy it? Does it contain many of the foods I like? Will I have to eat things I don't enjoy?

✳ How restrictive is it?

✳ How expensive is it? Can I afford it?

✳ Does it seem to fit in with what I now know is a healthy way to eat?

✳ How user friendly is it? Will it fit in with my lifestyle?

✳ How much time will it take up? Do I want to be juicing and spiralizing all the time or do I want something quick and easy?

✳ Does it tell me to eat foods I can't eat for medical or other reasons?

✳ If I use this diet to get down to my target weight, what will happen then – how will it help me for the future?

If a named plan can fit in with your lifestyle, seems healthy, and is something you can do long-term, it might just be worth trying.

But first, read on and consider giving yourself three weeks to retrain your brain and body into real positive, long-lasting weight-loss and weight control mode.

RETRAIN YOURSELF IN THREE WEEKS

For all those people who have battled with their weight for some time, yet another quick-fix diet really isn't ever going to be the answer. What you need

instead is to retrain your brain so that you can alter your eating habits for good.

So now we examine different aspects of eating for weight control, including strategies for behaviour modification and practical dietary advice. All you will need is some time – I suggest three weeks – to absorb the strategies, a notebook, and a degree of motivation!

✳ WEEK ONE
GETTING STARTED
Goals:

✳ Read Section One and understand what makes a healthy diet.
✳ Decide on sensible targets.
✳ Check out motivation (see box).
✳ Cut calories and fat in snack foods.

Take a week or so to achieve these goals. At the moment, don't think about 'dieting' as such at all. All you need to do is read through Section One, and spend the week preparing practically and mentally to begin adjusting your eating accordingly. Sort out your larder and shop for a healthier range of foods;

MOTIVATING YOURSELF

Make a list of all the reasons why you would like to be a reasonable body weight. Divide them into health reasons (for instant motivation, check Section Two for all the ailments linked with overweight), practical reasons (e.g. getting into favourite clothes, being able to do your favourite sport better) and social and other reasons. Most people should be able to come up with a list of at least ten reasons they would like to lose weight.

If you have tried and failed previously to lose weight and/or keep it off, agree with the following three statements:

✳ I didn't fail on past diets, the diets failed me.
✳ I will not dwell on my past disappointments.
✳ Now I am willing to take responsibility for what I eat.

look through the recipe section and find a few recipes that appeal to your taste-buds. Try one or two.

Meanwhile, also work out your own BMI (see Question 1, page 201), work out what weight will achieve a sensible BMI, then decide on a sensible time-scale for achieving your ideal BMI.

LOOK AT YOUR SNACKING HABITS

Take a look at your snacking habits – use your notebook to write a list of all the 'non-meal' foods you eat this week. Analyse your reasons for eating that particular food (e.g., nothing else available when hungry, speed, ease of eating) and think of better alternatives for each occasion – it's not totally necessary to give up snacks altogether in order to lose weight. One or two mini-meals a day could help keep hunger at bay (see Week 2) and can provide useful nutrients. Small amounts of unsalted nuts are an ideal snack as are small pots of natural full fat yogurt, oatcakes, and low GI fruits (see table page 210).

Whether or not your body responds well to meals plus snacks or two or three meals a day and no snacks is partly genetic – learn to listen to your body and see how its weight responds.

When tempted by high-fat, high-sugar snacks, try non-food alternatives, diversionary tactics such

as phoning a friend, having a bath or going for a walk. The fact is that you could eat a whole small, healthy meal for the same calories as a caramel-filled chocolate bar; so it really will pay to get control of unhealthy snacking habits.

✳ WEEK TWO
TAKING CONTROL

Goals:

- ✳ Learn when to say 'no' to food.
- ✳ Examine your breakfast eating habits.
- ✳ Learn how to avoid hunger.
- ✳ Begin to build more activity into your life.

Often it seems that almost everyone and everything is trying to influence what, when, where and how much you eat, and it is for precisely that reason that you need to make that positive decision that you are going to eat what YOU want, what is good for YOU.

Here are some of the occasions when you may have been eating due to outside influences – you'll be surprised how often it happens.

✳ *You're offered food or drink* – in the office, at someone's house, by someone else in your own home, for example. Nine times out of ten, even when they are not hungry or thirsty, people accept food and drink when it is offered, whether through politeness or not clicking in to their own voice that says, 'you're not hungry; you're not thirsty.' Listen to your inner voice. It's fine to say 'no', politely.

✳ *Hunger took you by surprise*. You grabbed a confectionery bar or cake because you didn't plan ahead and bring a piece of low GI fruit or a few

nuts. Plan ahead, 'be prepared!'. If you can't bring food when you are out and about, try to plan where you're going to eat, and what time. These days you can find out all you want with a few clicks on the screen.

✳ *Impulse buying.* You go into the newsagents for a magazine and come out with a magazine and a supersize bar of chocolate. You walk through the market, smell a newly-baked loaf, and buy it before you've realised. Being aware and being prepared with an avoidance strategy is the key to beating this.

✳ *Nibbling without realising.* The bowl of crisps someone else left in the sitting room. The leftover toast from your child's meal. Leftovers in the cooking dish. Things have a habit of going from hand to mouth without you even thinking about it, several times a day. Again, be aware – practise asking yourself every time you're around food that isn't part of your planned menu – 'I don't need this. I don't want this. It isn't wasteful to throw leftover away if it will mean less fat on me.'

Now - start to say 'no' to food you don't want, food you don't need and food that isn't going to do your body much good. Keep a diary and note your achievements.

BETTER BREAKFAST

Go back to pages 58–61 in Section Two and get yourself a healthy breakfast strategy. As we've seen, there is no one definitive answer to whether or not you should eat breakfast whether or not you are trying to lose weight. For some people, avoiding it is a good weight loss strategy. Others will lose well by eating breakfast and then

just one other meal a day. But most of us eat breakfast, lunch and dinner – and as that is the case, it's as well to know a good weight-loss promoting breakfast from a fattening one.

Because you don't want to succumb to the mid-morning doughnut and latte, you need to build your breakfasts around what will keep your hunger pangs at bay for as long as possible – and this means a breakfast containing enough fibre, some fat, and some protein (see more on anti-hunger foods overleaf). There is nothing wrong with carbs but the carbs need to be the healthy sort – wholegrain or whole fruits and vegetables and preferably those with a low or moderate GI (see chart overleaf).

So if you're eating breakfast, please forget the lowish-calorie slice of white toast with jam, honey or marmalade and get yourself a nutritious, if small, plateful to see you through. The breakfasts in the diet plan on pages 74–75 are all good examples. And if you are skipping breakfast – that small portable pack of nuts may be more important than ever.

AVOIDING HUNGER

All day long, you can help avoid hunger pangs and beat food temptation by ensuring that when you do eat, you're eating items that actually help control your hunger. As we've just seen, a breakfast with fibre, fat and protein does just that. And so will every meal of the day. You want maximum nutrients

FACT

If you removed from your diet all food that you didn't actually eat through genuine hunger and pre-planned decision, most people would save enough calories in a week to lose weight steadily without doing one other thing.

THE GLYCAEMIC INDEX

Low-GI foods (long-term energy; try to include plenty of these in your diet):

* All pulses including lentils, soya beans, kidney beans, chickpeas, butter beans, baked beans.
* Barley.
* Apples, dried apricots, peaches, grapefruit, plums, cherries.
* Avocado, courgettes, spinach, peppers, onions, mushrooms, leafy greens, leeks, green beans, broad beans, Brussels sprouts, mange-tout peas, broccoli, cauliflower.
* Natural yoghurt, sweetened yoghurt, milk, peanuts.

Medium-GI foods (medium-term energy; eat freely):

* Sweet potatoes, boiled potatoes, yams, raw carrots, sweetcorn, peas.
* White pasta, wholewheat pasta, oats, porridge, oatmeal biscuits, All Bran, noodles.
* Whole-grain rye bread (pumpernickel), pitta bread, buckwheat, bulgar, white and brown rice.
* Grapes, oranges, kiwi fruit, mangoes, beetroot, fresh dates, figs, apple-and-date bars.

High-GI foods (quick-release, short-term energy; eat as part of a meal containing protein/fat/low-GI foods):

* Glucose, sugar, honey, pineapple, bananas, raisins, watermelon.
* Baked potatoes, mashed potatoes, parsnips, cooked carrots, squash, swede.
* Rye crispbreads, wholemeal bread, white bread, rice cakes, couscous, bread sticks.
* Cornflakes, Bran Flakes, instant oat cereal, puffed cereal, popcorn, wheat crackers, muffins, crumpets. Orange squash, watermelon, dried dates.

and fibre for the amount of calories that your meal contains. So it's even more important to eat healthily (see Section 1) when you want to lose weight than at any other time in your life, perhaps.

Avoid at all costs, meals and snacks that contain only highly-refined carbs, especially those very high on the GI Index, and very little else. Always add in protein foods which are either low in fat or high in healthy fats (see page oo). And if you're having low-fat protein food (white fish, soya, skinless chicken for example) then always add a healthy fat (eg olive oil, avocado, nuts).

GET ACTIVE

Now it's time to remember to build a little activity into every day. Start with a 15-minute walk. Try to build up to longer, or increase your pace, or do more up hills as the days and weeks progress. Humans were meant to walk – that's one reason they didn't get fat, back in the day.

Build more other activity into your life. At home, at work, out enjoying yourself. There are always ways to move a little more, walk a little more, push, lift, pull. Always. This isn't an exercise book so I won't say more – but there is so much help out there, so many ideas – use them! You will come across people saying that exercise doesn't help you lose weight – but I disagree. It can help you, especially if you combine aerobic exercise like walking or cycling with strength work like lifting weights to build muscle which burns many more calories than does other body tissue.

And it's also very important for maintaining your new, slimmer weight. Vital, I'd say.

✳ WEEK THREE
EATING TO SLIM

Goals:

- ✳ Learn to listen to body signals about food.
- ✳ Retrain taste-buds to prefer less sugar and salt.
- ✳ Rebalance your main meals for painless slimming.

Few of us actually feel genuine hunger any more – mealtimes and snack-times come around well before real hunger has time to set in. Now see if, instead of eating exactly by the clock, you can get that slightly hungry feeling before tucking in. If you find it is lunchtime and you don't have that hunger, but you can't eat later because of, say, your work, just have a little and save some more for mid-afternoon.

Also, few of us are truly in tune with the moment when we feel full and should stop eating. Instead, we just eat all that is on the plate because it is there, and usually there is more of it than we would genuinely need to satisfy hunger.

So perhaps the absolute simplest way to control your food intake is to plate yourself up what you would consider a small portion (especially of the more dense, higher-calorie foods). Be aware when you eat. Chew thoroughly, take your time – and decide to stop when you feel full enough.

If you don't override or ignore your body signals, soon you will get back in tune with your real needs and weight-loss will become a natural consequence.

REDUCING YOUR SALT AND SUGAR INTAKE

Most of us eat much more salt than we need and while salt itself is calorie free,

many of the high-salt foods are also those that contain a lot of fat – often, the less healthy saturates – and refined carbs. In order to give your taste-buds a better chance to enjoy natural foods, which are often less calorific, you need to retrain them to need less salt. This is surprisingly easy to do.

Stop adding salt to food at the table and cut down by half all the salt that you add in cooking. Check out the list of high-salt foods on page 45 and start cutting back on the amount of those that you eat.

You will find within days your taste for salt diminished. Now go further by cutting the amount you add while cooking to just a few grains. The addition of fresh herbs, seasonings and spices will help you miss the salt even less.

Similarly, you can retrain a sweet tooth in just two weeks. First cut back on sugar added to drinks and cereals, then on sweet drinks themselves, then on sugary items such as cakes, biscuits and confectionery. High-calorie desserts are best avoided by slimmers except now and then. Nutritious desserts based on low GI fruit and dairy produce are ideal. Artificial sweeteners save calories by replacing sugar, but do little to help a sweet tooth – or weight control – in the long-term, much recent research finds.

YOUR HEALTHY SLIMMER PLATE

Now let's go back to your plates or bowls of lunch and supper. You've learnt now to dish yourself a smaller portion and eat it slowly. But for successful weight loss it's important always to balance what you have on your plate.

Make sure to have at least half of the plate items such as vegetables and salad (excluding starchy root veg such as potatoes). Have up to a quarter of the plate a healthy carb, such as sweet potato, whole grains, and the final quarter as a protein food. Your plate should contain adequate fat which will come at least in part from the foods already on your plate – vegetables, carbs and protein foods almost always contain a proportion of fat. Healthy fat can be added in small amounts as a dressing, sauce, and in some of your foods, e.g. avocados, nuts, seeds. For all you need to know about the healthy plate read Section One.

This isn't written in stone – some days you may have a plate that's mostly vegetables with just a bit of protein and virtually no carb, other days you may have a vegetable and carb dish with hardly any protein. You need to begin to trust yourself and devise a flexible way of eating that, over the course of a week or so, still fits the blueprint.

CALORIE LEVELS

Calories do count – there is a huge body of evidence to show that if you reduce the amount of calories you eat, and create a 'negative calorie balance' so that you take in fewer than you use up in energy, then weight loss will happen.

But if you follow all the advice above, then calorie control should happen quite naturally without you having to do calculations. However, for interest, experts say that an ideal calorie reduction to lose weight steadily is about 5–600 a day. So if you have been eating around 2,500 a day and are overweight, then reducing to 1,900 should see loss, for example. Then as you lose weight, the calories need to go down to keep that deficit steady. (See question 7 page 204 for more on this.)

The thing to do is weigh yourself once a week and if you are still losing, you are doing fine. If your weight sticks for more than a week, see question 7. If you are losing more than about 2lb a week (after the first two weeks on any slimming plan as you always lose more to start with, including fluid), you may be restricting your food intake too much, which is not a good idea – if you are too hard on yourself, you may not continue.

WEEK FOUR ONWARDS

By following the guidelines in the previous pages, you should be losing weight naturally and steadily – but not rapidly. Now you simply need to stay with it and continue to your own suitable weight.

And when you get there, the Basic Healthy Diet and all the information in Section One will help you to maintain that weight for good. For many people, this is the hardest thing to achieve.

WEIGHT MAINTENANCE

Many people put their lost weight back on after losing it – but the simple truth is that if you continue with the ideas we've discussed already in this section, then you will keep your brain happy with your 'correct' amount of food and you will keep it stable.

A FEW WORDS ABOUT WEIGHT GAIN

Despite the huge increase in obesity in the UK and other countries of the world in the past few decades, there is still a minority of people who feel they are, or are, too thin and would like to put on weight.

Sometimes being thin is a genetic thing, other times it is through over-exercise, illness or an eating disorder.

But if being thin is a worry and in all other respects you are healthy, the best strategy for weight gain is to simply increase portion sizes of healthy meals like those explained in Section One a little, so you are doing a reverse slimming diet.

Some people who need to gain weight have a problem with appetite. Ways to get round this include taking more calories in liquid form – e.g. a formula milk drink instead of a cup of tea a couple of times a day, or full fat milk instead of water.

And many people find it easier to cope with several small meals a day rather than two large ones, so snacking, preferably on healthier items such as nuts, fruits and dark chocolate, is a good idea. Eating more refined carbs such as white bread and white pasta can be a good strategy – although you will get less fibre this may not be a bad point, as fibre fills you up and can make you eat less.

Lastly, don't forget that fat contains double the calories per gram of either carbs or protein, so getting extra fat into the diet is helpful, particularly items that don't seem that fatty (which may be off-putting for some people). For example, Greek yogurt; hard cheese, nuts and seeds. ■

TIPS TO KEEP YOUR 'FOOD BRAIN' HAPPY

✳ Keep busy, occupied. Boredom is a significant enemy of moderate eating.

✳ Remember food is important. What you eat is for you, for your body. You deserve more than to fill your body with rubbish food.

✳ A natural, minimally-processed diet will help you beat hunger and weight gain much more easily than a diet of highly-processed foods.

✳ There is so much variety in food today – don't be unhappy choosing healthy foods you hate – choose the ones you love!

✳ Don't aim to keep too low a bodyweight. This a bit like the 'tightly wired spring'. It may well spring out of control one day. Aim for moderate – there is a great deal of room for manoeuvre within the ideal BMI ranges. And as you get older, a higher BMI up to 26 or 27 may indeed be the healthy way to go.

✳ Never forget the motivations that helped you lose weight in the first place.

TREAT FOODS AND DRINKS

Most people's idea of a 'treat' food or drink is something tinged with guilt – so it might be a slice of cake, a bar of milk chocolate, a sugar-rich dessert, or some wine. While, if you've followed the retrain programme, your taste for most so-called treats will have diminished, there is no harm at all in having an occasional treat.

The only rule is not to feel guilty, and to recognise that it is only a treat if you don't have it very often. You could also make it a small treat – the mini-bar rather than the 150g version for example. The fact is that if you have treats too often they become commonplace, and not really a treat at all. Just one more thing to beat yourself up about.

But don't forget – some 'treats' are healthy. Dark chocolate is. Red wine in strict moderation can be. Natural peanut butter is. Strawberries are. Cheese is coming out as a healthy food. A treat is what you like – so make yourself a treat list based on your favourite things, and you just might find they are healthier than you realised.

Lastly, you can make some treats healthier. For example – you love cake. Rather than a slice of the highly-refined sponge cake, how about a piece of fruit cake made with wholemeal flour, masses of fruits and nuts? Yes it will contain more calories as it is denser, but a small piece will keep your brain – and stomach – happy for a long while.

SECTION FIVE

Food for Health and Pleasure

Knowing what foods to eat for your continuing good health is, of course, what this book is all about. Almost as important, however, is knowing how to put it all together. Apart from those occasions when you eat out or bring a ready meal or takeaway home, as everyone does from time to time, the kitchen is where you put all your knowledge into practice.

Cooking well is important for two main reasons. Firstly, it is quite possible to turn decent healthy basic ingredients into less than healthy meals, and so a basic knowledge of healthy cooking is vital. Secondly, you need to provide meals you and your family actually want to eat. No amount of healthy eating theory will work unless you can convert it into tempting dishes that you really enjoy and which fit into your lifestyle and budget.

This section sets out to provide you with enough good ideas in the form of tips, guidelines and carefully thought-out recipes to do just that.

Healthy Cooking Guidelines

USING THE RECIPES THAT FOLLOW

The recipes give you a wide selection of ideas on how to incorporate very many healthy foods into your regular diet and that of your family. Most of the recipes are also featured within the various specialised diet plans.

COMMON COOKING METHODS COMPARED

The nutritional content of healthful ingredients and basic foods can be enhanced by careful cooking – or debased by poor cooking. For example, some cooking methods rob food of vital vitamins while others help to retain them. Here I summarise the main benefits and drawbacks of each common cooking method.

Raw: Retains maximum nutrients normally lost through cooking, with the main exceptions of carrots and tomatoes which contain nutrients better absorbed after cooking. Not suitable for wide range of foods (such as raw potatoes) which may be indigestible. Cut surfaces quickly lose vitamin C, so prepare at the last minute.

Boiling: No added fat needed. Boiled vegetables lose up to 70% of their water-soluble vitamins B and C. Retain more vitamins by using minimum water and cooking until only just tender. Don't leave to soak before cooking.

Steaming: Retains more nutrients than boiling. Still 30% or more water-soluble vitamin losses. Use cooking water in sauces, etc., to put back the vitamins.

Microwaving: Retains most water-soluble nutrients if minimum water used. Quite easy to over-cook or undercook unless care taken. Useful for reheating. Reheated food should be stirred and served piping hot.

Baking/roasting: No added fat necessary with meat – use foil; brush vegetables with olive oil. Heat destroys vitamin C. Poultry needs thorough cooking to avoid any likelihood of food poisoning. Meat juices from roasting contain B vitamins – use in sauce.

Braising/casseroling/stewing: Tenderizes low-cost meats; vitamins retained within dish. Can be high in meat fats unless cooled and skimmed of surplus. Ideal method for root vegetables and pulses.

Grilling/barbecuing: Low-fat way to cook meat; no added fats, plus fats melt and drip out of meat. Overgrilled, charred meat linked with several types of cancer. Don't serve burned food.

Frying (deep or shallow): Frying at very high temperatures releases carcinogens – particularly true of carb foods such as chips. Foods are best fried occasionally or at moderate temperatures. Use oils with a high smoke point (see chart). Use fresh cooking oil every time – much-used oils oxidize and may be carcinogenic.

Stir-frying: Retains water-soluble vitamins; little fat used. Suitable method for only 2–3 people at a time as not much food can be stir-fried correctly in one batch. Cut surfaces of vegetables quickly lose vitamin C – prepare shortly before use.

THE NUTRITION PANELS

Each recipe has a nutrition panel giving information on the nutrient content per serving or per item. All recipes are low in salt and dietary cholesterol, unless otherwise stated.

THE SMOKE POINT OF OILS AND FATS

All values approximate. When frying at high temperatures, choose an oil with a higher smoke point.

Avocado oil	270C
Sunflower oil, refined	250C
Ghee (clarified butter)	250C
Soya bean oil (refined)	240C
Olive oil (pale cooking type)	240C
Coconut oil (refined)	230C
Peanut (groundnut) oil	230C
Corn oil	225C
Blended vegetable oil	220C
Rapeseed oil (refined)	200C
Lard	190C
Olive oil (extra virgin)	190C
Margarine	180C
Coconut oil (extra virgin)	175C
Sesame oil (unrefined)	175C
Butter	120-150C
Rapeseed oil, extra virgin	110C
Flax seed oil	110C

SYMBOLS

Dairy-free

Gluten and wheat free

Vegetarian

Vegan (some non-vegan recipes which contain instructions on how to adapt to become vegan will have this symbol)

Low-calorie

Quick (20 minutes or less prep/cook time)

Budget

Starters, Snacks, Sharing

All nutrients are per serving as described within each recipe. For a sharing table, meze or tapas style, each recipe may serve up to 8 people, and so the nutrients per portion will decrease accordingly.

AVOCADO AND CRAYFISH SALAD

SERVES 2

CALORIES: 357

TOTAL FAT: 25.8G

SATURATED FAT: 3.7G

FIBRE: 9.3G

PROTEIN: MEDIUM-LOW

CARBOHYDRATE: LOW

A pretty supper party starter (or light lunch if you add in some rye bread or similar) that is an excellent source of good fats, vitamin C and antioxidants. You can use prepared crab or prawns instead of the crayfish for a change.

1½ tbsp extra virgin olive oil
Juice of ½ large ripe lime
1 red chilli, mild to moderately hot (or to taste), de-seeded and chopped
½ tbsp white wine vinegar
¼ tsp salt
Black pepper
10cm piece cucumber
1 ripe avocado
8 leaves crisp lettuce, e.g. cos
125g fresh mango chunks
100g ready cooked crayfish
2 handfuls wild rocket

Combine the oil, lime juice, chilli, vinegar, salt and pepper in a bowl, whisking thoroughly. Quarter the cucumber lengthways, cut out and discard the seeds, then dice.

Halve the avocado and remove the stone. Use a shallow spoon to scoop out the flesh of each half, then chop.

Arrange the lettuce on a serving plate followed by the cucumber, avocado and the mango chunks, then sprinkle over the crayfish and rocket. Whisk the dressing again and spoon over the top.

BEETROOT HUMMUS

SERVES 4

CALORIES: 189

TOTAL FAT: 10.9G

SATURATED FAT: 1.4G

FIBRE: 5.1G

PROTEIN: MEDIUM

CARBOHYDRATE: MEDIUM–HIGH

Traditional hummus is delicious but for a change try this version – the beetroot adds anti-oxidants and a lovely sweet earthy flavour and looks stunning. Ideal served with crudites such as celery, spring onions and cucumber.

> 1 beetroot, about 150g, trimmed and scrubbed
> 400g can chickpeas, drained and rinsed
> 2 cloves garlic, peeled and roughly chopped
> Juice of half a lemon
> 1½ tbsp light tahini
> ½ tsp salt
> Black pepper
> Approx 2 tbsp extra virgin olive oil

Wrap the beetroot in foil and roast it for 30-40 minutes or until tender. Slip off skin using your thumbs then roughly chop and add to food processor.

Add the chickpeas and garlic and blend to a rough puree, then add the tahini, lemon juice, seasoning and a tablespoon of the oil and blend again, adding a little more olive oil as necessary, until you have a fairly smooth puree still with a bit of texture. Check seasoning. Spoon into a serving bowl – will keep, well covered, for 3-4 days in the fridge.

MUSHROOM AND RED PEPPER SKEWERS

SERVES 2

CALORIES: 111

TOTAL FAT: 6.4G

SATURATED FAT: 1G

FIBRE: 3.2G

PROTEIN: MEDIUM–LOW

CARBOHYDRATE: MEDIUM–LOW

Quick and easy – turn into a higher-protein supper by adding cubed tofu or halloumi.

> 2 medium red peppers, halved and deseeded (about 200g)
> 1 tbsp olive oil
> 1 fresh juicy clove garlic
> 1 tsp sea salt
> ½ small fresh red chilli, deseeded and chopped
> 2 tsp balsamic vinegar
> 8 small chestnut mushrooms (about 115g)

Preheat the grill to medium-hot and place the pepper halves on the grill tray, skin side up. Brush them with a little of the olive oil, and grill on both sides until softened but not black.

Remove the pepper halves from the grill and, when they have cooled a little, cut them into bite-sized squares. Using a pestle and mortar, pound the garlic with the salt until well combined and creamy.

Beat in the remaining olive oil, chilli and the vinegar. Thread the pepper squares and mushrooms alternately on 2 skewers (soaked 30 minutes in water if wooden) and brush with the garlic oil mixture.

Grill under a medium heat, turning a few times and basting with remaining sauce until the mushrooms are cooked through, about 5 minutes. Serve hot.

MUSHROOM, SPINACH AND CHICKPEA SLIDERS

SERVES 8

CALORIES: 75

TOTAL FAT: 4.7G

SATURATED FAT: 0.6G

FIBRE: 1.7G

PROTEIN: MEDIUM

CARBOHYDRATE: MEDIUM

These mini burgers are packed with healthy ingredients and flavour. They freeze well, too.

> 2½ tbsp extra virgin olive oil
> 1 small onion, about 75g, very finely chopped
> 100g chestnut mushrooms, finely chopped
> 2 cloves garlic, well crushed
> ¼ tsp turmeric
> ½ tsp season-all
> ¼ tsp ground cumin
> 50g baby spinach leaves
> 2 tbsp fresh wholemeal breadcrumbs
> Juice of ½ lemon
> ¼ tsp salt
> Black pepper
> 150g cooked drained chickpeas

Heat 1½ tbsp of the oil in a non-stick frying pan and sauté the onions over medium heat for 5 minutes until soft and transparent. Add the mushrooms and garlic and stir for a minute, then add the spices and stir through.

Add the spinach to the pan, turn the heat up a little and stir until wilted. Take the pan off the heat and add the breadcrumbs, lemon juice, salt and pepper.

Mash the chickpeas in a bowl, removing the papery outer skins as you do so. Stir the mushroom mix into the bowl, combine everything thoroughly and then shape into eight small patties. Fry in the remaining oil over medium high heat for 3 minutes each side or until lightly golden.

FETA AND PEPPER DIP

SERVES 4

CALORIES: 190

TOTAL FAT: 15.8G

SATURATED FAT: 8.2G

FIBRE: 0.7G

PROTEIN: HIGH

CARBOHYDRATE: LOW

This calcium-rich simple dip is great with toasted flatbread slices. It also makes a great topping for toast or a sandwich filling.

> 1½ tbsp olive oil
> 1 red pepper, deseeded and chopped
> ½ fresh red chilli, deseeded and chopped
> Dash of chilli sauce
> 200g Greek feta cheese, roughly mashed

Heat the oil in a non-stick frying pan and stir-fry the pepper and chilli until soft but not browned. Add the chilli sauce.

Place the cheese in a blender or food processor followed by the contents of the pan and blend until you have a smooth spread. Serve at room temperature.

BUTTER BEAN AND BASIL SPREAD

SERVES 4

CALORIES: 98

TOTAL FAT: 3.7G

SATURATED FAT: 0.5G

FIBRE: 3.2G

PROTEIN: MEDIUM–HIGH

CARBOHYDRATE: HIGH

Spread on to crackers or mini toasts, spoon into destalked mushrooms and warm through, or use as a dip or side. The butter beans can be replaced with any cooked white bean and the canned beans can be replaced with dried, thoroughly boiled and drained beans.

> 400g can butter beans, drained and rinsed
> 2 cloves garlic, crushed
> 1 tb olive oil
> 1 tb lemon juice
> ½ tsp sea salt
> Black pepper
> 2 handfuls basil leaves

Place all ingredients except the basil in a blender or food processor and blend until you have a pâté which is still slightly rough – don't over-blend.

Add the basil leaves, fork them through and blend for 2 seconds. Check seasoning.

CANNELLINI BEANS WITH HOT TOMATO VINAIGRETTE

SERVES 2

CALORIES: 223

TOTAL FAT: 12G

SATURATED FAT: 1.8G

FIBRE: 8G

PROTEIN: MEDIUM–HIGH

CARBOHYDRATE: HIGH

This very high-fibre dish has all the flavours of tasty baked beans but with virtually no cooking and can be served warm or at room temperature. Great tapas dish and also excellent served with lamb.

> 400g can cannellini beans, drained and well rinsed
> 100g ripe beef tomato
> 2 tbsp olive oil
> 2 tsp red wine vinegar
> Pinch English mustard powder
> Pinch caster sugar
> ¼ tsp salt
> Black pepper
> 2 tsp chopped fresh basil

Put the beans in a saucepan. Blanch the tomato and skin it; halve it and deseed, then chop, retaining any juices that come out during this process.

In a bowl, mix together the oil, vinegar, tomato (with juices), mustard, sugar and seasoning.

Pour this over the beans in the pan and heat gently, stirring, until all is warmed through. Add the basil.

LENTIL AND FETA KOFTAS

MAKES 12 KOFTAS

CALORIES: 86

TOTAL FAT: 5.8G

SATURATED FAT: 2G

FIBRE: 1.8G

PROTEIN: HIGH

CARBOHYDRATE: MEDIUM

Rich-tasting and vegetarian, these koftas make a good addition to a meze table. For a vegan dish, use non-dairy feta-type cheese which is now available in supermarkets.

200g ready-cooked Puy lentils
120g feta cheese
1 tbsp chickpea flour
3 tbsp olive oil
2 tbsp chopped parsley
2 tbsp chopped coriander leaf
1 tbsp chopped mint
2 tbsp dukkha
½ tsp salt
Black pepper

Add the lentils to a mixing bowl and mash with a fork to make a rough puree. Crumble the feta finely and stir in, mix well.

Add the chickpea flour, 2 tbsp of the olive oil and the rest of the ingredients, combine thoroughly. Make 12 balls. If the balls seem a bit dry, add a little more oil.

Heat the remaining oil in a non-stick frying pan and fry the koftas over medium heat until golden, turning from time to time.

CHEESE AND COURGETTE MUFFINS

MAKES 6

CALORIES: 126

TOTAL FAT: 8.1G

SATURATED FAT: 2.3G

FIBRE: 0.7G

PROTEIN: HIGH

CARBOHYDRATE: LOW

Ideal as a snack or breakfast, these muffins are an excellent source of protein and many important vitamins and minerals.

½ tbsp cold-pressed extra virgin rapeseed oil plus ¼ tbsp for greasing
1 small courgette, grated
6 large eggs
3 tbsp grated Manchego or Gruyere cheese
4 spring onion, chopped
½ tsp turmeric
2 tbsp chopped basil
¼ tsp salt
Black pepper

Preheat the oven to 180C. Brush ¼ tbsp oil over the inside of a 6-hole muffin tin. Put the grated courgette on a thick piece of kitchen paper, cover with another, roll up and wring thoroughly with your hands until the paper is wet. Unroll – the grated courgette should be dry.

Whisk the eggs in a bowl with the rest of the oil then stir in the courgette and remaining ingredients and combine thoroughly. Pour the mixture into the six muffin holes then carefully put the tin in the middle shelf of the oven.

After 20 minutes the muffins should be puffed up and golden. If not leave them a few minutes longer, then remove from the oven to cool in the tin for 5 minutes (they will collapse a little).

Remove carefully with a broad blunt knife and serve warm.

Salads, Soups, Light Meals

SQUASH AND SWEET POTATO SOUP

SERVES 2

CALORIES: 252

TOTAL FAT: 6.5G

SATURATED FAT: 0.8G

FIBRE: 7.3G

PROTEIN: MEDIUM-LOW

CARBOHYDRATE: HIGH

A beautiful warming soup for the winter months with plenty of colour. Try grating a mature hard cheese over for extra calories and protein.

1 tbsp olive oil
1 small onion, finely chopped
400g butternut squash, peeled and cut into cubes
1 medium sweet potato (about 200g), peeled and cut into cubes
1 clove garlic, peeled and well crushed
1 tsp fresh thyme leaves
Black pepper
300ml gluten and wheat free vegetable stock
100g drained, canned butter beans
A little salt as necessary

Heat the oil in a non-stick frying pan and sauté the onion over medium-low heat until soft. Add the vegetables, garlic and thyme, stir, then add the stock, bring to a simmer and cook for 30 minutes, adding the butter beans towards the end of cooking time.

When the vegetables are tender, purée the soup in a food processor. Taste and add a little salt as necessary. If the soup is too thick, add a little water and blend again. Reheat gently to serve.

ROAST TOMATO, GARLIC AND PEPPER SOUP

SERVES 2

CALORIES: 257

TOTAL FAT: 16.3G

SATURATED FAT: 2.7G

FIBRE: 5.3G

PROTEIN: LOW

CARBOHYDRATE: HIGH

A great soup to make when there is a glut of ripe tasty local tomatoes in early autumn.

8 fresh juicy cloves garlic, peel-on, lightly crushed
8 ripe tomatoes (about 450g), halved and deseeded
1 medium red pepper, quartered and deseeded
2 tbsp olive oil
½ tsp salt
Black pepper
400ml vegetable stock
35g slice wholemeal bread, cut into 1.5cm squares

Preheat the oven to 190°C. Arrange the garlic, tomatoes and red pepper quarters on a baking dish and drizzle half the oil over them, then sprinkle on the salt and pepper. Bake for 20-30 minutes, or until the vegetables are soft. Press the garlic flesh out of the skins and discard the skin.

Toss the bread squares in the rest of the oil, arrange on another baking tray, and add to the oven for the last 10 minutes of cooking time, or until they are golden and crisp.

Now transfer the cooked vegetables and garlic to a blender with a little of the stock and purée until smooth, then add the remaining stock and blend again. Pour into a pan and reheat. Serve in bowls and sprinkle the croutons over the top.

SPICED LENTIL AND VEGETABLE SOUP

SERVES 2

CALORIES: 305

TOTAL FAT: 8.9G

SATURATED FAT: 2.2G

FIBRE: 8.2G

PROTEIN: MEDIUM-HIGH

CARBOHYDRATE: MEDIUM-HIGH

A chunky fibre-rich soup for any time of year – it is easy to make vegan by using coconut yogurt or soya cream instead of the dairy yogurt.

1 tbsp olive oil
1 medium red onion, peeled and finely chopped
1 garlic clove, peeled and well crushed
½ tsp ground coriander
¼ tsp ground cumin
500ml gluten-and wheat-free vegetable stock
100g (dry weight) brown lentils
1 large carrot, peeled and finely chopped
Black pepper
¼ tsp salt as necessary
2 tbsp fresh coriander leaves
2 tbsp natural yogurt

Heat the oil in a saucepan and sauté the onion over medium low heat until soft – about 10 minutes. Add the garlic, coriander and cumin and stir for a minute. Add the stock, lentils and carrot and bring to simmer.

Cook for 30 minutes or until the lentils are tender. Add the pepper, taste and add salt if necessary, and serve with the yogurt drizzled over the top and garnished with the coriander leaves.

COURGETTE SOUP

SERVES 2

CALORIES: 345

TOTAL FAT: 19.9G

SATURATED FAT: 6.8G

FIBRE: 5.8G

PROTEIN: MEDIUM-LOW

CARBOHYDRATE: MEDIUM-HIGH

A soup that is more delicious than you may think from reading the simple list of ingredients – and very easy to make, too.

1 medium onion, finely chopped
1½ tbsp olive oil
2 cloves garlic, peeled and well crushed
1 medium potato, peeled and chopped
600ml vegan vegetable stock
3 medium courgettes, topped, tailed and chopped
Salt, black pepper
½ tbsp each fresh chopped mint, parsley and oregano
40g grated extra mature hard cheese or vegan cheese
1 tbsp Greek or thick soya yogurt
A little extra chopped mint to serve

Sauté the chopped onion in the oil over low heat to soften but not colour; add garlic for last minute and stir in then add chopped potatoes and half the stock. Bring to simmer and cook for 15 minutes.

Add chopped courgettes, seasoning, herbs and the rest of the stock. Simmer for 10 minutes then cool slightly and blend in electric blender. Add a little water if too thick. Re-heat, check the seasoning, add the cheese and spoon on the yogurt and sprinkle over the mint to serve.

HOME BAKED BEANS

SERVES 2

CALORIES: 361

TOTAL FAT: 13G

SATURATED FAT: 1.6G

FIBRE: 12G

PROTEIN: MEDIUM

CARBOHYDRATE: HIGH

Making your own proper baked beans is easy to do and the result is worth it. For a vegetarian or vegan recipe, use soy sauce instead of the Worcestershire sauce.

400g can haricot beans, drained and rinsed
1 tbsp extra virgin rapeseed oil
1 medium onion, finely chopped
1 tsp English mustard powder
2 tsp soft brown sugar
1 tsp black treacle
2 tsp lemon juice
1 tsp Worcestershire sauce
½ tsp salt
1 recipe-quantity Tomato Sauce (see page xxx)

Preheat the oven to 150°C. Add the beans to an ovenproof lidded dish.

Heat the oil in a non-stick frying pan and sauté the onion over medium low heat until soft and just turning golden. Add the rest of the ingredients to the pan and stir well to heat through.

Pour the sauce over the beans, stir, put the lid on and bake in the oven for 1 hour, stirring once or twice. If the mixture begins to look dry at any time, stir in a little water.

TURKISH AUBERGINES

SERVES 2

CALORIES:	320
TOTAL FAT:	11.3G
SATURATED FAT:	1.6G
FIBRE:	14.3G
PROTEIN:	MEDIUM-LOW
CARBOHYDRATE:	HIGH

An easy and light very high- fibre supper or weekend lunch. For a change try using orzo pasta instead of the bulgur wheat.

1 large aubergine
1½ tbsp olive oil
30g bulgur wheat (dry weight)
30g red lentils (dry weight)
1 red pepper, deseeded and chopped small
1 red onion, finely chopped
1 level teaspoon ground cumin
Salt and black pepper
2 canned plum tomatoes, chopped

Preheat the oven to 180°C/ 350°F/ gas 4 and lightly oil a baking tray.

Halve the aubergine and scoop out all but the last 1cm of flesh. Turn the shells upside down on the baking tray and bake for 25 minutes, or until the shells are just tender.

Meanwhile, cook the bulgur wheat and lentils in a pan until soft – about 25 minutes – then drain thoroughly.

Heat the olive oil in a non-stick frying pan. Chop the aubergine flesh and add it to the pan, together with the red pepper, onion, cumin and seasoning. Stir-fry for a few minutes until soft then add the chopped tomatoes to the mix and stir in the wheat and lentils. Taste and add more seasoning as necessary.

Pile the mixture into the aubergine shells and return to the oven to warm through. Serve at once.

CHILLI LENTILS WITH GREENS

SERVES 2

CALORIES:	272
TOTAL FAT:	7.8G
SATURATED FAT:	1.5G
FIBRE:	8.5G
PROTEIN:	HIGH
CARBOHYDRATE:	MEDIUM

It is easy to make this dish vegan by using coconut or soya yogurt instead of the bio yogurt.

1 tbsp groundnut oil
1 medium onion, thinly sliced
1 tsp each freshly ground cumin seeds and fresh ginger
1 small red chilli, deseeded and finely chopped
Salt and black pepper
400g can green lentils, well drained and rinsed
200g mixed young dark green leafy vegetables (such as spinach, kale,
chard or spring greens), torn
Juice of ½ lemon
2 tbsp natural bio yogurt

Heat the oil in a non-stick pan and sauté the onion until soft. Add the spices, chilli and seasoning and sauté for a further minute.

Add the lentils and stir for a minute or two, then add the leaves and stir again for a minute until slightly wilted. Add the lemon juice and drizzle over the yoghurt before serving slightly warm or at room temperature.

SWEET POTATO HASH WITH POACHED EGGS

SERVES 2

CALORIES: 461

TOTAL FAT: 20.4G

SATURATED FAT: 3.8G

FIBRE: 10.6G

PROTEIN: MEDIUM

CARBOHYDRATE: HIGH

Packed with carotenes and other plant chemicals, this is a more-ish dish you'll make time and again

2 tbsp extra virgin olive oil
1 small onion, peeled and finely chopped
1 small red pepper, de-seeded and chopped
1 clove garlic, peeled and crushed
1 red chilli, de-seeded and finely chopped
400g sweet potato, peeled and cut into 1.5cm cubes
½ tsp salt
½ tsp smoked paprika
100g young tender curly kale, de-stalked and chopped
2 extra large eggs
Dash of sriracha sauce (optional)
Black pepper

Heat half the oil in a large lidded frying pan and sauté the onion and red pepper over medium low heat for 5 minutes, unlidded. Add the garlic and chilli and cook for a further 2 minutes.

Meanwhile, put the sweet potato in a microwaveable bowl with 2 tbsp water, cover and microwave on high for 4 minutes. (Otherwise, steam in a covered saucepan.) Drain and dry on kitchen paper.

Add the rest of the oil to the frying pan with the potato chunks, salt and paprika, stir well, put on the lid and cook over medium low heat for 10 minutes.

Turn the heat up to medium high for 2-3 minutes and stir occasionally until the potatoes are beginning to turn golden. Add the kale and stir for a minute.

Break the eggs into the pan, put the lid back on and cook on low for 7-8 minutes or until the eggs look lightly poached with runny yolks.

Sprinkle on the sriracha if using, and some black pepper.

ASPARAGUS, EGG AND QUINOA SUMMER SALAD

SERVES 2

CALORIES: 391

TOTAL FAT: 25.3G

SATURATED FAT: 3.3G

FIBRE: 5.5G

PROTEIN: MEDIUM-HIGH

CARBOHYDRATE: MEDIUM-HIGH

A substantial yet refreshing salad packed with fresh baby vegetables and herbs and ideal for early summer days.

50g (dry weight) white quinoa
1 tbsp chopped parsley
¼ tbsp fresh chopped tarragon
¼ tsp fresh chopped dill weed
2½ tbsp cold-pressed extra virgin rapeseed oil
Juice of one small lemon
Salt and black pepper
10 spears baby asparagus
30g mangetout
50g petit pois
4 spring onions, finely chopped
2 large eggs
Extra chopped parsley to garnish

Put the quinoa in a pan with water and simmer for 25 minutes or until soft; drain well and set aside until cool and stir in the herbs. Make a dressing by whisking together 2 tbsp of the rapeseed oil, the lemon juice and salt and pepper to taste and stir half of this into the quinoa.

Cut each asparagus spear in two and blanch in minimal boiling water with the mangetout and peas for 1½ minutes, drain and rinse in cold water; dry thoroughly.

Heat a frying pan half-filled with water until simmering and break the eggs into the pan. Cook until the whites are opaque and the yolks still runny, then remove using a large spatula and drain on kitchen paper.

While the eggs are cooking, heat the remaining oil in a small frying pan and gently stir the onions and blanched vegetables over medium heat until just tender – 2-3 minutes.

Divide the quinoa between two serving dishes, top with the vegetables and the eggs, drizzle over the rest of the dressing and sprinkle on a little parsley to serve.

WARM WINTER COLESLAW WITH WALNUTS AND CHICKEN

SERVES 4

CALORIES: *357*

TOTAL FAT: 23.5G

SATURATED FAT: 3.9G

FIBRE: 4.6G

PROTEIN: HIGH

CARBOHYDRATE: MEDIUM-LOW

A pretty salad that can be eaten with several other foods as well as chicken – try it with cheese, any cold meat, or with some more nuts, such as almonds and hazelnuts, stirred in, or a little ready-made dukkha.

150g each thinly-sliced raw red and white cabbage

1 medium raw carrot, peeled and very thinly sliced

1 small red onion, peeled and very thinly sliced

50g walnut pieces

50g semi-dried apricots, chopped

For the dressing:

2 tbsp cold pressed extra virgin rapeseed oil

2 tbsp walnut oil

Juice of half a large orange

1 tbsp sherry or white wine vinegar

½ tbsp aged balsamic vinegar

1 tbsp maple syrup

1-2 large cloves garlic, peeled and very well crushed (or to taste)

Salt and black pepper

2 handfuls coriander leaves

150g cooked skinless chicken breast, sliced

First make the dressing by shaking all the ingredients in a lidded jar until thoroughly combined. Taste and adjust seasoning if necessary. If you can make the dressing a day in advance it will be even better.

Tip the vegetables, nuts and apricots into a large dish and stir well to mix up. Add two-thirds of the coriander and stir again. Stir in the dressing. Warm the salad slightly in a microwaveable dish in the microwave at medium low for 2 minutes if you like – it tasted good cold but even better slightly warm. When it's time to serve the salad, arrange the chicken slices on top and sprinkle on the rest of the coriander leaves.

The salad will keep, covered (without chicken) in the fridge for several days and actually tastes even better after a day or two.

ROAST BEETROOT, FETA AND POMEGRANATE SALAD

SERVES 2

CALORIES: 353

TOTAL FAT: 24.9G

SATURATED FAT: 5.9G

FIBRE: 6.4G

PROTEIN: MEDIUM-HIGH

CARBOHYDRATE: MEDIUM

Another superb winter salad packed with flavour and texture. Vegans can easily use feta-style vegan cheese instead of the feta. The salad is nice served with crusty sourdough bread.

2 medium beetroots, trimmed and scrubbed

1½ tbsp extra virgin olive oil

25g red onion, peeled and chopped

4 radishes, sliced into rounds

50g feta cheese or vegan feta cheese

25g pecan nuts, halved lengthways

2 tbsp pomegranate seeds

2 handfuls rocket leaves

1 tbsp aged balsamic vinegar

2 tsp maple syrup

½ tsp Dijon mustard

Salt and black pepper

Brush the beets with a little of the olive oil and put in a small baking dish. Bake at 180C for 45 minutes or until tender, allow to cool then rub the skins off and slice.

Combine the rest of the oil with the vinegar, maple syrup, mustard and seasoning and whisk well to combine. Arrange the beet slices in two serving dishes then scatter over the onion, radish slices, nuts, rocket and pomegranate seeds.

Crumble over the feta and finally spoon over the dressing.

ARTICHOKE, AUBERGINE AND SPELT SALAD

SERVES 2

CALORIES: 511
TOTAL FAT: 27G
SATURATED FAT: 4.6G
FIBRE: 16.7G
PROTEIN: MEDIUM
CARBOHYDRATE: HIGH

A very fibre-rich dish for any time of year – try substituting the aubergine with squash or cauliflower for a change.

80g (dry weight) pearled spelt grain
80g ready cooked Puy lentils
1 large aubergine, about 400g
3 tbsp extra virgin olive oil
2 cloves garlic, peeled and well crushed
½ tsp each ground cumin, turmeric and coriander
100g ready chargrilled artichokes from a jar
Juice of half a lemon
2 tbsp chopped parsley plus extra for garnish
4 spring onions, chopped
Salt and black pepper
½ tsp smoked paprika

Cook the spelt in boiling water until tender, about 20 minutes. Meanwhile, cut the aubergine into bite-sized pieces. Heat the olive oil in a large frying pan over medium heat and quickly sauté the garlic and spices for a minute until you have a good aroma and the garlic is slightly softened. Add the aubergine pieces and sauté for 10 minutes, turning once, until golden and tender.

Tip the spelt and lentils into a bowl and combine the aubergine and all the remaining ingredients, cutting the artichokes as necessary. Serve warm or at room temperature.

Suppers

SPEEDY HERBED SWORDFISH

SERVES 2

CALORIES: 260

TOTAL FAT: 13G

SATURATED FAT: 2.4G

FIBRE: 0.4G

PROTEIN: HIGH

CARBOHYDRATE: LOW

A simple high-protein supper – if you want some carb, add new potatoes or crusty bread.

2 mild shallots, finely chopped
1 tbsp each of chopped fresh flat-leaved parsley and dill
1 tsp fresh thyme leaves
Juice of ½ a lemon
1 tbsp olive oil
2 medium swordfish steaks, each about 175g
1 tbsp fresh breadcrumbs

In a small blender or using a hand blender, mix together the shallots, herbs, lemon juice and olive oil. Place the fish steaks in a shallow dish and cover with the blended mixture. Leave for 1-2 hours.

When you are ready to eat, preheat the grill with a good-quality baking tray underneath it. Remove the swordfish steaks from the marinade (using a knife to scrape off most of the marinade back into the dish) and place on the hot baking tray.

Quickly mix the remaining marinade with the breadcrumbs and use to coat the tops of the swordfish steaks. Grill for a few minutes until the steaks are cooked and the topping browned. (If the baking tray is good and hot, the underside of the fish will cook nicely so there's no need to turn it.)

SCALLOPS AND MUSSELS IN THE PAN

SERVES 2

CALORIES: 361

TOTAL FAT: 9.5G

SATURATED FAT: 1.9G

FIBRE: 3.3G

PROTEIN: HIGH

CARBOHYDRATE: MEDIUM

A vitamin and mineral-rich dish for shellfish lovers.

1 red onion, finely chopped
1 green chilli, deseeded and chopped
1 yellow pepper, deseeded and chopped
2 tomatoes, deseeded and chopped
1cm piece fresh root ginger, peeled and grated
Handful of fresh coriander leaves
Juice of a lime
Salt and black pepper
150ml vegetable or fish stock
50g (dry weight) couscous
1 tbsp groundnut oil
250g fresh scallops
1 clove garlic, peeled and well crushed
200g shelled mussels

In a bowl, combine the onion, chilli, pepper, tomatoes, ginger, coriander, lime juice, salt and pepper. Set aside for at least 30 minutes. Heat the stock and place in a bowl with the couscous. Set aside.

Heat the oil in a non-stick frying pan over a medium heat and cook the scallops (halved to make two smaller discs if very big) and garlic for a minute or two. Add the mussels and onion mixture and stir for 2 minutes.

Fluff up the couscous and serve with the scallops and mussels.

BAKED SARDINES WITH PINE NUTS AND RAISINS

SERVES 2

CALORIES: 565

TOTAL FAT: 35.2G

SATURATED FAT: 6.2G

FIBRE: 2.9G

PROTEIN: HIGH

CARBOHYDRATE: MEDIUM-LOW

This easy dish is rich in omega-3s and other healthy fats and tender, sweet sardines are an excellent low-cost alternative to salmon. Try serving with new potatoes and broccoli or green beans.

2 tbsp raisins
8 filleted sardines
2 tbsp pine nuts
2 shallots, peeled and finely chopped
2 tbsp extra virgin olive oil
100g fresh baby spinach leaves
4 tbsp breadcrumbs
Juice of a small lemon
Salt and black pepper

Put the raisins in a small bowl and cover them with warm water. Leave to plump up. Make sure there are no scales on the sardine skins, pat dry and place half in a lightly oiled shallow oblong baking dish, opened up and skin side down.

Heat a non-stick frying pan dry over medium high heat – when hot, add the pine nuts and toast until golden, stirring once or twice. As soon as they start to change colour, take the pan from the heat as they will quickly burn otherwise. Remove from the pan and set aside.

Wipe out the pan then add a little of the olive oil; sauté the shallots over medium heat for a few minutes until soft and beginning to turn golden. Add a little more oil to the pan with the spinach and stir for a minute until lightly wilted. Add half the pine nuts, the drained raisins, the lemon juice, a little salt and plenty of black pepper, and stir to combine.

Spoon the mixture evenly over the sardines then place the remaining sardines, skin side up, on top to make a 'sandwich'. Toss the breadcrumbs in the rest of the oil with the remaining pine nuts and sprinkle the mix over the top. Bake at 180C for 15 minutes or until the sardines are cooked through when pierced with a sharp knife and the topping is lightly golden.

MISO-MARINATED SALMON

SERVES 2

CALORIES: 311

TOTAL FAT: 17.3G

SATURATED FAT: 13.9G

FIBRE: 1.3G

PROTEIN: HIGH

CARBOHYDRATE: LOW

A tasty Japanese-influenced way to serve salmon and great served with pak choi or other oriental greens and stir-fried beansprouts.

2 salmon fillets, each about 125g
1 tbsp white miso paste
½ tbsp mirin
1 tbsp coconut aminos or reduced-salt soya sauce
Juice of ½ a lime
1 mild green chilli, de-seeded and finely chopped
2 spring onions, finely chopped
Pinch sugar

Combine all the ingredients except the salmon in a small bowl. Brush the salmon with the mixture and leave to marinate for half to one hour.

Place the salmon on a lightly oiled baking tray and bake in the oven for 12 minutes at 180C or until the fish is just cooked through in the centre.

WINTER SQUASH WITH LENTILS AND GINGER

SERVES 2

CALORIES: 388

TOTAL FAT: 7.8G

SATURATED FAT: 1.3G

FIBRE: 13G

PROTEIN: MEDIUM-HIGH

CARBOHYDRATE: HIGH

A delicious very high-fibre supper suitable for everyone and rich in plant chemicals, vitamins and minerals.

500g orange-fleshed squash or pumpkin
1 tbsp groundnut oil
1 onion, thinly sliced
1 clove garlic, peeled and well crushed
3cm piece of fresh root ginger, grated
1 tbsp gluten-free black bean sauce
400g can green or brown lentils, drained and rinsed
150ml vegan vegetable stock
2 tbsp chopped fresh coriander

Peel the squash, deseed it and cut the flesh into medium chunks. Heat the oil in a flameproof casserole or heavy-lidded frying pan and sauté the onion until just turning golden. Add the garlic and ginger and stir for a minute. Add the squash and sauté until the chunks are tinged golden, then add the black bean sauce and lentils and give everything a good stir. Pour in enough stock barely to cover the squash, bring to a simmer and cook, covered, for 20 minutes or until squash is tender. Serve garnished with the coriander.

RICE AND BEANS

SERVES 2

CALORIES: 359

TOTAL FAT: 3.4G

SATURATED FAT: 1G

FIBRE: 5.5G

PROTEIN: MEDIUM

CARBOHYDRATE: HIGH

A well balanced, magnesium and potassium-rich meal for non-meat eaters – but if you enjoy meat and are very hungry you can add some strips of cooked chicken to the dish before serving.

125g (dry weight) brown Basmati rice
250ml gluten-free vegan vegetable stock
½ tsp ground turmeric
4 tbsp coconut milk
1 green chilli, deseeded and chopped
1cm piece fresh root ginger, chopped
1 red pepper, deseeded and chopped
2 spring onions, finely chopped
½ x 400g can mixed beans, drained and rinsed
Black pepper
1 tbsp chopped fresh coriander

Cook the rice and turmeric in the stock in a lidded pan for 30 minutes or until tender and all the liquid is absorbed (adding a little extra hot water towards the end if the rice is not tender and the pan is dry).

Meanwhile, put the coconut milk, chilli, ginger, pepper and spring onions in a small saucepan and simmer for a few minutes. When the rice is cooked, toss the rice, coconut sauce, mixed beans, seasoning and coriander together and serve.

POTATO AND MEDITERRANEAN VEGETABLE BAKE

SERVES 2

CALORIES:	497
TOTAL FAT:	23.6G
SATURATED FAT:	3.8G
FIBRE:	13.8G
PROTEIN:	LOW
CARBOHYDRATE:	HIGH

An easy high-fibre bake that all the family will enjoy. If you want to increase the protein content, you could add in some soya or pork mince.

350g waxy potatoes cut into 0.5cm thick rounds
2 courgettes (about 200g)
2 red peppers (about 250g)
1 aubergine (about 275g)
2 tbsp olive oil
1 recipe-quantity Tomato Sauce (see recipe page 246)
2 tsp chopped fresh oregano leaves
Salt and black pepper
2 tbsp grated Parmesan cheese

Preheat the oven to 200C; parboil the potatoes in lightly salted water until almost tender. Drain and reserve.

Meanwhile, top and tail the courgettes and slice them thinly at an angle. Deseed the pepper and cut it into quarters, then halve these. Top and tail the aubergine and slice it into 1cm rounds then halve these. Place all the vegetables except the potatoes on a baking tray, brush them with a third of the olive oil, sprinkle on a little salt and bake for 25 minutes, or until soft and turning golden.

Brush a suitable baking dish (small lasagne dish or similar) with a little of the remaining olive oil and put half the potato slices in the bottom. Arrange the baked vegetables over the potatoes, then pour on the tomato sauce to coat evenly and sprinkle on the oregano.

Arrange the remaining potatoes evenly on top, sprinkle with pepper and cheese, and drizzle over the last of the oil. Return to the oven for 20 minutes or until lightly browned.

ALMOND, CHICKPEA AND RAISIN PILAF

SERVES 2

CALORIES: 714	
TOTAL FAT: 30G	
SATURATED FAT: 4.6G	
FIBRE: 7.3G	
PROTEIN: MEDIUM	
CARBOHYDRATE: HIGH	

275ml gluten-free vegan vegetable stock
1 tsp saffron threads
150g (dry weight) brown rice
1 tbsp groundnut oil
35g unsalted cashews
35g flaked almonds
1 onion, finely chopped
½ tsp each ground coriander and cumin seeds
100g cooked chickpeas
40g raisins
1 tbsp chopped fresh coriander

Heat the vegetable stock in a saucepan and add the saffron. Add the rice, bring to simmer and cook, covered, for 30 minutes or until the rice is tender and all the stock absorbed (add more stock or water if rice dries out before it is tender).

Heat a non-stick frying pan and brush the base with a little of the groundnut oil. Add the cashews and almonds and stir-fry until golden. Remove from the pan and reserve.

Add the rest of the oil to the pan and sauté the onion until soft and just turning golden. Add the ground coriander and cumin and stir-fry for a minute, then add the chickpeas and raisins and stir-fry for another minute. Add the rice, toasted nuts and chopped coriander and stir together gently to combine.

CHICKEN CACCIATORE

SERVES 2

CALORIES: 214	
TOTAL FAT: 12G	
SATURATED FAT: 2.4G	
FIBRE: 1G	
PROTEIN: HIGH	
CARBOHYDRATE: LOW	

An easy to put together, low fat summer casserole – good served with green vegetables, and new potatoes or pasta if you want some carbs.

1 tbsp olive oil
4 chicken thighs, part-boned and skinned
2 cloves garlic, well crushed
Few sprigs of fresh thyme, tarragon and oregano or 2 tsp dried mixed Italian herb blend
100ml dry white wine
200g can chopped tomatoes
Salt and black pepper
6 stoned black olives, halved
6 capers, rinsed and drained

Heat the oil in a flameproof casserole or heavy frying pan with a lid and brown the chicken on all sides. Turn the heat down a little and add the garlic, herbs and wine. Stir for a minute or two.

Add the tomatoes with their liquid and some seasoning to taste. Bring to simmer and cook, covered, for 20 minutes or until the chicken is tender. Add the olives and capers, stir well and cook for a further 2-3 minutes, uncovered, until you have just a little thick sauce left. Adjust the seasoning as necessary.

SPICED CHICKEN AND GREENS

SERVES 2

CALORIES: 332

TOTAL FAT: 13G

SATURATED FAT: 3.7G

FIBRE: 4.3G

PROTEIN: HIGH

CARBOHYDRATE: LOW

A light and refreshing summer chicken dish rich in B vitamins, iron and plant chemicals

200g tender young green leaves of choice (e.g. chard, kale, spring cabbage)

2 x 125g chicken breast fillets, skinned

1 tbsp groundnut oil

1 onion, finely chopped

2 cloves garlic, peeled and well crushed

1 fresh green chilli, deseeded and finely chopped

1/2 teaspoon each ground turmeric and cumin seeds

1/4 tsp freshly ground nutmeg

150g tomatoes halved and deseeded

100ml Greek yogurt or full-fat natural bio yogurt

3 tbsp gluten and wheat free chicken stock

Salt and black pepper

Chop the green leaves into thin slices. Slice each chicken breast across the grain into 4 pieces.

Heat the oil in a non-stick frying pan and sauté the onion until soft. Move the onion to the edges of the pan and add the chicken pieces. Cook until they have turned slightly golden – if the onion is also slightly golden by now that is fine.

Reduce the heat and add the garlic, chilli and spices, stirring everything in well for a minute or two. Chop the tomatoes and add to the pan, then cook for a further 2 minutes. Add the greens and stir for 2 minutes more, then spoon in the yoghurt and bring to simmer.

Using the chicken stock, thin the sauce down a little. Add a little salt and black pepper to taste.

CHIPOTLE LIME CHICKEN

SERVES 2

CALORIES: 278

TOTAL FAT: 13.6G

SATURATED FAT: 1.4G

FIBRE: 1.1G

PROTEIN: HIGH

CARBOHYDRATE: LOW

Delicious served with corn on the cob and cucumber and lettuce salad, this is one of the easiest recipes you could try. You can also cut the breasts into four pieces each, marinade then thread onto skewers and grill to cook through.

2 skinless chicken breast fillets each cut into two
Lime wedges

For the marinade:
Juice of a lime
Zest of a lime
1½ tbsp extra virgin olive oil
1 tbsp fresh coriander leaves, roughly chopped
1 small red medium-hot fresh chilli, finely chopped
2 tsp smoked chipotle chilli paste
2 cloves garlic, peeled and well crushed
1 tsp agave nectar or maple syrup
½ tsp ground coriander seed
¼ tsp salt
Black pepper

Put the chicken fillets in a shallow non-metallic heatproof bowl, up. Whisk all the marinade ingredients together and pour over the chicken pieces to coat everything evenly. Cover and marinate for two hours.

Bake the fillets in their bowl at 190C for 20 minutes, basting with the marinade in the dish at least once. Check the fillets are cooked through (when pricked with a sharp knife or skewer the juices should run clear) and if not, cook a little longer.

Serve the chicken with lime wedges.

LAMB TAGINE
SERVES 2

CALORIES: 441

TOTAL FAT: 20.6G

SATURATED FAT: 4.5G

FIBRE: 6.1G

PROTEIN: HIGH

CARBOHYDRATE: MEDIUM-LOW

Try serving the tagine with wholemeal flatbreads, bulgur wheat or any grain of your choice.

275g leg or neck of lamb, cut into chunks
1½ tbsp olive oil
1 onion, peeled, halved and sliced
1 carrot, peeled and chopped
3 cloves garlic
1 tbsp ras el hanout spice mix
1 tsp harissa paste
1 tbsp tomato puree
2 preserved lemons, chopped OR juice and zest of 1 small fresh lemon
250ml lamb stock
50g dried apricots, chopped
40g round green beans, diced
Chopped flat parsley, mint or coriander
1 tbsp toasted flaked almonds
1 dessert spoonful of dried rose petals (optional)

Heat oil in large lidded frying pan and brown the lamb lightly over high heat for a minute or two. Remove meat using slotted spatula and reserve. Add onion and carrot to the pan and cook over medium low heat for 15 minutes, stirring occasionally, until onion is transparent and soft. Peel and crush the garlic, stand for a few minutes then add to the onion mix with the spices. Stir for a minute then add the harissa, tomato puree, preserved lemon and stock and stir again.

Return the lamb to the pan with the apricots, bring to simmer, put lid on and cook for an hour, stirring from time to time. Add the beans for the last 15 minutes of cooking time. To serve, sprinkle over chopped flat leaf parsley, mint and/or coriander leaf, the almonds and the rose petals if using.

CHILLI BEEF FAJITAS

SERVES 2

CALORIES: 662

TOTAL FAT: 34.2G

SATURATED FAT: 7.9G

FIBRE: 16.9G

PROTEIN: MEDIUM-HIGH

CARBOHYDRATE: MEDIUM-HIGH

An ideal way to enjoy your beef steak, without eating too large a portion; there is so much else in this hearty wrap filled with healthy fats and fibre that you won't want more!

200g beef steak, whichever cut you prefer

A little salt; black pepper

1 tbsp olive oil

2 large wholemeal wraps

2 tbsp guacamole (see recipe page 249)

3 tbsp cooked black beans, well drained

6 cherry tomatoes, halved

6 pieces grilled yellow pepper

1 tsp sriracha sauce or to taste

½ tsp smoked paprika

½ tsp ground cumin

Crisp lettuce leaves

2 tbsp thick natural yogurt or coconut or soya yogurt

2 mild red chillies, thinly sliced into rings, de-seeded

Season the steak, rub with 1 tsp of the olive oil and cook on a hot griddle for 4 minutes, turning once. Remove to a warm plate to rest.

Lay wraps out flat then spread them with the guacamole. Slice steaks into thin strips then divide between the wraps. Lay on the beans, tomatoes and yellow pepper, add the sriracha sauce, seasoning, paprika and cumin.

Drizzle with remaining olive oil and the steak resting juices. Top with a dollop of yogurt, some chilli slices and the lettuce, then wrap up, folding in the sides, then the base, then the top, and cut with sharp knife down the centre.

ARTICHOKE, AUBERGINE AND SPELT WARM SALAD

SERVES 2

CALORIES: 511

TOTAL FAT: 27G

SATURATED FAT: 4.6G

FIBRE: 16.7G

PROTEIN: MEDIUM-LOW

CARBOHYDRATE: HIGH

Spelt makes a lovely change from rice or pasta and the addition of lentils boosts the protein content of this hearty warm salad. If there is any over, store it in the fridge for up to two days – it reheats well or can be eaten cold.

80g (dry weight) pearled spelt grain
80g ready cooked Puy lentils
2 tbsp chopped parsley plus extra for garnish
4 spring onions, chopped
1 large aubergine
3 tbsp extra virgin olive oil
2 cloves garlic, peeled and well crushed
½ tsp each ground cumin, turmeric and coriander seed
100g ready chargrilled artichokes from a jar, well drained and cut into bite-sized pieces as necessary
Juice of half a lemon
Salt and black pepper
½ tsp smoked paprika

Simmer the spelt in a covered saucepan in lightly salted water for 25 minutes or until soft, drain well, stir in the lentils, 2 tbsp parsley and half the chopped spring onions. Put the lid back on and leave on the hob (turned off) to keep somewhat warm.

Cut the aubergine into 2cm chunks, heat half the oil in a large frying pan and cook over medium high heat, turning from time to time, until the pieces are tender and lightly browned. Add the garlic and spices to the pan with a small drizzle more of oil and stir for a minute or two. Turn the heat off and leave the pan on the hob.

Make a dressing with the remainder of the olive oil, the lemon juice, a little salt and plenty of black pepper. Stir half of this into the spelt and lentil mixture, then spoon it into a serving bowl.

Arrange the aubergine and artichoke pieces on top, stirring a few lightly into the grain mixture. Sprinkle over the rest of the spring onions and parsley, then the rest of the dressing, and garnish with the smoked paprika.

Side dishes, Sauces and Accompaniments

ANCHOÏADE

SERVES 4

CALORIES: 207

TOTAL FAT: 21.2G

SATURATED FAT: 3G

FIBRE: 0.3G

PROTEIN: MEDIUM

CARBOHYDRATE: LOW

This very healthy spread is good as a dip, as a quick sauce for a pasta starter, as a topping for crostini or as a side sauce with eggs.

> 4 cloves garlic, peeled
> 12 canned anchovy fillets in oil, drained
> 12 good plump green olives, stoned
> About 75ml extra-virgin olive oil
> Dash of white wine vinegar

Put the garlic, anchovies and olives in a blender or food processor and blend until puréed. Pour in half the oil and the vinegar and blend again.

Add as much more of the oil as you need to make a paste or purée or sauce, depending upon its intended use.

TOMATO SAUCE

SERVES 4

CALORIES: 72

TOTAL FAT: 3.8G

SATURATED FAT: 0.5G

FIBRE: 0.9G

PROTEIN: LOW

CARBOHYDRATE: MEDIUM-HIGH

A versatile and flavour packed sauce useful in very many recipes.

> 1tb olive oil
> 1 onion, finely chopped
> 1 clove garlic, peeled and well crushed
> 400g can chopped tomatoes (with their liquid)
> 2 tsp tomato paste
> 1 tsp soft brown sugar
> 2 tsp lemon juice
> Salt and black pepper

Heat the oil in a non-stick frying pan and sauté the onion until soft. Add the garlic and stir for a minute. Add the tomatoes, tomato paste, sugar and lemon juice, bring to a simmer and cook, uncovered, for 30 minutes or more, until you have a rich sauce. If too much liquid evaporates, add a little water or tomato juice. Taste, and add a little salt and some black pepper as necessary.

TOFU MAYONNAISE

MAKES 6 TABLESPOONS

CALORIES: 207

TOTAL FAT: 21.2G

SATURATED FAT: 3G

FIBRE: 0.3G

PROTEIN: MEDIUM

CARBOHYDRATE: LOW

You can use this tasty egg and dairy free mayo to replace ordinary egg-based mayonnaise for salads, and to accompany salmon, chicken and plenty of other meals.

100g silken tofu, mashed
1 small clove garlic, peeled and crushed
2 tsp white wine vinegar
1 tsp gluten-free Dijon mustard
Pinch black pepper
Little salt to taste

Blend the tofu, garlic, vinegar, mustard and pepper together in a blender or food processor or combine very well with a fork in a small bowl. Taste and add a little salt as necessary.

Try varying the mayonnaise by adding chopped fresh herbs, such as dill, tarragon or chives. Lemon juice can be used instead of the vinegar.

SAUCE VERDE

MAKES 4 TABLESPOONS

CALORIES: 67

TOTAL FAT: 6.8G

SATURATED FAT: 0.9G

FIBRE: 0.4G

PROTEIN: LOW

CARBOHYDRATE: LOW

A good piquant sauce rich in plant chemicals and ideal for grilled meat and fish dishes or as a dip.

2 cloves garlic, crushed
½ tsp salt
1 tsp gluten-free Dijon mustard
2 tbsp chopped fresh flat-leaved parsley
2 tbsp chopped fresh mint or basil
Juice of ½ a lemon
2 tbsp extra-virgin olive oil
Black pepper

Blend together the garlic and salt. Then, using a blender or food processor on slow, blend in the mustard, herbs and lemon juice. With the machine still running, slowly add the olive oil, blending as you do, until you have a green sauce. Add black pepper to taste.

MANGO SALSA

SERVES 4

CALORIES: 63

TOTAL FAT: 0.4G

SATURATED FAT: 0.1G

FIBRE: 2G

PROTEIN: LOW

CARBOHYDRATE: HIGH

A pretty salsa, very rich in vitamin C and carotenes – try serving it with spicy chicken, game or fish dishes.

1 ripe mango
1 small red onion
Juice of ½ a lime juice
2 tsp chopped fresh mint
Pinch of salt

Peel and stone the mango flesh, then chop the flesh, reserving any juice. In a bowl, combine this with all the remaining ingredients and leave in the fridge for 30 minutes.

SUMMER VEGETABLES WITH MINT

SERVES 2

CALORIES: 169

TOTAL FAT: 8.9G

SATURATED FAT: 1.9G

FIBRE: 5.8G

PROTEIN: MEDIUM

CARBOHYDRATE: MEDIUM

Broad beans can be double-podded by removing the beans from the long pods, and then removing the pale green-grey shells to reveal the tender bright green beans inside.

> 100g broad beans, double-podded
> 100g peas
> 50g fine beans, topped and tailed
> 1 tbsp extra-virgin olive oil
> 1 tbsp chopped fresh mint
> 2 tsp lemon juice
> A little salt and black pepper
> 30g lettuce leaves
> 2 tbsp freshly shaved Parmesan cheese

Simmer the broad beans, peas and beans in a little lightly salted water until just tender. Drain and add to a small frying pan with the oil, mint, lemon juice and seasoning. Stir for a minute so that the flavours combine.

Add the lettuce leaves and stir for a few seconds. Serve with the cheese shavings sprinkled over.

TABBOULEH

SERVES 2

CALORIES: 243

TOTAL FAT: 14.2G

SATURATED FAT: 1.8G

FIBRE: 5.6G

PROTEIN: LOW

CARBOHYDRATE: HIGH

Delicious salad to serve with falafel or meat or halloumi skewers, and also good as a filling for baked sweet pepper halves or aubergines.

> 50g bulgar wheat
> 1 beef tomato, skinned, deseeded and chopped
> Half a cucumber, chopped
> 2 handfuls of chopped fresh flat-leaved parsley
> 3 tbsp chopped fresh mint
> 2 spring onions, chopped
> 2 tbsp olive oil
> ½ tsp salt
> Black pepper
> Juice of a lemon

Put the bulgar in a large bowl, pour over boiling water and leave to soak for 30 minutes, or according to packet instructions, until plumped up. Drain.

Mix the bulgar with all the other ingredients in the bowl. Allow to stand, covered, for up to an hour at room temperature before serving.

GUACAMOLE

SERVES 4

CALORIES: 180

TOTAL FAT: 14.9G

SATURATED FAT: 2.1G

FIBRE: 7.7G

PROTEIN: LOW

CARBOHYDRATE: MEDIUM

One of the very best dishes to include in a tapas-style meal. Serve on toast or with toasted flatbreads, or use to liven up any sandwich or wrap, guacamole is rich in healthy fat and plant compounds.

1 large ripe tomato
2 avocados, properly ripe
Juice of a lime
Good handful coriander leaves
Half a small red onion, finely chopped
1 mild green chilli, e.g. Jalapeno, de-seeded and finely chopped
Salt and black pepper

Halve the tomato, scoop out the seeds with a teaspoon and discard, then chop the flesh well and add to a bowl. (You can peel the tomato if you like, by making a cross in the stalk end, then microwaving it for a minute on high then stripping off the peel, but I don't bother.)

Halve and stone the avocados and use a tablespoon to scoop out the flesh. Roughly chop it and add to the bowl with the lime juice, most of the coriander leaves, the onion, chilli and some seasoning to taste.

Combine everything well with a spoon then mash it a little with a fork so that the avocado is somewhat mashed but also with plenty of chunks. Scatter with the remaining coriander to serve.

If you want to keep the guacamole for a few days, level the top out well using a knife and then pour olive oil over the top. Store in the fridge. When you want to use it, pour the olive oil off (can be used for something else) and fluff up again to serve.

ROASTED TURMERIC CAULIFLOWER

SERVES 3

CALORIES: 124

TOTAL FAT: 9.9G

SATURATED FAT: 0.9G

FIBRE: 3.2G

PROTEIN: LOW

CARBOHYDRATE: MEDIUM-LOW

The cauliflower steaks are a great side with any lamb or beef dish or are good as the main event served with grains or lentils and green salad.

> 1 cauliflower
> 2 tbsp extra virgin rapeseed oil
> 1 tsp ground turmeric
> ½ tsp ground cumin
> Salt

Trim the cauliflower off its leave and cut the base straight. Sit the cauliflower on a board on its base and, using a carving knife, cut down through the cauliflower (starting at the florets end and finishing at the stalk end) in 2cm slices – the outer parts will fall away in small florets but when you get nearer the centre you will have thick cauliflower 'steaks' – an average cauliflower should make three.

Preheat the oven to 190C. Heat half the oil in a large frying pan and cook the steaks for 2 minutes a side over medium high heat. Remove the steaks from the pan with a slotted spatula and arrange on foil in a roasting tray.

Add the rest of the oil to the frying pan and stir in the spices and a little salt until well combined. Now brush all of this mixture over the steaks and roast in the oven for 20–25 minutes or until golden and just tender when pierced with a sharp knife.

CATALAN PEPPER AND ALMOND SAUCE

SERVES 4

CALORIES: 106

TOTAL FAT: 8G

SATURATED FAT: 0.9G

FIBRE: 1.7G

PROTEIN: LOW

CARBOHYDRATE: MEDIUM

This traditional, and very healthy, Spanish sauce is often served with meaty fish steaks such as tuna or swordfish, and is also good with grilled vegetables, pork and chicken. If you don't thin it, it makes a great dip for toasted wholewheat flatbreads.

1 large sweet red pepper, de-seeded and roughly chopped
1½ tbsp extra virgin olive oil
2 cloves garlic, peeled and crushed
1 red chilli, medium-hot, de-seeded and sliced
½ tsp sweet paprika
¼ tsp smoked paprika
200g canned chopped tomatoes
1 tbsp sherry vinegar
Pinch sugar
Salt and black pepper
2 tbsp ground almonds

Sauté the red pepper in a frying pan with the oil for a few minutes over medium high heat, stirring from time to time, until softened and beginning to turn golden at the edges.

Add the garlic, chilli and paprikas to the pan and stir for another half minute, then tip in the chopped tomatoes, vinegar, sugar and some seasoning. Stir well to combine and allow to cook gently over medium-low heat for a few minutes.

Take off the heat and allow to cool slightly then transfer to an electric blender and blend until smooth. Add the ground almonds to the blender with a tablespoon of water, and pulse for a few seconds just to combine. Look at the mix – if it is not of a thick pouring consistency, add a little more water and blend again.

Return to the pan to re-heat. Taste and adjust seasoning if necessary. The sauce freezes well in a strong freezer bag or container.

SMOKY AUBERGINE SALSA

SERVES 4

CALORIES: 135

TOTAL FAT: 9.5G

SATURATED FAT: 1.3G

FIBRE: 5.1G

PROTEIN: LOW

CARBOHYDRATE: MEDIUM

This is similar to a baba ghanoush but of chunkier texture. It goes very well with lamb dishes, falafel, vegetarian burgers and plenty more.

2 aubergines
2 tbsp extra virgin olive oil
1 tbsp light tahini paste
Juice of 1 lemon
3 cloves garlic, peeled and crushed
½ tsp ground cumin
Salt and black pepper
1 tbsp dukkha
½ tbsp chopped mint leaves
½ tsp smoked paprika

Preheat the oven to 180C. Cut each aubergine in quarters lengthways, brush all over with olive oil and put on a baking tray. Bake for 20 minutes until the quarters are browned and the aubergine is soft when pierced with a sharp knife. Allow to cool, then peel the skin off each quarter and discard.

Chop half the aubergine flesh and put in a bowl, and put the other half in an electric blender with the tahini, lemon juice, garlic, a little salt and the black pepper. Blend to a rough puree. Taste and add a little more seasoning if necessary.

Spoon the mixture into the bowl with the chopped aubergine and combine. Top with the dukkha, mint and smoked paprika. Serve at room temperature.

Desserts and Bakes

STIR-FRIED FRUIT SALAD

SERVES 2

CALORIES: 214

TOTAL FAT: 6.6G

SATURATED FAT: 3.1G

FIBRE: 3.4G

PROTEIN: LOW

CARBOHYDRATE: HIGH

Good served with Greek or coconut yogurt.

1 large barely ripe banana
1 tsp cold pressed extra virgin rapeseed oil
7½g unsalted butter
2 slices of fresh pineapple, each cored and cut into four
1 small ripe papaya, peeled, de-seeded and cut into large chunks
2 tsp lime juice
1 tbsp sweet dessert wine

Peel the banana and cut it into wedges. Heat the oil and butter in a non-stick frying pan and, when very hot, add the fruit. When it starts to brown, stir gently.

Add the lime juice, stir again and add the dessert wine. When the wine has bubbled for a few seconds, spoon into serving dishes and serve warm.

MANGO FILO TARTS

SERVES 2

CALORIES: 232

TOTAL FAT: 1.5G

SATURATED FAT: NEGLIGIBLE

FIBRE: 4.5G

PROTEIN: LOW

CARBOHYDRATE: HIGH

This easy carotene-rich dessert is good served with a raspberry coulis.

3 oblong sheets of filo pastry
Approx 18 sprays of sunflower cooking oil spray
1 large ripe mango
2 tsp maple syrup
Juice of ½ a lime
Pinch each of ground cinnamon and ginger
1 tbsp sultanas

Preheat the oven to 200°C. Cut the filo sheets in half to make six squares. Spraying each sheet with the cooking oil spray as you go, arrange three sheets at angles to each other to produce a decorative edge in 2 patty tins, or similar, to make 2 pastry shells. Bake for 10 minutes, or until just turning golden. Remove from the oven.

Meanwhile, peel, stone and chop the mango. Mix this with the remaining ingredients. Heat through in a small saucepan or microwave to combine the flavours.

When the pastry cases are ready, fill them with the mango mixture and serve immediately.

NECTARINE AND BANANA FOOL

SERVES 2

CALORIES: 174

TOTAL FAT: NEG

SATURATED FAT: 4G

FIBRE: 1.4G

PROTEIN: MEDIUM-LOW

CARBOHYDRATE: HIGH

An extremely quick and simple creamy dessert – you can use peach or apricot instead of the nectarine.

> 1 ripe nectarine
> 1 medium just-ripe banana
> 2 tsp icing sugar
> 1 tbsp orange juice
> 150ml Greek yogurt

Peel and chop the nectarine and banana and place them in a blender or food processor with the icing sugar and orange juice. Blend until fairly smooth.

Fold the fruit mixture into the yogurt, divide between 2 glass dessert bowls or glasses and chill if you have time, for at least 30 minutes.

RUSTIC LEMON AND BLUEBERRY SCONES

MAKES 12

CALORIES: 170

TOTAL FAT: 6.1G

SATURATED FAT: 1.2G

FIBRE: 3.5G

PROTEIN: MEDIUM

CARBOHYDRATE: HIGH

These nutrient-packed scones contain less than 4g sugar each and are delicious spread with a little unsalted butter for a treat.

> 250g wholegrain multi-seed flour
> 90g fine oatmeal
> 1 tbsp milled linseeds
> 2 tsp baking powder
> ½ tsp bicarbonate of soda
> 1 tsp salt
> 2 tbsp light soft brown sugar
> 125g blueberries
> Zest and juice of half a lemon
> 250ml natural yogurt
> 2 tbsp cold pressed extra virgin rapeseed oil plus extra for oiling
> 100ml whole milk

Preheat the oven to 200C. Put the flour, oatmeal, linseeds, baking powder, bicarbonate of soda, salt and sugar into a bowl and thoroughly combine with a fork. Stir in the blueberries and lemon zest.

Put the yogurt, oil, lemon juice and milk into a jug and whisk together.

Pour the yogurt mix into the flour mix and stir until you have a rough dough.

Flour your hands and divide the mix into 12 rough balls. Brush a baking tray with a little rapeseed oil and put the balls on the tray. Bake for 15 minutes or until the scones are golden and firm. Leave to cool down for 10 minutes – eat warm or cold.

SUMMER BERRY GRATIN

SERVES 2

CALORIES: 149	
TOTAL FAT: 3G	
SATURATED FAT: 1.2G	
FIBRE: 4.2G	
PROTEIN: MEDIUM	
CARBOHYDRATE: MEDIUM-HIGH	

You can alter the berries to suit what is in season – blackberries are nice too.

200g fresh raspberries and strawberries
3 tsp light brown soft sugar
100ml Greek yogurt
100ml Quark

Preheat the grill. Halve any larger strawberries and divide the berries between two individual soufflé dishes. Sprinkle on half the sugar.

Beat together the yogurt and Quark and spoon evenly over the top of the raspberries. Sprinkle the rest of the sugar on top.

Put the soufflé dishes underneath the grill. Grill the gratins until the tops begin to bubble and brown. Serve at once.

OAT BREAD

MAKES 2 X 450G LOAVES

PER 35G SLICE:	
TOTAL FAT: 2G	
SATURATED FAT: 0.4G	
FIBRE: 2G	
PROTEIN: MEDIUM	
CARBOHYDRATE: HIGH	

This wheat-free bread is high in soluble fibres and a good source of protein. It is gluten-free if the oat flour is guaranteed free from gluten contamination (and should say gluten-free on the pack label).

475g gluten-free oat flour
40g soya flour
7½g sachet of quick-blend dried yeast
1 tsp salt
1 tbsp soft brown sugar
1 tbsp sunflower oil

Put the flours into a mixing bowl with the yeast, salt and sugar. Add the oil and 400ml water and mix thoroughly. When a dough has begun to form, knead it thoroughly for 5-10 minutes.

Divide the dough between 2 lightly oiled 450g (1lb) loaf pans and leave in a warm place, covered with a tea towel, for 30 minutes until well risen. Preheat the oven to 180°C. Bake the loaves for 50 minutes, or until they sound hollow when tapped on the base.

Turn out on racks and leave to cool well before serving. The bread will keep for a day in an airtight container, or freeze.

APPLE FLAPJACKS

MAKES 10

CALORIES: 198

TOTAL FAT: 6.6G

SATURATED FAT: 0.7G

FIBRE: 4.6G

PROTEIN: MEDIUM-LOW

CARBOHYDRATE: HIGH

Our soft and chewy, easy to make flapjacks, packed with oats, sunflower seeds, fruit and nuts, make a tasty guilt-free snack. They contain plenty of soluble fibre as well as healthy fats and compared with most flapjacks you can buy, these are very moderate in sugar.

3 dessert apples
300ml good quality apple juice
75g sultanas
225g gluten-free porridge oats
30g sunflower seeds
50g crushed walnuts
2 tsp ground cinnamon
½ tsp salt
6 sprays sunflower oil cooking spray

Slice and core the apples, put in a saucepan with the juice and sultanas and bring to the boil. Reduce the heat and simmer, uncovered, stirring from time to time for 20 minutes or until you have a fairly thick mixture. Puree in an electric blender.

Stir the oats, sunflower seeds, and walnuts into the apple and sultana puree and mix well.

Heat the oven to 180C and line a 22cm cake tin with baking parchment. Spray with cooking oil spray to coat. Tip the oat mixture into the tin and spread out evenly with a spatula.

Bake for 25 minutes or until firm and golden. Cool slightly, cut into wedges then leave the flapjacks to cool completely in the tin before removing. Store in an airtight tin.

AVOCADO AND DARK CHOCOLATE MOUSSE

SERVES FOUR

CALORIES: 276

TOTAL FAT: 20.5G

SATURATED FAT: 6G

FIBRE: 8.6G

PROTEIN: LOW

CARBOHYDRATE: MEDIUM

If you've not yet tried a chocolate mousse made creamy and moreish with the addition of ripe avocado, do try this. The mousse doesn't taste of avocado but it is unctuous and rich, and packed with heart-friendly plant chemicals and healthy fats too.

2 medium perfectly ripe avocados
2½ tbsp maple syrup
2 tbsp canned coconut milk
2 tbsp cocoa powder
40g dark chocolate
1 tsp vanilla extract
Pinch salt
1/3 tsp ground cinnamon

Peel and stone the avocados, roughly chop and add to a small electric blender; pulse to a puree. Add the maple syrup, coconut milk, cocoa powder, vanilla, salt and cinnamon. Blend again.

Melt ¾ of the chocolate in a small dish in the microwave and stir into the mix; blend for a couple of seconds then pour the mix into four small glass dishes.

Chill for 30 minutes then grate the remaining dark chocolate over the top to serve.

SECTION SIX

Food at a Glance

The charts that follow list the nutrient breakdown of more than 300 common and not-so-common foods. Whenever you want to know what is in the food that you eat – for instance, the amount of saturated fat or fibre, this is the section that will help. Where appropriate, there are also additional notes.

The nutrient information is calculated from published official analysis and, where necessary, from manufacturers' data. However, individual foods vary in their precise nutrient content for various reasons – time of year (especially with fresh fruits and vegetables), method of storage (poor storage loses vitamins, for example), and there are also sometimes quite significant variations in nutritional content of various brands of similar foods, in which case I've given an approximate average.

Notes

THE FIGURES ARE taken from the USDA Nutrient Database when possible. Other figures are taken from the UK Composition of Foods or from supermarket data or manufacturers' food labels.

FIBRE

The charts list total fibre content for a wide range of foods. Neither the UK Composition of Foods database or the USDA Nutrient Database list soluble fibre figures for foods. This seems to be because recent research finds that accurate measures aren't possible. For this reason, I haven't included soluble fibre, but I've flagged up good sources in the special notes, as well as good sources of resistant starch, another type of fibre.

VITAMINS AND MINERALS

The vitamin and mineral columns list all the vitamins and minerals most likely to be in shortfall in an average Western diet, and which appear in the portion size of food listed in good quantities or above. This in most instances is about a fifth or more of the daily UK RNI (reference nutrient intake). If a food contains less than this but still, if eaten regularly or in larger portions size, is likely to provide a reasonable or good contribution of a vitamin or mineral to your diet, this is often pointed out in the special notes as having a useful amount of that vitamin or mineral.

When Vitamin A is listed, this includes pro-vitamin A (converted from plant foods). Calcium is abbreviated to calc, magnesium to mag, potassium to pot, phosphorous to phos and selenium to sel.

For more advice on vitamins, minerals and how much of them we need in our diets, turn to Section One, where you will also find charts listing many principal sources for all major vitamins and minerals.

SALT

Although salt consists of the minerals sodium and chloride, it has its own column showing the amount in g in a product, as many people need or want to know the exact amount of salt they are eating. The sodium content is 40% of the salt total.

CLASSIFICATION OF THE FOODS

To help you find your way about the charts, the foods are classified under the following headings in the order given:

Breads, crispbreads
Breakfast cereals
Condiments, sauces
Dairy products, plant alternatives, eggs
Biscuits, cakes, desserts
Drinks
Fats, oils
Fish, seafood
Fruit
Grains
Meat, poultry, and alternatives
Nuts, seeds
Pasta, noodles, pastry
Pulses
Spreads, dips, pâtés
Snack foods
Store cupboard items
Sugar, sweeteners, confectionery
Vegetables

	Cals	Fat g	Sats g	Carbs g	Sugar g	Fibre g	Protein g	Chol mg	Salt g
Breads, crispbreads									
Ciabatta loaf, 100g	278	4.3	0.7	47	2.9	3.1	11	0	0.9
Croissant, one	231	12	3.9	26	6.4	1.5	4.7	4.5	0.7
French stick, 100g	325	6.1	0.5	55	6.9	4.7	11	0	0.8
Granary bread, 100g	256	2.4	0.7	46.4	3.4	3.7	10.3	0	1
Pitta bread, white, one	165	0.7	0.1	33.4	0.8	1.3	5.5	0	0.8
Pitta bread, wholewheat, one	168	1.1	0.1	35.8	1.8	3.9	6.3	0	0.8
Rye, German-style 100g	177	1	0.2	34.4	0.9	8.3	6.1	0	1.1
Soda bread, 100g	290	5	1.1	56	1	2.6	6.6	0	1
Sourdough bread, 100g	250	2.8	0.3	45.1	2.6	2.4	9.8	0	1

Vitamins	Minerals	Special Notes
B3	cal, iron, phos, sel	
B3, folate	sel	
B3	cal, iron, sel	
B1, B3, folate	mag, phos	
	iron	
B1	iron, mag, phos	
B1, B2, B3, folate	iron, phos, zinc	Breads with a high level of rye flour (rye loaves do vary considerably) are a good source of soluble fibres. They are also lower on the glycaemic index. Check label as many 'rye' loaves are higher in wheat than rye.
B1, B2, B3, folate	iron	No yeast used as a raising agent.
B1, B2, B3, folate	iron, phos	A traditionally made sourdough is yeast-free, may help prevent bloating and is easier to digest as its enzymes neutralise phytic acid in wheat. People who are gluten-intolerant may be able to eat sourdough though it does contain gluten.

	Cals	Fat g	Sats g	Carbs g	Sugar g	Fibre g	Protein g	Chol mg	Salt g
White wheat bread, 100g	266	3.3	0.7	49.4	5.7	2.7	8.8	0	1.2
Wholewheat bread, 100g	278	5.4	0.8	51.4	3.8	6	8.4	0	0.9
Oatcake, round, one/10g	45	1.8	0.4	5.8	0.1	1.1	1.1	0	0.2
Corn thins, two/12g in all	46	0.4	0.1	8.5	tr	1.2	1.2	0	0.1
Rice cakes, round, two/15g in all	58	0.4	tr	12	tr	0.4	1.2	0	0.1
Dark rye crispbread, one/10g	34	0.1	tr	6.7	0.3	1.5	0.9	0	0.1

Breakfast Cereals

	Cals	Fat g	Sats g	Carbs g	Sugar g	Fibre g	Protein g	Chol mg	Salt g
All Bran, 30g	100	1	0.2	14	5.4	8.1	4.2	0	0.3
Bran flakes, 30g	108	1	0.2	19	4.2	4.5	3.6	0	0.2
Cornflakes, 30g	113	0.3	0.1	25	2.4	0.9	2.1	0	0.3

Vitamins	Minerals	Special Notes
B1, B2, B3	calc, iron, phos	When fortification of flour with folate becomes law in the UK (set for 2019), white bread will be an excellent source.
B1, B2, B3, folate	iron, mag, phos, zinc	Source of plant sterols.
		Good source of soluble fibre.
		Gluten and wheat free.
		Gluten and wheat free.
B1, B2, B3, B6, B12, folate, D	iron	Commercial breakfast cereals in the UK are fortified with vitamins.
B1, B2, B3, B6, B12, folate, D	iron	
B1, B2, B3, B6, B12	iron	

	Cals	Fat g	Sats g	Carbs g	Sugar g	Fibre g	Protein g	Chol mg	Salt g
Fruit and Fibre, 30g	114	1.8	1	20.7	7.2	2.7	2.4	0	0.3
Granola, 50g	213	6.9	2.2	32.1	14.2	3.3	4.1	0	tr
Muesli, no added sugar, 50g	187	3.1	0.4	32	8	3.9	5.5	0	0.1
Porridge made with water, 200g	142	3	0.6	24	0.5	3.4	5.1	0	tr
Rice Crispies, 30g	115	0.3	0.1	26	3	0.3	1.8	0	0.3
Shredded Wheat, two biscuits	158	0.9	0.2	37	0.4	5.8	5.3	0	tr
Weetabix, two biscuits	136	0.8	0.2	26	1.7	3.8	4.5	0	0.1

Condiments, Sauces

	Cals	Fat g	Sats g	Carbs g	Sugar g	Fibre g	Protein g	Chol mg	Salt g
Burger relish, 1 tb	14	tr	0	3.3	2.9	0.1	0.2	0	0.3
Mayonnaise, full fat, 1 tb	94	10.3	1.6	0.1	0.1	0	0.1	11	0.2

Vitamins	Minerals	Special Notes
B1, B2, B3, B6, B12, folate, D	iron	
B1, folate	mag, phos, zinc	Contains much more sugar than most other breakfast cereals.
B1, B2, B6	calc, iron, mag, phos, zinc	
	mag, phos, zinc	¼ tsp salt will add 1.5g salt to the porridge.
B1, B2, B3, B6, B12, folate, D	iron	
B1, B3, folate	iron, zinc	
B1, B2, B3, folate	iron	
		Real mayo, made with olive oil and eggs, is a healthy condiment!

	Cals	Fat g	Sats g	Carbs g	Sugar g	Fibre g	Protein g	Chol mg	Salt g
Pesto, basil, 1 tb/20g	84	7.5	1.4	2	1.3	0.4	2	6	0.3
Salad cream, 1 tb	52	4.7	0.6	2.5	2.5	0	0.2	6	0.3
Soya sauce, 1 tb	8	0.1	tr	0.8	0.1	0.1	1.3	0	2.2
Sweet pickle, 1 tb	20	0.1	tr	5.3	4.8	0.2	0.1	0	0.3
Tomato ketchup, 1 tb	15	tr	tr	3.5	3.4	0.1	0.2	0	0.3
Worcestershire sauce, 1 tb	10	tr	tr	3.3	2.7	0	0.6	0	0.3
Vinegar, wine, 1 tb	3	0	0	tr	0	0	tr	0	tr
Vinegar, balsamic, 1 tb	14	0	0	2.7	2.4	0	0.1	0	tr

Dairy Products, Plant Alternatives, Eggs

	Cals	Fat g	Sats g	Carbs g	Sugar g	Fibre g	Protein g	Chol mg	Salt g
Cow's milk, whole, 100ml	66	3.9	2.4	4.8	4.8	0	3.2	14	0.1

Vitamins	Minerals	Special Notes
K		
		High salt item.
		If tomato ketchup and tomato puree are eaten regularly they can make a useful contribution to carotene intake.
		May help to control appetite. Red wine vinegar contains resveratrol to protect against cancer and heart disease.
		Aged balsamic vinegar makes a good alternative to an oil-based salad dressing.
A, B2, B12	calc, pot, phos	Dairy milk is one of our most important calcium sources, and latest research sheds some doubt on the link between full-fat dairy and heart disease.

	Cals	Fat g	Sats g	Carbs g	Sugar g	Fibre g	Protein g	Chol mg	Salt g
Cow's milk, semi-skimmed, 100ml	46	1.6	1	5	5	0	3.3	7	0.1
Cow's milk, skimmed, 100ml	33	0.1	0.1	5	5	0	3.3	2	0.1
Goat's milk, 100ml	69	4.1	2.7	4.4	4.4	0	3.6	10	0.1
Almond milk, 100ml	13	1.1	0.1	0	0	0.3	0.4	0	0.1
Coconut milk, 100ml	27	2	1.9	1.9	1.6	0.1	0.2	0	0.1
Rice milk, 100ml	50	1	0.1	9.9	7.1	0	0.1	0	0.1
Soya milk, unsweetened, 100ml	39	1.8	0.3	2.5	2.5	0.5	3	0	0.1
Cream, single, 30ml	55	5.4	3.4	0.6	0.6	0	1	17	tr
Cream, double, 30ml	133	14.3	8.9	0.8	0.8	0	0.5	65	tr
Crème fraiche, 30ml	89	9.3	6.5	0.6	0.6	0	0.6	53	tr

Vitamins	Minerals	Special Notes
B2, B12	calc, pot, phos	
B2, B12	calc, pot, phos	
A, B2, B12	calc, pot, phos	For some people easier to digest than cow's milk.
B12, E		Can also make a reasonable contribution to Vitamin D and calcium intake.
B12		This refers to the type of coconut milk sold in cartons rather than the thicker milk sold in cans.
B12		Reasonable source of vitamin D and calcium.
B12		Reasonable source of vitamin D and calcium.
A		
A		
A		

	Cals	Fat g	Sats g	Carbs g	Sugar g	Fibre g	Protein g	Chol mg	Salt g
Soya cream, single, 30ml	37	3.1	0.4	1.3	0.5	0.1	0.7	0	tr
Yogurt, natural, wholemilk, 100g	61	3.2	2.1	4.7	4.7	0	3.5	13	0.1
Yogurt, natural, low-fat, 100g	63	1.5	1	7	7	0	5.2	6	0.2
Yogurt, natural, Greek, 100g	97	5	2.4	4	4	0	9	13	0.1
Soya yogurt, plain, 100g	50	2.3	0.4	2.1	2.1	1	4	0	0.2
Coconut yogurt, dairy and soya free, 100g	151	11.5	10.3	10.8	2.2	0.3	1.3	0	0.1
Brie, 50g	167	13.8	8.7	0.2	0.2	0	10.4	50	0.8
Cheddar cheese, 50g	202	16.7	9.4	1.5	0.2	0	11.4	50	0.8
Cottage cheese, standard, 50g	53	2.5	1.6	1.9	1.9	0	5.6	7	0.2
Cream cheese, standard, 50g	220	24	15	tr	tr	0	1.5	48	0.4

Vitamins	Minerals	Special Notes
B12	calc, phos	'Live' yogurt (which has not been heated or pasteurised) is a rich source of probiotics that can improve digestive health.
B2, B12	calc, phos	
B2, B12	phos	
B12		
		Brands made mainly from cultured coconut milk will be high in calories, fat and saturates. Some 'coconut' yogurts are soya-based with some added coconut and will be lower in all these - check the labels for the type you require.
A, B2, B12		Aged cheese contains butyrate consumption of which can reduce blood cholesterol.
A, B2, B12	calc, phos	Aged cheddars are a good source of probiotics, as are many other cheeses.
B12		
A, B12		Mascarpone has a similar nutrient profile.

	Cals	Fat g	Sats g	Carbs g	Sugar g	Fibre g	Protein g	Chol mg	Salt g
Feta cheese, 50g	125	10	6.7	0.8	0.8	0	7.8	35	1.1
Gruyere cheese, 50g	205	17	10.7	0.2	0.2	0	14	55	0.7
Mozzarella cheese, soft, full fat, 50g	150	11.2	6.6	1.1	0.5	0	11.1	40	0.8
Parmesan cheese, 50g	196	12.9	8.2	1.6	0.4	0	17.9	34	1.7
Stilton cheese, 50g	206	18	11.2	0.1	0.1	0	11	53	1
Egg, hen's, one medium	72	4.7	1.6	0.4	0.2	0	6.3	186	0.2
Dairy-free Cheddar-style cheese, 50g	153	12.3	10.2	8.5	tr	0.8	1.8	0	0.9

Biscuits, Cakes, Desserts

	Cals	Fat g	Sats g	Carbs g	Sugar g	Fibre g	Protein g	Chol mg	Salt g
Chocolate Chip Cookie, large/75g	362	17.6	8.5	46.3	28	1.7	3.8	0	0.2
Digestive biscuit, milk chocolate	83	3.9	2.1	10.4	4.9	0.5	1.1	tr	0.2

Vitamins	Minerals	Special Notes
B12	calc, phos	
A, B12	calc, phos, zinc	
B12	calc, phos, zinc	
B2, B12	calc, phos, zinc	
A, B2, B12	calc, phos, zinc	Rich in probiotics.
A, B12, D		Eggs contain a reasonable amount of B2, B3, folate. The iron in eggs is not well absorbed. Yolks are source of lutein and zeaxcanthin for eye health. Only $1/3$ of the fat in most eggs is saturated.
		Sizes and recipes of choc chip cookies vary a lot so read the nutrition panel.

	Cals	Fat g	Sats g	Carbs g	Sugar g	Fibre g	Protein g	Chol mg	Salt g
Digestive biscuit, plain	71	3.1	1.5	9.2	2.4	0.5	1.1	0	0.2
Shortbread biscuit, oblong	104	5.8	3.8	11.9	3.7	0.5	1	5	0.1
Chocolate cake with buttercream, 75g slice	292	15	4.5	39.6	30	1.7	2.6	16	0.6
Doughnut, ring/55g	217	13.6	6.3	19.5	2.5	2.4	3.2	6	0.3
Fruit cake, rich, 75g	250	7	2.8	41.8	30.3	1.8	3.2	5	0.2
Scone, sultana, one, 60g	190	5.2	1.8	42	14.2	1.5	4.9	5	1.1
Sponge, Victoria, jam/cream-filled, 75g	210	8.2	2.2	33	25.3	0.7	3.1	44	0.4
Cheesecake, lemon, 100g	290	15	9	35	23	1	3	30	0.2
Chocolate ganache pot, 50g	200	17	10	12	10	1	1.5	50	0.1
Custard, dairy, full fat, 100ml	100	3	1.7	15	11	0	3	11	0.1

Vitamins	Minerals	Special Notes
		The calculation is for an all-butter shortbread; brands vary.
folate	phos	
A, D, E		Vitamin E content applicable only if non-dairy fat is used.
		Average values.
		Average values.
		Average values.

	Cals	Fat g	Sats g	Carbs g	Sugar g	Fibre g	Protein g	Chol mg	Salt g
Ice-cream, dairy, vanilla, 100g	204	10.8	6.8	23	19	0	3.6	45	0.2

Drinks, alcohol

	Cals	Fat g	Sats g	Carbs g	Sugar g	Fibre g	Protein g	Chol mg	Salt g
Beer, standard, half pint/ 285ml	94	0	0	6.3	6.3	tr	0.8	0	tr
Cider, dry, half pint/ 285ml	103	0	0	7.1	7.1	0	tr	0	tr
Spirits, 25ml	48	0	0	tr	tr	0	tr	0	0
Stout, e.g. Guinness, half pint/ 285ml	85	0	0	4.3	4.3	tr	1.1	0	tr
Wine, white, dry, 150ml glass	123	0	0	3.2	1.4	0	0.1	0	tr
Wine, red, dry, 150ml glass	122	0	0	3.7	0.9	0	0.1	0	tr

Drinks

	Cals	Fat g	Sats g	Carbs g	Sugar g	Fibre g	Protein g	Chol mg	Salt g
Coffee, instant, black, 225ml	4	0	0	0.8	0	0	0.2	0	tr

Vitamins	Minerals	Special Notes
	calc, phos	Average values.
B3, B6*		5% ABV * Vitamin B content varies according to brand – 'premium' beers usually contain useful amounts while mass-market beers contain less.
B3		
		This value is for a chardonnay; values vary depending on type of grape.
		Red wines often contain useful levels of flavonoids which may help protect against cardio-vascular disease.

	Cals	Fat g	Sats g	Carbs g	Sugar g	Fibre g	Protein g	Chol mg	Salt g
Coffee, fresh ground, 225ml	4	0	0	0.5	0	0	0.7	0	tr
Cola, standard, 330ml can	139	0	0	35	35	0	0	0	0
Lemonade, standard, 330ml can	59	0	0	14	14	0	0	0	0.1
Apple juice, 180ml/individual carton	81	0	0	19	16	1.6*	0.6	0	0
Grape juice, purple, 180ml	122	0	0	29.7	29.7	0	0.2	0	tr
Orange juice, 180ml	77	0	0	16	16	1.1	1.4	0	0
Smoothie, strawberry and banana, 180ml	95	0	0	21.6	18	1.3	1.1	0	0
Tea, black, 225ml	2	0	0	0.7	0	0	0	0	tr
Tomato juice, 180ml	38	0	0	5.9	5.9	1	2	0	0.3

Vitamins	Minerals	Special Notes
		Rich in plant chemicals and compounds that can protect health.
C		* Fibre content varies from brand to brand, from nil to 1.6g/180ml.
C		Red and purple grape juice is a good source of flavonoids to help protect against cardio-vascular disease.
C		
C		Based on pure fruit smoothie – those containing milk or yogurt will have a different profile.
		Rich in antioxidants including catechin and quercetin, and believed to protect against heart disease. Green and white tea have similar nutrient profile and even higher levels of protective plant chemicals.
C, E		Good source of carotenes.

	Cals	Fat g	Sats g	Carbs g	Sugar g	Fibre g	Protein g	Chol mg	Salt g
Fats, Oils									
Butter, salted, 25g	179	20.3	12.8	tr	tr	0	0.2	54	0.4
Butter, spreadable blend, 25g	176	19.5	8.7	0.1	0.1	0	0.1	25	0.2
Low-fat (light) spread, 25g	70	7.5	1.6	0.7	0.1	0	tr	0	0.3
Vegetable baking block, 25g	169	18.7	7	0	0	0	0	0	0.3
Olive oil spread, 60% fat	125	13.5	3.2	0.2	tr	0	tr	tr	0.3
Coconut oil, 25g	225	25	21.7	0	0	0	0	0	0
Groundnut (peanut) oil, 25g	225	25	5	0	0	0	0	0	0
Olive oil, 25g	225	25	3.6	0	0	0	0	0	0
Rapeseed oil, 25g	225	25	1.6	0	0	0	0	0	0

Vitamins	Minerals	Special Notes
A, D		
A		Blend of butter and oil, type of oil varies and so may the nutrition.
A, D, E		
A, D		
A,D,E		
		Very high in saturated fat, much of which is lauric acid which may have health benefits.
E		Contains around 44% monounsaturated fats.
E		Around 73% of its fat is monounsaturated.
E		Around 60% of its fat is monounsaturated

	Cals	Fat g	Sats g	Carbs g	Sugar g	Fibre g	Protein g	Chol mg	Salt g
Sesame oil, 25g	225	24.9	3.6	0	0	0	0	0	0
Sunflower oil, 25g	225	25	3	0	0	0	0	0	0
Walnut oil, 25g	225	25	2.3	0	0	0	0	0	0

Fish, Seafood

	Cals	Fat g	Sats g	Carbs g	Sugar g	Fibre g	Protein g	Chol mg	Salt g
Cod fillet, raw, 100g	82	0.7	0.1	0	0	0	17.8	43	0.1
Haddock fillet, raw, 100g	74	0.4	0.1	0	0	0	16.3	54	0.2
Haddock fillet, smoked, 100g	116	1	0.2	0	0	0	25.2	77	1.9
Mackerel fillet, raw, 100g	205	13.9	3.3	0	0	0	18.6	70	0.2
Salmon fillet, raw, 100g	208	13.4	3	0	0	0	20.4	55	0.1
Swordfish, steak, raw, 100g	144	6.6	1.6	0	0	0	19.7	66	0.2

Vitamins	Minerals	Special Notes
		Around 38% of its fat is monounsaturaates and 38% polyunsaturates.
E		Very high in polyunsaturates at around 63% of its total fat content.
		Very high in polyunsaturates at around 70% of its total fat content.
B3, B12	phos, sel	
B3, B6, B12	phos, sel	
B3, B6, B12	Mag, phos, sel	
B3, B6, B12, D	Mag, phos, sel	For omega-3 (EPA & DHA) content of oily fish see page 22.
B1, B3, B6, B12, D, E	Phos, sel	Farmed. Smoked salmon is much higher in salt – around 3g/100g.
B3, B6, B12, D	Phos, sel	

	Cals	Fat g	Sats g	Carbs g	Sugar g	Fibre g	Protein g	Chol mg	Salt g
Trout, rainbow, fillet, raw, 100g	119	3.5	0.7	0	0	0	20.5	59	0.1
Tuna, steak, yellowfin, fresh, 100g	109	0.5	0.2	0	0	0	24.4	39	0.1
Tuna, canned in water, 100g	128	3	0.8	0	0	0	23.6	42	0.8
Crabmeat, fresh, white and brown, 100g	97	1.5	0.1	0	0	0	19.3	53	2.7
Mussels, shelled, 100g	86	2.2	0.4	3.7	0	0	11.9	28	0.7
Oysters, shelled, 100g	65	1.3	0.2	2.7	0	0	11	50	0.3
Prawns, shelled, 100g	71	1	0.3	0.9	0	0	13.6	126	1.4
Scallops, shelled, 100g	69	0.5	0.1	3.2	0	0	12.1	24	1
Squid, raw, 100g	92	1.4	0.4	3.1	0	0	15.6	233	0.1

Vitamins	Minerals	Special Notes
B3, B6, B12	Phos, sel	
B3, B6, B12, D	Phos, sel	
B3, B6, B12, D	Phos, sel	
B3, B6, B12, folate	Mag, phos, zinc	Most types of shellfish are a particularly good source of zinc.
B1, B2, B12, folate	Iron, Phos, zinc	
B3, B12, D	Iron, zinc, phos, sel	
B3, B6, B12	Phos, zinc	
B12	Phos, zinc	
B2, B3, B12	Phos, zinc	

	Cals	Fat g	Sats g	Carbs g	Sugar g	Fibre g	Protein g	Chol mg	Salt g
Fruit									
Apple, dessert, with skin, medium/150g	77	0.2	tr	20.6	15.5	3.6	0.4	0	tr
Apple, cooking, peeled, 100g	35	0.1	tr	8.9	8.9	1.6	0.3	0	tr
Apricot, fresh, one	17	0.1	tr	3.9	3.2	0.7	0.5	0	tr
Apricots, soft dried, 50g	120	0.3	tr	31.3	26.7	3.6	1.7	0	tr
Banana, 1 medium	105	0.4	0.1	26.9	14.4	3.1	1.3	0	tr
Blackberries, 100g	43	0.5	tr	9.6	4.9	5.3	1.4	0	tr
Blackcurrants, 100g	28	tr	0	6.6	6.6	4.3	0.9	0	tr
Blueberries, 100g	57	0.3	tr	14.5	10	2.4	0.7	0	tr
Cherries, 100g	63	0.2	tr	16	12.8	2.1	1.1	0	0

Vitamins	Minerals	Special Notes
C	Pot	Vitamin C content of apples will diminish with storage and in warm, light conditions. Good source of polyphenols especially red skinned varieties, and prebiotics.
C	Pot	
		Apricots are a useful source of carotenes and soluble fibre.
	Pot	Useful source of iron and calcium, vitamin B3 and A .
B6, C		Useful source of potassium, resistant starch, probiotics.
C, K		Source of folate, quercetin and plant sterols, and one of the few fruits with a useful amount of vitamin E.
C		Rich in anthocyanins (members of the flavonoid group of plant chemicals see page 48), and one of the richest sources of vitamin C.
C, K		One of the best sources of anthocyanins and contain several other health-protecting plant chemicals.
		Useful source of vitamin C and rich in ellagic acid and anthocyanins.

	Cals	Fat g	Sats g	Carbs g	Sugar g	Fibre g	Protein g	Chol mg	Salt g
Coconut, flesh, raw	100g	354	33.5	29.7	15.2	6.2	9	0	tr
Dates, Medjool, one	66	tr	0	18	15.9	1.6	0.4	0	0
Fig, fresh, one medium	37	0.1	tr	9.6	8.1	1.4	0.4	0	0
Grapefruit, half	41	0.1	tr	10.3	8.9	1.4	0.8	0	0
Grapes, 100g		69	0.2	tr	18.1	15.5	0.9	0.7	0
Kiwifruit, one		42	0.4	tr	10.1	6.2	2.1	0.8	0
Lemon, one	17	0.2	tr	5.4	1.4	1.6	0.6	0	tr
Lime, one	20	0.1	tr	7.1	1.1	1.9	0.5	0	tr
Mango, 100g flesh	60	0.4	0.1	15	13.7	1.6	0.8	0	tr
Melon, canteloupe, 100g flesh	34	0.2	tr	8.2	7.9	0.9	0.8	0	tr

Vitamins	Minerals	Special Notes
folate	Iron, phos, zinc	One of the few fruits high in saturated fats.
B6		
C		Source of soluble fibre. Should not be eaten in combination with some medications including some statins - ask doctor.
tr	K	Red and black grapes are a good source of ppolyphenols which may help prevent heart disease.
tr	C, K	An average fruit contains a whole day's recommended intake of vitamin C for an adult.
C		The juice from a lemon will contain similar nutrition but with very little of the fibre.
C		See notes for lemon above.
A, C, folate		Rich source of carotenes and soluble fibre.
A, C		Orange and red-fleshed types are particularly good source of vitamin A and carotenes, while pale-fleshed varieties are not.

	Cals	Fat g	Sats g	Carbs g	Sugar g	Fibre g	Protein g	Chol mg	Salt g
Nectarine, one	62	0.4	tr	15	11.2	2.4	1.5	0	0
Orange, one	62	0.2	tr	15.4	12.2	3.1	1.2	0	0
Papaya, 100g flesh	43	0.3	0.1	10.8	7.8	1.7	0.5	0	tr
Peach, one	58	0.4	tr	14.3	12.6	2.2	1.4	0	0
Pear, one	101	0.2	tr	27.1	17.4	5.5	0.6	0	tr
Pineapple, fresh, 2 rings/100g	50	0.1	tr	13.1	9.8	1.4	0.5	0	tr
Plum, one	30	0.2	tr	7.5	6.5	0.9	0.5	0	0
Prunes, stoned, 50g	120	0.2	tr	31.9	19.1	3.5	1.1	0	tr
Raisins/sultanas, 50g	150	0.2	tr	39.6	29.6	1.9	1.5	0	tr
Raspberries, 100g	52	0.6	tr	11.9	4.4	6.5	1.2	0	tr

Vitamins	Minerals	Special Notes
C		Also a useful source of vitamin B3.
folate, C		One fruit contains over a day's supply of vitamin C and is a good source of soluble fibre.
A, C, folate		Very high vitamin C content.
C		Useful amount of vitamin E.
C		
		Contains some vitamin C and potassium.
K		Useful source of a range of vitamins and minerals.
		Useful source of calcium, iron and potassium.
C, K		Useful source of vitamin E, iron and zinc.

	Cals	Fat g	Sats g	Carbs g	Sugar g	Fibre g	Protein g	Chol mg	Salt g
Rhubarb, 100g	21	0.2	tr	4.5	1.1	1.8	0.9	0	tr
Strawberries, 100g	32	0.3	tr	7.7	4.9	2	0.7	0	tr

Grains and pseudograins All dry weight per 100g

	Cals	Fat g	Sats g	Carbs g	Sugar g	Fibre g	Protein g	Chol mg	Salt g
Amaranth	371	7	1.5	65.2	1.7	6.7	13.6	0	tr
Barley, pot (hulled, not pearled)	354	2.3	0.5	73.5	0.8	17.3	12.5	0	tr
Buckwheat	343	3.4	0.7	71.5	tr	10	13.2	0	tr
Bulgur wheat	342	1.3	0.2	75.9	0.4	12.5	12.3	0	tr
Cornflour	359	0.6	tr	88	tr	tr	tr	0	0.2
Couscous	376	0.6	0.1	77.4	tr	5	12.8	0	tr
Freekeh, cracked, roasted	369	3.3	0	72	2	17.4	15.2	0	0

Vitamins	Minerals	Special Notes
K		Useful source of vitamin C and calcium.
C, folate		Very rich source of vitamin C. Relatively low GI fruit and rich in polyphenols for heart health.
B1, B2, B6, folate	Cal, iron, mag, phos, zinc	Pseudograin - useful source of vitamin E and potassium.
B1, B2, B3, B6	Iron, mag, phos, zinc	Useful source of potassium and pre-biotics.
B2, B3	Mag, phos, zinc	Pseudograin, useful source of B6 and potassium.
B1, B3, B6, folate	Mag, phos, zinc	Useful source of iron and potassium.
B1, B3	Phos	Not strictly a grain as it is a manufactured product, from wheat.
		Useful source of iron.

	Cals	Fat g	Sats g	Carbs g	Sugar g	Fibre g	Protein g	Chol mg	Salt g
Millet	378	4.2	0.7	72.8	tr	8.5	11	0	tr
Oats, rolled	379	6.5	1.1	67.7	1	10.1	13.1	0	tr
Polenta, quick cook	82	0.6	tr	16.3	tr	1.8	2.3	0	tr
Quinoa	368	6.1	0.7	64.2	tr	7	14.1	0	tr
Rice, brown	367	3.2	0.6	76.2	0.7	3.6	7.5	0	tr
Rice, white	365	0.7	0.2	79.9	0.1	1.3	7.1	0	tr
Rye	338	1.6	0.2	75.9	1	15.1	10.3	0	tr
Spelt	338	2.4	0.4	70.2	6.8	10.7	14.6	0	tr
Sorghum	329	3.5	0.6	72.1	2.5	6.7	10.6	0	tr
Teff	367	2.4	0.4	73.1	1.8	8	13.3	0	tr

Vitamins	Minerals	Special Notes
B1, B2, B3, B6, folate	Iron, mag, phos, zinc	
B1	Iron, mag, phos, zinc	Useful source of potassium, resistant starch and the soluble fibre beta-glucans to lower blood cholesterol.
		Pre-cooked ground maize (corn).
B1, B2, B6, folate, E,	Iron, mag, phos, zinc	Pseudograin, useful source of potassium and calcium.
B1, B3, B6, folate	Mag, phos, zinc	
	phos	
B1, B2, B3, B6, folate	Iron, mag, phos, zinc	
B1, B3, B6, folate	Iron, mag, phos, zinc	
B1, B3, B6	Iron, mag, phos, zinc	
B1, B2, B3, B6	Cal, iron, mag, phos, zinc	

	Cals	Fat g	Sats g	Carbs g	Sugar g	Fibre g	Protein g	Chol mg	Salt g
Wheat, rolled	342	2	0.3	75.2	0.4	9.5	11.2	0	tr
Wheat, flour, whole	340	2.5	0.4	72	0.4	10.7	13.2	0	tr
Wheat flour, white	341	1.3	0.2	77.7	1.5	3.1	9.4	0	tr

Meat, Poultry and meat-free alternatives

	Cals	Fat g	Sats g	Carbs g	Sugar g	Fibre g	Protein g	Chol mg	Salt g
Bacon, back, 2 fat-trimmed rashers/ 75g raw weight	102	5	1.9	tr	tr	tr	14.1	23	2.5
Beef, minced, 10% fat, 100g	176	10	3.9	0	0	0	20	65	0.2
Beef, steak, raw, fat band removed, 100g	117	2.7	1	0	0	0	23.1	55	0.1
Beefburger, one, quarterpounder grilled	251	19	6.5	3.1	1.2	tr	17	48	0.8
Meat-free burger, plain, one quarterpounder grilled	232	12.5	0.9	10.3	1.8	2.5	18.2	0	1
Falafels, chick-pea, baked, four/100g	270	14	1.8	25	4	6	8	0	1.5

Vitamins	Minerals	Special Notes
B1, B2, B3, B6, folate	Iron, mag, phos, zinc	Useful source of calcium and potassium. Wholegrains are a good source of plant sterols. Useful source of calcium and potassium. Wholegrains are a good source of plant sterols.
B1, B2, B3, B6, folate	Iron, mag, phos, zinc	
B1	Cal, phos	Will contain excellent level of folate in UK when it is fortified by law.
B1, B3, B6	Phos, zinc	
B3, B6, B12	Phos, zinc	Useful source of iron.
B3, B6, B12	Phos, zinc	Useful source of iron.
B3, B6, B12	Phos, zinc	Average values.
B1, B2, B3, B6, B12, folate	Cal, iron, mag, phos, zinc	These figures are for an average soya-based burger, most of which are also wheat-free. Other vegetable burgers may be made from a range of ingredients; check label.
Folate	Iron, mag, phos, zinc	Some brands contain wheat.

	Cals	Fat g	Sats g	Carbs g	Sugar g	Fibre g	Protein g	Chol mg	Salt g
Ham, lean, 100g	107	3.3	1.1	1	1	0	18.4	58	3
Ham, Parma, 2 slices/27g	70	4.3	1.5	tr	tr	0	7.9	16	1.2
Lamb, leg, raw, lean, 100g	128	4.5	1.6	0	0	0	20.6	64	0.2
Liver, lamb's, raw, 100g	136	4.9	1.5	2.2	0	0	20.7	386	0.1
Pork fillet, raw, 100g	109	2.2	0.7	0	0	0	20.9	65	0.1
Sausage, chorizo, 100g	455	38	14.5	2	0	0	24	90	3.1
Sausage, pork, fresh, 1 large/56g, grilled	100	6.8	2.6	2.8	0.6	tr	6.6	50	0.7
Sausage, vegetarian, one/50g, grilled	70	2.5	0.9	3.4	0.6	2.3	8.2	0	0.7
Veal, fillet, raw escalope, 100g	107	1.8	0.5	0	0	0	21.3	78	0.2
Venison, fillet, raw, 100g	116	2.7	0.6	0	0	0	21.5	18	0.1

Vitamins	Minerals	Special Notes
B1, B2, B3, B6, B12	Phos, zinc	
B1, B2, B3, B6, B12	Phos, zinc	
B2, B3, B6, B12	Phos, zinc	Also a useful source of iron.
A, B1, B2, B3, B12	Iron, phos, zinc	Extremely high in vitamin A and should be avoided in excess in pregnancy.
B1, B2, B3, B6, B12	Phos, zinc, sel	
B1, B2, B3, B6, B12	Phos, zinc	
		Based on average vegetarian sausage with high soya content. Useful source of B vitamins and several minerals.
B2,B3, B6, B12	Phos, zinc	
B1, B2, B3, B6, B12	Iron, Phos, zinc	

	Cals	Fat g	Sats g	Carbs g	Sugar g	Fibre g	Protein g	Chol mg	Salt g
Chicken breast fillet, skinless, raw, 100g	120	2.6	0.6	0	0	0	22.5	73	0.1
Quorn fillet, 100g, raw	84	1.6	0.7	1.9	0.7	5.5	12.5	0	0.8
Chicken thigh fillet, skinless, raw, 100g	121	4.1	1.1	0	0	0	19.7	94	0.2
Chicken, roast, meat and skin, average serving 150g	358	19	5.7	0	0	0	41	132	0.3
Duck, breast, lean meat, raw, 100g	135	5.9	2.3	0.9	0	0	18.3	77	0.2
Duck, roast, meat and skin, average serving 150g	506	42.5	14.5	0	0	0	28.5	126	0.2
Pheasant, roast, meat and skin, average serving 150g	358	18.1	5.9	0	0	0	48.6	134	0.1
Rabbit, meat, raw, 100g	114	2.3	0.7	0	0	0	21.8	81	0.1
Turkey breast, raw, 100g	114	1.5	0.3	0.1	tr	0	23.7	57	0.3

Vitamins	Minerals	Special Notes
B3, B6	Phos	
	phos, sel, zinc	Quorn is a mycoprotein, lab-made using Fusarium venenatum fungus which can, rarely, cause allergic reaction.
B3, B6, B12	Phos, zinc	
B2, B3, B6, B12	Phos, sel, zinc	Also useful source of iron.
B1, B2, B3, B6, B12	Phos, sel, zinc	Also useful source of iron.
B1, B2, B3, B6, B12	Iron, phos, sel, zinc	High in monounsaturated fats.
B2, B3, B6, B12	Phos, sel, zinc	Also useful source of iron. Farmed pheasant higher in fat than you may imagine.
B3	Iron, phos, sel	Very low-fat source of animal protein.
B3, B6, B12	Phos, sel, zinc	

	Cals	Fat g	Sats g	Carbs g	Sugar g	Fibre g	Protein g	Chol mg	Salt g
Nuts, Seeds All nuts shelled, unsalted, per 50g									
Almonds, blanched	295	26.3	2	9.3	2.3	5	10.7	0	tr
Brazil nuts	330	33.5	8.1	5.9	1.2	3.8	7.2	0	tr
Cashew nuts	276	21.9	3.9	15.1	3	1.6	9.1	0	tr
Hazelnuts	314	30.4	2.2	8.3	2.2	4.8	7.5	0	0
Peanuts	284	24.6	3.1	8.1	2.4	4.2	12.9	0	tr
Pecans	346	36	3.1	6.9	2	4.8	4.6	0	0
Pistachios	280	22.7	2.9	13.6	3.8	5.3	10.1	0	0
Walnuts	327	32.6	3.1	6.9	1.3	3.4	7.6	0	tr
Chia seeds	243	15.4	1.7	21.1	tr	17.2	8.3	0	tr

Vitamins	Minerals	Special Notes
B2	Mag, phos, zinc	Useful source of calcium, iron and potassium. Skin-on almonds contain 6.2g fibre.
B1, E	Mag, phos, sel, zinc	For Brazil nuts and selenium, see page 42. Can be toxic in excess.
B1, B3	Iron, mag, phos, sel, zinc	
B1, B6, folate, E	Mag, phos, zinc	Very useful source of iron.
B1, B3, folate, E	Mag, phos, zinc	Useful source of iron and calcium.
B1, B6	Mag, phos, zinc	
B1, B6, folate	Mag, phos	Useful source of vitamin E, iron and zinc.
B1, B6, folate	Mag, phos, zinc	Useful source of iron.
B1, B3	Cal, iron, mag, phos, sel, zinc	Very rich in soluble fibre.

	Cals	Fat g	Sats g	Carbs g	Sugar g	Fibre g	Protein g	Chol mg	Salt g
Flaxseeds	267	21.1	1.8	14.4	0.8	13.7	9.1	0	tr
Pine kernels	336	34.2	2.4	6.5	1.8	1.9	6.8	0	tr
Pumpkin seeds	280	24.5	4.3	5.4	0.7	3	15.1	0	tr
Sesame seeds	286	24.8	3.5	11.7	0.1	5.9	8.9	0	tr
Sunflower seeds	292	25.7	2.2	10	1.3	4.3	10.4	0	tr

Pasta, Noodles, Pastry

	Cals	Fat g	Sats g	Carbs g	Sugar g	Fibre g	Protein g	Chol mg	Salt g
Pasta, white, all shapes, dried uncooked, 100g	371	1.5	0.3	75	2.7	3.2	13	0	tr
Pasta, white, fresh, uncooked, 100g	288	2.3	0.3	54.7	tr	1.9	11.3	73	0.1
Pasta, white, dried, boiled with salt, average 225g portion (weight after cooking and draining)	353	2.1	0.4	68.8	1.3	4	13	0	0.7

Vitamins	Minerals	Special Notes
B1, B6, folate	Cal, iron, mag, phos, sel, zinc	The nutrients in flaxseeds are much better absorbed in the body if they are consumed ground. Good source of soluble fibre and plant sterols.
B1, E, K	Iron, mag, phos, zinc	
B3	Iron, mag, phos, zinc	
B1, B6, folate	Calc, iron, mag, phos, zinc	
B1, B2, B3, B6, E, folate	Iron, mag, phos, sel, zinc	Very rich source of vitamin E.
	Phos, sel, zinc	
B1, B2, B3, B12, folate	Iron, mag, phos	Fresh pasta, unlike dried, usually contains eggs.
	phos	

	Cals	Fat g	Sats g	Carbs g	Sugar g	Fibre g	Protein g	Chol mg	Salt g
Pasta, wholewheat, all shapes, dried, uncooked, 100g	352	2.9	0.4	73.4	2.7	9.2	13.9	0	tr
Pasta, wholewheat, all shapes, dried, boiled with salt, average 225g portion (weight after cooking and draining)	335	3.8	0.5	68	1.7	8.8	13.5	0	0.7
Noodles, egg, dried, 100g	384	4.4	1.2	71.3	1.9	3.3	14.2	84	0.1
Noodles, rice, dried, 100g	364	0.6	0.1	80.2	0.1	1.6	5.9	0	0.5
Noodles, soba, dried, 100g	336	0.7	0.1	74.6	1.5	3	14.4	0	2
Noodles, cellophane (mung bean) dried, 100g	351	0.1	tr	86.1	0	0.5	0.2	0	tr
Pastry, filo, packet, 100g uncooked	283	0.9	0.3	58.9	5.9	2.2	8.7	0	0.6
Pastry, puff, packet, 100g uncooked	387	23.9	11.4	36.8	0.8	1.1	5.7	0	0.6
Pastry, shortcrust, packet, 100g uncooked	444	28.5	11	40	1.6	1.4	6	0	0.5

Vitamins	Minerals	Special Notes
B1, B2, B3, B6, folate	Iron, mag, phos, sel, zinc	
B1, B2, B3, folate	Iron, mag, phos, sel, zinc	
B1	Mag, phos, sel, zinc	
	Phos	
B1, B3, B6, folate	Iron, mag, phos, zinc	Made from buckwheat flour.
B1	Cal, phos	
B1, B2, B3, folate	Iron	Cholesterol free if made with vegetable fats rather than, eg, lard.
B1		

	Cals	Fat g	Sats g	Carbs g	Sugar g	Fibre g	Protein g	Chol mg	Salt g
Pulses All cooked (or canned in water) pulses are for well-drained weight.									
Baked beans in tomato sauce, canned, 100g	79	0.2	tr	12.9	5	3.7	4.7	0	0.6
Black beans, cooked, 100g	132	0.5	0.1	23.7	0.3	8.7	8.9	0	tr
Blackeye beans, 100g	97	0.4	0.1	20.3	3.2	5	3.2	0	tr
Borlotti beans, cooked, 100g	100	0.6	tr	12.9	0.6	7.7	6.9	0	tr
Butter beans, cooked, 100g	108	0.7	tr	14.8	tr	7.3	6.9	0	tr
Cannellini beans, cooked, 100g	101	0.6	tr	13.3	tr	6.4	7.5	0	tr
Chick peas, cooked, 100g	164	2.6	0.3	27.4	4.8	7.6	8.9	0	tr
Flageolet beans, cooked, 100g	64	tr	tr	9.4	0.6	4.2	3.6	0	0.1
Haricot beans, cooked, 100g	140	0.6	0.1	26	0.4	10.5	8.2	0	0

Vitamins	Minerals	Special Notes
	phos	Useful source of carotenoids, iron, calcium and magnesium.
B1, folate	Mag, phos	Useful source of iron, potassium zinc.
folate, K	Cal, mag	Useful source of iron and potassium.
B1, folate	Mag	Useful source of calcium, iron and potasium.
B1, folate		Useful source of calcium, iron, magnesium, potassium and zinc.
folate	Iron	Useful source of magnesium.
folate	Iron, phos, zinc	All pulses are a good source of resistant starch, soluble fibre and prebiotics and contain plant sterols.
		Useful source of iron.
B1, folate	phos	Useful source of cal, iron, mag, zinc.

	Cals	Fat g	Sats g	Carbs g	Sugar g	Fibre g	Protein g	Chol mg	Salt g
Lentils, brown/black, cooked, 100g	105	0.7	0.1	16.9	1.2	8	8.8	0	tr
Lentils, red, cooked, 100g	86	0.9	0.3	9.6	tr	4.5	7.5	0	tr
Red kidney beans, cooked, 100g	103	0.5	0.1	17.4	1	7.8	8.4	0	tr
Soya beans, cooked, 100g	141	7.3	0.9	5.1	2.1	6	14	0	tr
Soya flour, full fat, 100g	434	20.6	3	31.9	7.5	9.6	37.8	0	tr
Split peas, cooked, 100g	118	0.4	tr	21.1	2.9	8.3	8.3	0	tr
Tofu, firm, 100g	118	7.1	1.2	1	0.7	1.9	12.6	0	tr
Tofu, silken, soft, 100g	55	2.7	0.4	2.9	1.3	0.1	4.8	0	tr

Spreads, dips, pates

	Cals	Fat g	Sats g	Carbs g	Sugar g	Fibre g	Protein g	Chol mg	Salt g
Cashew butter, 25g	157	12.8	2.5	4.7	1.4	1.1	5.1	0	0

Vitamins	Minerals	Special Notes
B6	Iron, sel	All pulses are a good source of resistant starch, soluble fibre and prebiotics and contain plant sterols.
		Useful source of folate and iron.
B1, folate	phos	Useful source of cal, mag, iron, zinc.
folate	Iron, mag, phos	Useful source of vitamin E, potassium, calcium, zinc.
B1, B2, B3, B6, folate, K	Cal, iron,mag, phos, zinc	Useful source of vitamin E, pot.
B1, folate		Useful source of iron, mag, potassium, zinc.
B1	Cal, mag, phos, zinc	High calcium content only if prepared using calcium sulphate.
		Most nut butters are a good source of plant sterols.

	Cals	Fat g	Sats g	Carbs g	Sugar g	Fibre g	Protein g	Chol mg	Salt g
Fruit conserves, average, 25g	63	0.1	tr	15	15	0.2	tr	0	0.1
Hummus, plain, 25g	70	5.5	0.7	2.6	0.2	1.3	1.7	0	0.1
Mushroom pate, average, 25g	37	3	1	1.5	0.1	1	1	tr	0.1
Liver pate, average, 25g	90	8	3	1.2	0.6	tr	2.2	40	0.5
Peanut butter, no added sugar, 25g	160	13.6	1.8	2.3	1	1.6	6.6	0	0.2
Taramasalata, 25g	115	11.5	0.8	2.1	0.4	tr	0.8	9	0.5
Yeast extract, 1 tsp	9	tr	0	0.7	tr	tr	1.5	0	0.3

Snack Foods

	Cals	Fat g	Sats g	Carbs g	Sugar g	Fibre g	Protein g	Chol mg	Salt g
Crisps, potato, plain salted, 25g	132	8	0.7	12.9	tr	1.1	1.5	0	0.3
Crisps, mixed vegetable, salted, 25g	126	8.9	1	9.6	5.6	3	1.2	0	0.3

Vitamins	Minerals	Special Notes
		Source of resistant starch, soluble fibre and prebiotics.
B2, B12, folate		
B3		Useful source of vitamin E, magnesium and zinc as well as soluble fibre.
B1, B3, B12, folate		

	Cals	Fat g	Sats g	Carbs g	Sugar g	Fibre g	Protein g	Chol mg	Salt g
Popcorn, plain, salted, popped, 25g	122	6.4	0.7	12.5	0.1	2	2	0	0.3
Salted mixed nuts, 25g	160	13.8	2	2.3	1	2.5	5.4	0	0.2
Tortilla chips, salted, 25g	118	5.2	0.7	17	0.2	1.4	1.8	0	0.2

Storecupboard items

	Cals	Fat g	Sats g	Carbs g	Sugar g	Fibre g	Protein g	Chol mg	Salt g
Coconut milk, canned, per 100ml	180	18.2	15.4	2.9	2.4	tr	0.9	0	tr
Coconut, creamed block, 25g	175	17	15.3	2.4	1	tr	2	0	tr
Curry powder, 1 tb	20	0.9	0.1	3.5	0.2	3.4	0.9	0	tr
Miso paste, 1 tb	34	1	0.2	4.3	1	0.9	2.2	0	1.6
Mustard, Dijon, 1 tsp	8	0.6	tr	0.2	tr	0.2	0.2	0	0.3
Olives, black, stoned, in brine, drained, per 15g	24	2.4	0.3	tr	tr	0.7	tr	0	0.4

Vitamins	Minerals	Special Notes
	Mag, phos	
		For information on coconut and health see page 19.
		Good source of plant compounds including curcumin and usually capsaicin, for health protection and antibacterial action.
		Good source of probiotics as are all fermented foods.

	Cals	Fat g	Sats g	Carbs g	Sugar g	Fibre g	Protein g	Chol mg	Salt g
Tahini, 1tb	89	7.9	1.1	3.2	tr	0.7	2.6	0	tr
Tomato paste, 1tb	13	0.1	tr	3	1.9	0.7	0.7	0	tr
Tomato sauce for pasta, 100ml	60	1.5	0.2	8	7	2	2	0	0.7

Sugar, Sweeteners, Confectionery All 100g/ml

	Cals	Fat g	Sats g	Carbs g	Sugar g	Fibre g	Protein g	Chol mg	Salt g
Agave nectar (syrup)	310	0.4	0	76.4	68	0.2	0.1	0	tr
Brown rice syrup	310	0	0	76.2	47.6	0	2.4	0	0.2
Date sugar	330	0	0	88	66	2	2	0	tr
Date syrup	320	0	0	85	65	0	0	0	0.1
Coconut palm sugar	383	0.5	0	92.8	87.5	0	2.6	0	0.1
Honey	304	0	0	82.4	82.1	0.2	0.3	0	tr

Vitamins	Minerals	Special Notes
B1	Phos	
		Useful source of vitamin A.
A		
C, B2, B6, K		High fructose syrup made by extraction from agave plant often using high temperatures.
		Glucose-based sweetener, low GI, contains small amount of some minerals.
B1	Pot	Made by grinding dried dates; sometimes with added flour to aid flow - check ingredients label. Should contain some plant chemicals.
		Made by soaking, boiling with water and purifying/extracting the syrup.
		Made from the nectar of coconut tree blossom. Low GI.
		Minimally processed honeys may contain beneficial phenols and may have antibacterial function. Honey contains small amounts of various vitamins and minerals.

	Cals	Fat g	Sats g	Carbs g	Sugar g	Fibre g	Protein g	Chol mg	Salt g
Maple syrup	260	0.1	0	67	60.5	0	tr	0	tr
Molasses	290	0.1	0	74.7	74.7	0	0	0	0.1
Palm sugar	337	0	0	84.2	84.2	0	0	0	0
Sugar, brown	380	0	0	98.1	97	0	0.1	0	0.1
Sugar, white	387	0	0	99.9	99.8	0	0	0	tr
Chocolate, milk	535	29.7	18.5	59.4	51.5	3.4	7.6	23	0.2
Chocolate, dark, 70% cocoa solids	598	42.6	24.5	45.9	24	10.9	7.8	3	tr

Vegetables

	Cals	Fat g	Sats g	Carbs g	Sugar g	Fibre g	Protein g	Chol mg	Salt g
Artichoke hearts, cooked, 100g	53	0.3	0.1	12	1	5.7	2.9	0	0.2
Artichoke, Jerusalem, 100g	73	tr	0	17.4	9.6	1.6	2	0	tr

Vitamins	Minerals	Special Notes
B2	Zinc	Produced by extracting the sap from maple trees and heating to temperatures up to 115C to produce syrup. High fructose.
	Calc, iron, Mag, pot.	Similar to black treacle, a by-product of processing refined sugars, contains some B3 and B6.
		Made from the sap of various varieties of palm trees. May contain useful amounts of calc, iron.
		Contains a small amount of minerals including calcium and iron.
B2	Calc, mag, phos, zinc	Useful source of iron.
B12	Iron, mag, phos, pot, zinc	Useful source of calcium, B3 and E.
folate, K	Pot	Contains cynarin, said to boost liver function and help regulate blood cholesterol. Good source of the soluble fibre inulin and prebiotics.
B1	Iron, pot	Good source of prebiotics.

	Cals	Fat g	Sats g	Carbs g	Sugar g	Fibre g	Protein g	Chol mg	Salt g
Asparagus, 100g		20	0.1	tr	3.9	1.9	2.1	2.2	0
Aubergine, 100g		25	0.2	tr	5.9	3.5	3	0.1	0
Avocado, half average, 125g	200	18.3	2.7	10.7	0.8	8.4	2.5	0	tr
Beans, broad, shelled, cooked, 100g	81	0.6	0.1	11.7	1.3	6.5	7.9	0	tr
Beans, French, cooked, 100g	35	0.3	0.1	7.9	3.6	3.2	1.9	0	tr
Beans, runner, cooked, 100g	18	0.5	0.1	2.3	2	1.9	1.2	0	tr
Beansprouts, 100g	30	0.2	tr	5.9	4.1	1.8	3	0	tr
Beetroot, 100g	43	0.2	tr	9.6	6.8	2.8	1.6	0	0.2
Broccoli, 100g	34	0.4	tr	6.6	1.7	2.6	2.8	0	0.1
Brussels sprouts, 100g	43	0.3	0.1	8.9	2.2	3.8	3.4	0	0.1

Vitamins	Minerals	Special Notes
tr	folate, A, K	Useful source of C, E, iron, zinc. And a good source of soluble fibre.
tr		
C, B2, folate, E, K		Rich in monounsaturated fat. Useful source of mag, pot, zinc.
C		Useful source of carotenes, folate, calc, mag, iron, zinc. Good source of soluble fibre, resistant starch and plant sterols.
C, A, K		
C, folate		Source of carotenes.
C, folate, K		Based on mung beans though other sprouts will be similar values. Useful source of iron.
folate		Contains plant compounds linked to a variety of health benefits including reduction of blood pressure.
A, C, folate		Useful source of calcium. Contains cancer-fighting glucosinolates and lutein and zeaxanthin for eye health.
A, C, folate		Very good source of glucosinolates, see broccoli. Good source of soluble fibre.

	Cals	Fat g	Sats g	Carbs g	Sugar g	Fibre g	Protein g	Chol mg	Salt g
Cabbage, green, 100g	25	0.1	tr	5.8	3.2	2.5	1.3	0	tr
Cabbage, red, 100g	31	0.2	tr	7.4	3.8	2.1	1.4	0	0.1
Carrots, 100g	41	0.2	tr	9.6	4.7	2.8	0.9	0	0.2
Cauliflower, 100g	25	0.3	0.1	5	1.1	2	1.9	0	0.1
Celeriac, 100g	42	0.3	0.1	9.2	1.6	1.8	1.5	0	0.2
Celery, 2 sticks/100g	16	0.2	tr	3	1.3	1.6	0.7	0	0.2
Chard, Swiss, 100g	19	0.2	tr	3.7	1.1	1.6	1.8	0	0.5
Chilli pepper, red, one 30g	12	0.1	tr	2.6	1.6	0.4	0.6	0	tr
Courgettes, 100g		17	0.3	0.1	3.1	2.5	1	1.2	0
Cucumber with peel, 100g	15	0.1	tr	3.6	1.7	0.5	0.6	0	tr

Vitamins	Minerals	Special Notes
C, folate, K		The darker green leaves contain good amounts of cancer-fighting plant chemicals and lutein and zeaxanthin for eye health. Cabbage is a good source of pre-biotics.
A, C, K		Contains cyanidins for heart health.
A		Richest source of carotenes.
C, folate, K		
C, K	phos	
A, folate, K		Rich in antioxidant phenols.
A, C, E, K	Mag	Contains various anti-inflammatory plant chemicals including betalain. Useful source of calcium and iron.
A, C		Rich in capsaicin which is strongly antiinflammatory.
tr	C	
K		

	Cals	Fat g	Sats g	Carbs g	Sugar g	Fibre g	Protein g	Chol mg	Salt g
Fennel bulb, 100g	31	0.2	0.1	7.3	3.9	3.1	1.2	0	0.1
Garlic, 1 bulb/30g	45	0.1	tr	9.9	0.3	0.6	1.9	0	tr
Ginger root, fresh peeled, 20g	16	0.1	tr	3.5	0.3	0.4	0.4	0	tr
Kale, 100g	49	0.9	0.1	8.7	2.2	3.6	4.3	0	0.1
Kimchi, jar, 100g	15	0.5	tr	2.4	1.1	1.6	1.1	0	1.2
Leek, one medium, trimmed, 100g	61	0.3	tr	14.1	3.9	1.8	1.5	0	tr
Lettuce, Cos type, 100g	17	0.3	tr	3.3	1.2	2.1	1.2	0	tr
Mangetout peas, 100g	42	0.2	tr	7.5	4	2.6	2.8	0	tr
Mushrooms, 100g	22	0.1	tr	4.3	1.7	0.6	2.5	0	tr
Onions, 100g		40	0.1	tr	9.3	4.2	1.7	1.1	0

Vitamins	Minerals	Special Notes
A, C, K		
B6, C		Contains a range of plant chemicals that are antibiotic, antifungal and health protective in several ways.
		Contains anti-inflammatory and pain-relieving gingerols and compounds soothing to the digestive system.
A, B6, C, K, folate		Useful source of vitamin E. Rich in glucosinolates (see broccoli) and lutein and zeaxanthin for eye health.
K, folate		Fermented cabbage dish from Korea: probiotic.
C, folate, A		Useful source of calcium and iron. Contains allicin.
A, folate, K		Dark and red lettuce leaves contain excellent levels of carotenes but pale leaved lettuce does not.
A, folate, K		Useful source of soluble fibre.
B2, B3		Dark gilled brown mushrooms contain cancer-fighting lentinan and canthaxanthin plant chemicals.
tr		Rich in flavonoids, and have antibiotic action. Good source of inulin, a type of soluble fibre which is prebiotic.

	Cals	Fat g	Sats g	Carbs g	Sugar g	Fibre g	Protein g	Chol mg	Salt g
Pak choi, 100g	13	0.2	tr	2.2	1.2	1	1.5	0	0.2
Parsnips, 100g	75	0.3	tr	18	4.8	4.9	1.2	0	tr
Peas, shelled, 100g	81	0.4	0.1	14.4	5.7	5.7	5.4	0	tr
Peppers, sweet, red/orange/yellow, one	37	0.4	tr	7.2	5	2.5	1.2	0	tr
Potatoes, peeled, boiled, 100g	86	0.1	tr	20	0.9	1.8	1.7	0	tr
Potato, baked, one, 200g	178	0.3	tr	39.2	2.9	3.6	4.6	0	0.1
Sauerkraut, 100g	19	0.1	tr	4.3	1.8	2.9	0.9	0	1.6
Spinach, 100g	23	0.4	0.1	3.6	0.4	2.2	2.9	0	0.2
Squash, butternut, peeled, 100g	45	0.1	tr	11.7	2.2	2	1	0	tr
Swede, peeled, 100g	24	0.3	tr	5	4.9	1.9	0.7	0	0.2

Vitamins	Minerals	Special Notes
A, C, folate, K		Useful source of calcium.
C, folate, K		
A, B1, folate, C, K		Contains resistant starch, soluble fibre.
A, B6, folate, C		Useful source of vitamin E. Green peppers are a little lower in calories, carbs and sugar.
B6		Useful source of vitamin C - new potatoes contain much more than old ones. Don't leave potatoes soaking in water as they will leach their vitamin C.
B3, B6, folate, C	Mag, pot	The skins contain the most fibre and the flesh just under the skin contains most vitamin C.
C, K		Fermented cabbage-based food, rich in probiotics.
A, C, folate, K	Iron, mag	Useful source of most B vitamins, E, calcium and potassium. Oxylates in spinach hinder calcium and iron absorption. Absorption is improved if spinach is cooked and is served with high vitamin C accompaniments. Drinking tea at the same time should be avoided as tannins also hinder absorption.
A, C		
A, C		

	Cals	Fat g	Sats g	Carbs g	Sugar g	Fibre g	Protein g	Chol mg	Salt g
Sweetcorn, 1 cob	88	1.4	0.3	19.1	6.4	2	3.3	0	tr
Sweet potato, peeled, 100g	86	tr	tr	20.1	4.2	3	1.6	0	0.1
Tomatoes, 100g	18	0.2	tr	3.9	2.6	1.2	0.9	0	tr
Watercress, 25g	3	tr	0	0.3	tr	0.1	0.6	0	tr

Vitamins	Minerals	Special Notes
B1		
A		Very good source of carotenes.
A, C		
A, C, K		Contains anti-cancer compounds.

Index